"The conquest of Canaan is arguably th
and to date no solution has garnered a consensus. These authors offer a g...
approach to mitigate the difficulties. Deeply rooted in ancient Near Eastern mores and reconsideration of key biblical words and texts, the arguments challenge many commonly held ideas. While provocative at times, this book deserves careful consideration."

John W. Hilber, professor of Old Testament, Grand Rapids Theological Seminary

"The violence in the book of Joshua has long vexed devoted Bible readers. The father and son authors of this fine volume offer a fresh, more pacific reading of the book in light of what they deem to be relevant ancient Near Eastern parallels. They present their case in a series of propositions that rebut inadequate (in their view) modern solutions and support their alternative view with impressive close rereadings of biblical and extrabiblical texts and illuminating Hebrew word studies. They argue, for example, that the Hebrew verb *herem* means 'to remove from use,' not 'to annihilate,' and that its application to human communities 'is intended to destroy identity, not to kill people.' Indeed, ancient cultural ideas of order (versus disorder), identity (not ethnicity), and the suzerain-vassal model of what the authors call 'covenant order' drive their argument. Ultimately, they demonstrate that to read the Bible from an ancient (versus modern) perspective may yield a clearer, less distorted understanding of its controversial topics. They have proffered a commendable, thorough, thought-provoking rethinking of violence in Joshua and its implications for Christian identity today."

Robert L. Hubbard Jr., professor emeritus of biblical literature, North Park Theological Seminary, Denver

"Into the many recent discussions concerning the ethical and moral problems of the Israelite conquest, Walton and Walton offer a much-needed corrective, effectively arguing that to properly understand these troublesome texts one needs to interpret them in light of their ancient context. They boldly challenge common assumptions regarding the conquest, carefully examine biblical and ancient Near Eastern texts, and helpfully guide readers to apply these lessons, using them as a template to make sense of the New Testament."

David T. Lamb, Allan A. MacRae Professor of Old Testament, Biblical Theological Seminary, author of *God Behaving Badly* and *Prostitutes and Polygamists*

Larry Thompson
(814) 873 6696

"For God
so loved ..."
John 3:16

Mr Lawrence Thompson
PO Box 8798
Erie, PA 16505

THE
LOST WORLD
OF THE
ISRAELITE
CONQUEST

Covenant, Retribution,
and the Fate of the Canaanites

JOHN H. WALTON
J. HARVEY WALTON

IVP Academic

An imprint of InterVarsity Press
Downers Grove, Illinois

InterVarsity Press
P.O. Box 1400, Downers Grove, IL 60515-1426
ivpress.com
email@ivpress.com

*InterVarsity Press® is the book-publishing division of InterVarsity Christian Fellowship/USA®, a
movement of students and faculty active on campus at hundreds of universities, colleges, and schools of
nursing in the United States of America, and a member movement of the International Fellowship of
Evangelical Students. For information about local and regional activities, visit intervarsity.org.*

Cover design: David Fassett
Interior design: Daniel van Loon
*Images: © Baker Publishing Group and Dr. James C. Martin, courtesy of the British Museum,
       London, England*

ISBN 978-0-8308-5184-3 (print)
ISBN 978-0-8308-9007-1 (digital)

Printed in the United States of America ♾

Library of Congress Cataloging-in-Publication Data
A catalog record for this book is available from the Library of Congress.

P	22	21	20	19	18	17	16	15	14	13	12	11	10	9	8	7	6	5	4	3	2	1
Y	34	33	32	31	30	29	28	27	26	25	24	23	22	21	20	19	18	17

Contents

PART 1: INTERPRETATION

PART 2: THE CANAANITES ARE NOT DEPICTED AS GUILTY OF SIN

PART 3: THE CANAANITES ARE NOT DEPICTED AS GUILTY OF BREAKING GOD'S LAW

PART 4: THE LANGUAGE AND IMAGERY OF THE CONQUEST ACCOUNT HAS LITERARY AND THEOLOGICAL SIGNIFICANCE

Preface

This book began, as all academic books should, as a conversation. My theologian son (J. Harvey) and I (John) were discussing the problem that people have today with the conquest of Canaan. "Is God some kind of moral monster that he would commit or condone genocide?" This has indeed become a major thorn in the flesh for many Christians . . . and not only because the skeptics of the world have positioned it as the major indictment against the Bible, the God of the Bible, and Christians who take the Bible seriously. It has also become a catalyst for Christians to begin to doubt the Bible, doubt their God, and doubt their faith. As I listened to my son's thoughts, I realized that he was formulating solutions that I had not encountered before as he brought new perspectives into the issue. He was building on the foundational work that I have done on the nature of law in the ancient world and in the Bible, and on the covenant, as well as using hermeneutical methods that I have taught. But then he was following them through to their logical conclusions to craft an overall understanding of what is going on in the conquest. I found it refreshing and paradigm shifting. It reshaped the conversation for me, as I hope it will for readers.

I suggested he write a paper about it. So he began. After writing nearly nonstop for several days, he had passed twenty thousand words and was not near finished. We realized that this was going to be too long for a journal article and began thinking about a book. At first we were concerned that it might not be long enough for a book, but as the writing process continued, it became clear that having enough for a book would be no problem. It was only after I talked to Dan Reid at IVP about whether he was interested in such a book (and gratefully he was) that it occurred to us all that it would be best as another Lost World book. By the time we were done, we had to pay attention to economy of words so that it would not become too long. It is a complicated topic, and as a result readers who have read other books in the series will find this a more difficult read. Nevertheless, we have tried to honor our commitment to accessibility. Several technical sections seemed apropos, but we decided to make them available on the InterVarsity Press website. The logic should flow around those so that readers who don't want to get entangled or waylaid in the technical details do not have to. Yet, at the same time, that information will be available to those who desire to get it all.

I never intended for Lost World to become a series. In fact, after each one, I state emphatically to friends, family, and students that this will be the last Lost World book! But in our Bible reading, all of us continually encounter portions that we find difficult to penetrate and understand. We need whatever help we can get to position ourselves in the ancient Israelite audience and hear the text as they heard it.

The foundational principles of the book are ones that I have developed over the course of my career, but the specific ideas, logic, and flow of the argument, as well as much of the writing, are the work of my son. My role has been that of consultant for Hebrew and for the ancient Near East, and editor and conversation partner as the ideas developed. This book represents in the main my son's ideas, but I don't say that to distance myself from them. Where I was not initially on board with one piece or another, we would hash it out until we came to agreement. The ideas in the book have been shaped along the way by our conversations, and I have provided the Hebrew details and pointed him to resources from the ancient Near East to make the case.

The stock in trade of the Lost World series is that it uses information from a close reading of the Hebrew text (whether the broad scope of literature and theology or the focused studies of lexical semantics) and combines that with perspectives and information from the ancient cultural context of the Old Testament. This process produces interpretations that help us to transcend the shackles of our modern worldview and traditional readings to recapture the text as it would have been understood by the original author and audience. Our hope is that through that process a world, and indeed a text, that has been lost to us can be found.

Supplemental material for this book can be found at ivpress.com /the-lost-world-of-the-israelite-conquest. Three appendixes available there are "The Holiness Spectrum and Its Flaws," "Syntactico-Semantic Analysis of *Qdš*," and "Joshua 10:12-15 and Mesopotamian Celestial Omen Texts."

Abbreviations

AB   Anchor Bible

ARAB   Daniel David Luckenbill. *Ancient Records of Assyria and Babylonia.* 2 vols. Chicago: University of Chicago Press, 1926–1927

BJS   Brown Judaic Studies

CAD   *The Assyrian Dictionary of the Oriental Institute of the University of Chicago.* Chicago: The Oriental Institute of the University of Chicago, 1956–2006

CHD L-N   *The Hittite Dictionary of the Oriental Institute of the University of Chicago.* Vol. L-N. Edited by Harry A. Hoffner and Hans G. Güterbock. Chicago: University of Chicago Press, 1989. Available at http://oi.uchicago.edu/sites/oi.uchicago.edu/files/uploads/shared/docs/chd_l-n.pdf

COS   *The Content of Scripture.* Edited by William W. Hallo. 3 vols. Leiden: Brill, 1997–2002

JPS   Jewish Publication Society Torah Commentaries

NICOT   New International Commentary on the Old Testament

NIDOTTE   *New International Dictionary of Old Testament Theology and Exegesis.* Edited by Willem A. VanGemeren. 5 vols. Grand Rapids: Zondervan, 1997

SAAS   State Archives of Assyria Studies

TDOT   *Theological Dictionary of the Old Testament.* Edited by G. Johannes Botterweck and Helmer Ringgren. Translated

by John T. Willis et al. 15 vols. Grand Rapids: Eerdmans,
1974–2015

ZIBBCOT   *Zondervan Illustrated Bible Background Commentary,
Old Testament.* Edited by John H. Walton. 5 vols. Grand
Rapids: Zondervan, 2009

Introduction

Christians and skeptics alike struggle with the God of the Old Testament. With images of Jesus fresh in their minds from the New Testament, they are baffled with the portrait of a God of war and retribution in the Old Testament. How can such a portrait be reconciled with the peaceful love of God proclaimed in the New Testament? What of forgiveness and loving one's enemies? The situation only gets worse when readers arrive at the account of the conquest of the Promised Land recorded in Joshua, set up in the five books that precede it. Here God looks not only harsh and demanding, but also as if he is actually driving the Israelites to genocide of the native population of the land. Skeptics and sensitive Christians all ask, "How can Christians worship such a God?"

One response to this conundrum is to conclude that God is not really like that at all—that somehow these accounts of the conquest are actually just Israel's own political agenda, which they shifted onto their God, as one commonly finds in the ancient Near East. In order to steer criticism away from God, well-meaning interpreters portray Israel as justifying their land grab by claiming covenant rights and a martial God who has grown offended by the native population—propaganda, plain and simple.

Others readers, willing to accept God as the actual mover of these events and justified in whatever he does, endorse the Israelite invasion and furthermore appropriate the whole scenario to a variety of situations beyond the time of Israel. They stand ready to justify war as holy war against the enemies of God and fight in his name, demolishing cities and people deemed worthy of God's punishment. In their minds the book of Joshua gives marching orders to wipe out the infidels.

The options look bleak. If we reject the biblical account as simply propaganda, describing what Israel did but having no teaching for us, we face the prospect of a flawed or inconsistent method of interpretation when we try to take other parts of the Bible seriously. If we reject select elements in the biblical portrait of God, we go against the claims of Jesus to actually be the God of the Old Testament, and we resign ourselves to picking and choosing from the biblical material to simply shape God as we want him to be. If we accept both God and conquest as providing marching orders, somehow providing guidelines for us today, how do we avoid the appropriation made by fanatics?

Some despair and just conclude that the Old Testament is no longer of any value to us today. Others resign themselves to the idea that morality has no internal logic but is based solely on the inscrutable and arbitrary commands of a higher power. Still others insist that God will always act justly, so he must have had warrant for the extermination of the people of the land, and they try to reconstruct that warrant in order to justify God (theodicy).[1] Apologists begin to explore the nature of good. Yet much that is revealed in the Bible is not good, even by its own admission. How do we tell which parts reveal the good and which do not? Is something only good if it conforms to what we already believe the good to be? But where did this prior belief come from? Not from the Bible, for we are applying that understanding *to* the Bible. But if not from the Bible, how do we know that it conforms to God? So around and around it goes, as we try to extract God from what seems an embarrassing situation. And through it all,

---

[1]This was a common explanation that I (John) regularly offered to classes: God gets the benefit of the doubt.

atheists declare that all rational persons must disavow any God less moral than themselves.

In this book, we are not going to follow any of those paths. We believe that the solution to the supposed problem is better reading of the biblical text and better understanding of the ancient world in which the biblical Israelites were embedded. Armed with that information and its resulting interpretation, we will try to understand the theological meaning of this material for today.

As described briefly above, there is no shortage of proposed interpretations or explanations of the conquest. When weighing these various options against the understanding of the Bible as an ancient text, however, it becomes clear that virtually every element that forms the basis of these interpretations is misunderstood. The words and ideas that modern interpreters use to describe, defend, or dispute the conquest do not correspond to what those words and ideas mean in the ancient context of the biblical text.

When we consider the broader issue of the conquest, we base our solutions on, among other things, the answers we give to the following questions:

- What is the law, and what does it mean that the Canaanites did not obey it?[2]

- What does it mean to be holy?

- What sin did the Canaanites supposedly commit?

- What is the purpose of the covenant?

- What does it mean for God to punish?

- What does the Hebrew word *ḥerem* ("put under the ban"; "devote to destruction"; "utterly destroy") actually mean, and what is accomplished by doing it?

---

[2]We will use *Canaanites* throughout the book to refer to the peoples of the land rather than use the full list of various peoples. The exception will be when we believe that the text is making more specific statements about one of the groups in particular.

Many readers have ready answers to most or all of these that are relatively consistent across the spectrum of proposed interpretations. So we commonly hear that the law represents a list of God's moral commandments; to obey them is to be holy, and to disobey is to sin; the purpose of the covenant is to bring salvation (a combination of morality and monotheism) to all people; punishment is retribution for the crime of failing to be perfectly moral; and *herem* is the carrying out of the (death) sentence for the worst offenders. These elements are relatively consistent, though their specific connotations vary depending on whether the Canaanites are depicted as heinous sinners, overprivileged oppressors, or (conversely) victims of vicious imperial expansionism or a fanatical religious pogrom. Yet despite the consistency of the answers, when we examine the text as an ancient document, we discover that every single one of them is open to serious question.

Without the accurate answers to these questions, it is impossible to develop any kind of accurate understanding of the conquest as an event, or of what that event says or does not say about the God who commanded it, or what significance that event has for people today. Discovering those accurate answers is the purpose of this book. However, this task is neither simple nor straightforward.

If we want to reach an understanding about how we should go about reading a particular passage in the Bible, we have to understand how we should go about reading the Bible more generally. In particular, we want to have a way to approach the biblical text that we are comfortable applying to any part of it, as opposed to selectively choosing an approach based on whether it produces the conclusions that we want. Consequently, before we can discuss how to go about interpreting the conquest account specifically, we have to discuss how to go about interpreting the Bible. Once we understand how to learn what *any* passage is teaching, and how to apply that teaching to expectations of our behavior today, we will be able to apply that understanding to the conquest and be confident in the conclusions that result.

PART 1

INTERPRETATION

Reading the Bible Consistently Means Reading It as an Ancient Document

The problem of the conquest is not about what a tribe of Semitic people did or did not do in the Levant in the Bronze Age. The issue is all about what the Bible says or does not say. If we really are interested in what the Bible says, we should take particular care that our interpretations do not simply result in us construing the text to say whatever we would prefer it to say or think that it should say. One of the ways we avoid doing this is to make sure that methods we use to derive our conclusions are applied consistently to any biblical text. In other words, we should adopt a method and accept whatever conclusions result from it; we should not adopt a conclusion and then apply whatever method will enable us to reach it in that particular instance. But how should we go about forming a method for interpreting the biblical text?

Central to our approach to how the conquest should be interpreted and understood is that the Bible, while it has relevance and significance *for* us, was not written *to us*. It was written in a language that most of us do not understand, to a culture very different from ours, and to people who thought very differently from how we do. If we want to understand what something in the Bible means, we have to first understand what it *meant* to the people to whom it was originally written.

The Cultural River

To illustrate the difference between the modern and ancient cognitive environments, we propose the metaphor of a cultural river. In our modern world there exists a cultural river that is widely known. Among its currents are various ideas and ways of thinking, such as natural rights, freedom, capitalism, democracy, individualism, globalism, postcolonialism, postmodernism, market economy, scientific naturalism, an expanding universe, empiricism, and natural laws, just to name a few. Though the culture of the United States may well be the primary source for the cultural river described above, the currents of this river flow around the globe (globalism is another current in the river) and affect many other cultures. Some may well wish to float in these currents, while others may struggle to swim upstream against them, but everyone draws from its waters. Though the extent to which each culture immerses itself varies, we are all in the cultural river. We are all aware of and affected by the ideas and ways of thinking listed here, whether or not we support any or all of them.

In the ancient world, the cultural river of the time flowed through all of the diverse cultures: Egyptians, Hittites, Phoenicians, Canaanites, Aramaeans, Assyrians, and Babylonians—and the Israelites. And despite the variations among cultures and across the centuries, certain elements remained static. But the point is that currents common to the ancient cultures are not the currents found in our modern cultural river. In the ancient cultural river we would find currents such as community identity, the comprehensive and ubiquitous control of the gods, the role of kingship, divination, the centrality of the temple, the mediatory role of images, the reality of the spirit world and magic, and the movement of the celestial bodies as the communication of the gods. The Israelites sometimes floated on the currents of that cultural river without resistance, while at other times the revelation of God encouraged them to wade into the shallows to get out of the currents or to swim persistently upstream. But whatever the extent and nature of the Israelites' interactions with the cultural river, it is important to remember that they were situated in the ancient cultural river, not immersed in the modern ideas or mindsets of our cultural river.

The Bible is written *for* us (that is, we are supposed to benefit from its divine message and expect that it will help us to respond to the currents in our cultural river by transforming us), but it is not written *to* us (not in our language or in response to our culture). The message transcends culture, but it is given in a form that is fully ensconced in the ancient cultural river of Israel. The communicators that we encounter in the Old Testament are not aware of our cultural river; they neither anticipate it nor address its elements directly. We cannot therefore assume any of the constants or currents of our cultural river in Scripture. This means that if we are to interpret Scripture so as to receive the full impact of God's authoritative message, we have to recognize our modern influences in order to do the best we can to realize when they are affecting our understanding of the text. The Bible was written to the people of ancient Israel in the language of ancient Israel, and therefore its message operates according to the logic of ancient Israel.

Since the Bible was not written in terms of our modern cultural river, its purpose is not to teach us how to be good Americans, where *good* is defined by the cognitive environment of America. But by the same token, it was not written to teach the ancient Israelites how to be good Americans either; that is, it does not necessarily affirm that the things Americans like are good, the things Americans value are valuable, and so on.

At the same time, it was not written to teach the ancient Israelites how to be good citizens of the ancient world; for the same reason, it does not teach *us* that we should be good citizens by the standards of the ancient world, either. The Bible was not written in order to transform ancient thought to resemble modern thought, and neither was it written in order to simply affirm the values and ideas of the ancient cognitive environment and stamp them with divine authority for all time. But its teaching *is* presented in the context of the ancient cognitive environment, just as it is presented through the medium of ancient language. That does not mean that God wants us to think like ancient Israelites any more than it means that God wants us to speak Hebrew. But it does mean that if we want to understand what the Bible is teaching we have to know what the ancient cognitive environment was, in the same way that if we want to know what the Bible is saying we have to be able to read Hebrew. This is what we mean when we say that the cultural river or cognitive environment must be *translated.* Since we don't come to the text with the same mindset as the ancient people to whom it was written, we have to work to understand the currents that were flowing in the cultural river of the time and how they affected the message of the Bible for its original audience.

TRANSLATING THE CONQUEST

Because the Bible was written for us—that is, its teaching is not confined to the context of the ancient world—it means that we can apply its teaching within our own cognitive environment. However, because the logic and culture must be translated, we cannot apply that teaching by simply reading the logic of our own culture onto the words of the text. In order to translate properly, we have to understand the internal logic of the source, apply *that* logic to the text (as opposed to our own), and then rephrase the *conclusion* in terms that correspond to *our* logic. The conquest is a war, but if we want to understand the event, we cannot do so by using our modern understandings about war—what it is, what it is for, whether it is good or evil, how it should be waged, and so on. Instead, we have to look at the account in light of ancient understandings about war.

When we read phrases like "destroy them totally . . . and show them no mercy" (Deut 7:2), the meanings of those (English) words combine with the logic of our cognitive environment to produce a meaning of "do a thing that should never be done." Consequently, when we translate the conquest event today, we are inclined to draw parallels to other things that our culture defines as things that should never be done: the Holocaust, jihad, colonial imperialism, the Crusades, and so on. But in the logic of the cognitive environment of ancient Israel, God was not commanding Joshua to do a thing that should never be done. Those parallels are therefore an example of *bad cultural translation*. Joshua is conducting a war in a generally similar manner to the way wars were conducted in the ancient world (for further discussion, see proposition 17). Whether or not *we* prefer to conduct wars that way is irrelevant; what matters is not what modern Westerners think about the methods, but what ancient Near Easterners would have thought.

The ancient world did not perceive of war as an irreconcilable evil in the way that some modern people do. When the narrator of Ecclesiastes laments the grievous evil that is done under the sun, he does not mention war, or plague, or tsunamis, or the deaths of innocent children, or any of the other things that modern Westerners are inclined to decry as the worst of all evils. On the other hand, he does mention things such as improper burial (Eccles 6:3) and being forgotten (Eccles 1:11), which were horrifying for the ancients but are matters of relative indifference for us. Thus we can understand that such threats as "Your carcasses will be food for all the birds and the wild animals" (Deut 28:26) should not be interpreted in light of modern (neutral or positive) ideas of returning to nature and providing for the needs of animals; in the ancient mindset, improper burial condemned the victim to an eternity of restlessness in the afterlife and thus was essentially the conceptual equivalent of modern hellfire. In the same way, we cannot understand the meaning of the conquest accounts by imposing our modern animosity toward war and human suffering onto the words.

The Israelites would not have understood Moses' command to *herem* the Canaanite communities as "do a thing that you are inclined to think should never be done," even though that is what we feel when we hear the words. In contrast, the command to Ezekiel in Ezekiel 4:12 ("bake it . . . using human excrement for fuel") *is* intended to be heard as "do a thing that should never be done," but many of us would be relatively indifferent to doing this ourselves; if someone developed a process to turn human waste into an energy source, we would *celebrate*. We can understand that this prophetic sign-act is intended to be shocking, regardless of whether we are actually shocked by it. Likewise, we should understand that the conquest was not intended to be outrageous, even if we are outraged by it. The purpose of prophetic sign-acts is not to communicate ideal sentiments about human feces; neither is the command to Israel here intended to communicate ideal sentiments about *herem* and war. We don't have to share the sentiments portrayed in the language and logic of the text, but if we want to understand the text properly we have to know what those sentiments were and interpret accordingly. That is what this study is intended to examine.

Proposition 2

We Should Approach the Problem of the Conquest by Adjusting Our Expectations About What the Bible Is

The difficulties that the conquest account presents in the modern mind do not arise only as a result of the words of the biblical text. We are not simply experiencing the culture shock of unfamiliar ideas, or even reacting emotionally to a depiction of "man's inhumanity to man." We can read a book such as the *Iliad*, with its glorification of ancient cultural values that differ from ours and its graphic depictions of the sack of cities, without experiencing visceral horror. This is because the modern difficulties with the conquest account derive as much from what the Bible *is* as they do from what the Bible *says*. In other words, because Christians view the Bible as intended to be prescriptive for today, reading it is different from reading something we view as merely descriptive of ancient times.

The Bible Is the Authoritative Word of God

The most common rationalization of the conquest by far is to construe the account as an act of divine judgment on the people of Canaan as punishment for spectacular crimes that together constituted a greater evil than the evils of the wars that destroyed their society. As we will discuss throughout this work, such an interpretation cannot be derived from the text itself. But the difficulties that arise for modern readers from the text as written are mostly derived from ideas about what the Bible is and how it is supposed to be used. Whatever else the Bible is, it is most importantly the authoritative Word of God. But if we want to regard the Bible's teaching as an *authority* (as opposed to literature, records of an ancient culture, insightful fables, stories for children, a collection of inspirational and emotionally uplifting platitudes, an instrument of social control, and so on), and if we want to respect that authority, then the thing we must absolutely *not* do is to change what it says. By the same token, if we do not regard the Bible as an authority, then we have no compelling reason to rationalize what it says, for the same reasons that we have no compelling reason to rationalize what the *Iliad* says.

Our first premise, then, is that the Bible is a source of authoritative teaching. That is, we (the readers) are supposed to adjust our thinking and/or behavior in more or less specific ways based on what it says. This in turn means that we cannot adjust what it says to match the ways that we would prefer to behave; we have to work from the text as it is written. These premises are foundational and nonnegotiable, but they themselves do not produce the problem of the conquest. The problem of the conquest arises from a further series of assumptions about how to convert the text's content into behavior, and consequently about what that behavior turns out to be. In light of the Bible's authority, we assert that these assumptions, rather than the content of the Bible's text, should be adjusted. But that adjustment in turn requires examining what the assumptions actually are.

WHAT DO WE MEAN BY "WHAT THE BIBLE SAYS"?

We should not think of what the Bible says as a list of sentences (or verses) read in isolation; we have to consider the significance of the ideas that the words and sentences contain in light of broader considerations such as theme and genre. So, if we want to understand what, for example, "the city and all that is in it are *ḥerem* for the LORD" (Josh 6:17) means, in terms of the thought and behavior that we are supposed to adopt as a result of reading it, we first have to understand what all the words mean in their context. We cannot draw conclusions based on the meaning of the English words "utterly destroy," because those words mean different things for us from what the word *ḥerem* meant for the Israelites (see proposition 15). The question, "What does the Bible say?" cannot be effectively answered by asking, "What does this [word or verse] mean?" Rather, the question we should ask is, "Why is this in here?" In the process of answering that question, we will have to consider what the words mean and what ideas are being conveyed by the various units of discourse, but we will also be able to consider the broader questions of context that are crucial to discerning meaning.

Of course, it is theoretically possible that the question, "Why is this in here?" will yield an answer of "So that you will do exactly what it tells you to do," but that possibility is yet another assumption that should not be simply taken for granted. If we want to know why any given passage is in the Bible, we must first have some understanding of why *any* passage is in the Bible; in other words, we must know why we have a Bible. We have accepted as a premise that the Bible is a source of authority that expects an adjustment in the thought and behavior of its readers. Therefore, at a superficial level we could conclude that God gave us the Bible because God wants particular thoughts or behaviors from those who read it. But thoughts and behaviors are desired for a purpose, and producing them is a means to an end. When we know *why* God wants us to think and behave in certain ways, we will understand why we have a Bible and, in turn, we will be in a position to understand how any particular part of the Bible, and the conquest in particular, serves that purpose.

We propose that the Bible is given to us not to provide a list of rules for behavior but to reveal God's plans and purposes to us, which in turn will allow us to participate with him in those plans and purposes. We believe that God's plans and purposes are good and that by our participation we will contribute to the manifestation of that goodness in some way. When we get to the conquest, it is easy to become confused about how God's plans and purposes represented there are good and how they should affect our thinking about his goodness and ours. We therefore must turn our attention briefly to the idea of God's goodness.

The Bible Does Not Define Goodness for Us or Tell Us How to Produce Goodness, but Instead Tells Us About the Goodness God Is Producing

When we read the conquest account today, we normally approach the text with the assumption that it will contain rules or demonstrations that we should follow or imitate in order to increase human happiness or decrease human suffering, because we believe that this is what God has always wanted to do because God is good. It is this assumption, and not the content of the text per se, that produces the problem we encounter with the conquest. Thus the solution to that problem must first be approached not by examining the words of the text, but by examining our assumptions about what the text is and what its teaching is supposed to accomplish.

One fundamental tenet of the Christian tradition is that God is good. Presumably, then, God's reasons for acting in particular ways are supposed to lead to some manifestation of goodness in the world. Since providing us with the Bible was one of God's actions, we can assume that the thoughts and behaviors that the Bible's teaching are intended to produce are supposed to lead, in turn, to some manifestation of goodness in the world. The primary difficulty with the conquest account is that it seems to advocate behaviors that, if carried out, did not produce goodness then and are incapable of doing so now. However, this difficulty arises from several further assumptions about how the words in the text are supposed to be converted into behaviors and also about what exactly goodness is. These assumptions must be examined before we can draw any conclusions about the Bible's teaching and the conquest.

The examination of the way that God's goodness is manifested in reality is called *moral theology*. There are several different approaches to the question of how God's goodness is manifested, but two in particular are of interest to us. The first is called *nomism* and teaches that God produces goodness in the world by providing rules for people to follow, then enforcing those rules either in real time, through the dispensing of blessing or calamity, or in eternity, by means of heaven and hell. Interpreters vary on their understanding of how these rules are conveyed; some think they are known innately by all people, and some think they are deduced through reason, but for our purposes the most important means of conveyance is that the rules are written down in the Bible. A nomistic approach to the Bible sees the text as a collection of commands, demonstrations, and illustrations of principles that, if obeyed or imitated, will produce goodness.

This approach creates an immediate difficulty with passages like the conquest account, since such passages contain commands or record actions that we do not think produce goodness. Consequently, the tendency of many nomistic interpreters is to infer all manner of horrific crimes committed by the Canaanites in order to make Joshua's actions *seem* good and thereby form the basis of a rule that we can feel comfortable imitating ("God commands us to remove evil from the world by taking action against evil people"). This interpretation is problematic because, as we will demonstrate in parts two and three, most specifically in proposition eight, the text does not support this indictment of the Canaanites. Reading an indictment of the Canaanites into the text requires changing what the text says, in which case we are not treating it as having authority.

Other nomistic interpreters decide that, since God issued commands to Joshua and the Bible records Joshua's actions in carrying them out, the outcome that transpired *must* have been good, even if it does not seem that way to us. Since God's commands produce goodness, Joshua's actions define what goodness is, and if we think otherwise, then our perception is wrong. This interpretation is problematic as well. Fortunately, nomism is not the only possible approach to moral theology.

An alternative view is that God produces goodness in the world by taking actions that serve a good purpose. This could theoretically consist of giving rules, but goodness in this conception is something that God produces, not something that God teaches us how to produce. The difference is most clearly demonstrated by Joseph's statement in Genesis 50:20: "You intended to harm me, but God intended it for good." God orchestrated Joseph's slavery, imprisonment, and elevation (Gen 45:8, "It was not you who sent me [to Egypt], but God") to serve a good purpose. It does not mean that Joseph's brothers, or Potiphar, or even Joseph himself (Gen 47:21) are demonstrating behavior that, if imitated, will produce goodness. The Joseph narrative exists to describe something that God did, not to illustrate things that God wants us to do, either specifically or even in principle. Joseph's brothers contributed to God's good purposes specifically by selling their brother into slavery; that does not mean that we can contribute to God's good purposes by selling our own siblings into slavery. It does not even mean broadly that we can do evil things that should never be done (of which the text offers selling a brother as an example) as long as they contribute to God's greater purpose of "the saving of many lives" (Gen 50:20). Neither the details of the particular methods nor the details of the purpose itself are provided by the text. Joseph was sent to Egypt to provide a means to preserve Jacob's bloodline (Gen 45:7, "to preserve for you a remnant on earth and to save your lives by a great deliverance"), but that in turn was a means to preserve the covenant with Abraham, which was made in service of a larger purpose that we can in no way reproduce. (For a further discussion of the covenant, see proposition eight.)

In this approach to moral theology, the same is true of the entire Bible. The Bible is a record of God's actions that we are supposed to understand, not a compilation of rules that we are supposed to obey. But this approach still has to explain how reading about God's actions is supposed to lead to any implications for our thought and behavior. In this approach, the actions of Joseph's brothers have no implications for us; the actions of Joshua and his army have no implications for us; why should the actions of God have any implications for us?

WHAT DOES IT MEAN TO BE GOOD?

That God does not tell us how (or expect us) to produce goodness does not therefore mean that goodness has nothing to do with us. We already understand this basic idea in the context of salvation. If we want to be saved, we have to make specific adjustments to our thoughts and behaviors, but those thoughts and behaviors do not themselves produce our salvation; Christ's death and resurrection does that (that is, what God does produces salvation, not what we do). Further, the Bible does not tell us what particular actions we have to take; we draw our understanding of these from our own religious tradition (that is, our own cognitive environment). The text does not specify anything beyond a generic "Believe in the Lord Jesus" (Acts 16:31) and baptism of water and the Spirit (Jn 3:5). It provides no specific creed or catechism and does not specify infant baptism, believer's baptism, the sacrament of chrismation, the sinner's prayer, or any other particular action. It certainly does not tell us that if we want to be saved we should do what Christ did.[1] God does not tell us how to produce our own salvation; instead, he tells us how we can participate in the salvation that he has produced. Goodness works the same way. God's actions are performed toward a good purpose; our expected actions are not intended to produce goodness but to allow us to participate in the goodness that God is producing. But then what exactly should we expect that participation to look like? This leads us to examine the question of what goodness is.

Our modern Western system of ideas, which historians and philosophers call *humanism*, is based on the belief that human happiness constitutes the highest value and therefore the highest good (since goodness is related to value). Happiness in turn is generally defined in terms of an absence of pain (physical, psychological, or existential), such that our word *evil* (the opposite of *good*) is synonymous with human suffering. Everyone who participates in the cognitive environment of the modern West, both Christian and non-Christian, shares this idea, although Christians and non-Christians often have different ideas of the means by which the greatest happiness might be achieved (power, pleasure, and material prosperity versus charity, simplicity, existential fulfillment, etc.) and also about the various institutions and social structures that can best bring it about. Religions normally advocate themselves as the means to human happiness, while what we call secular humanism advocates a combination of irreligious government and the sciences to achieve human happiness. Regardless of the means or particulars, human happiness remains the highest ideal.[2] It is part of our cognitive environment and is the substance of what we mean when we use the English word *good*.

---

[1]Even, for example, Arianism and Pelagianism, which say that Christ earned his own salvation by a moral life that we are intended to imitate, expect that imitation to follow extrapolations of general universal moral principles (that is, "show compassion to the sick and the poor") rather than specific instructions lifted from the text ("choose disciples, make a mess in a temple, ride a donkey, and get yourself executed for blasphemy").

[2]In education circles the current terminology is *human flourishing*.

The cognitive environment of the ancient Near East, however, did not hold human happiness as the highest ideal. Their highest ideal is probably best described by our English word *order*. For ancient Near Easterners, a thing was good not based on the extent to which it produced human pleasure or alleviated human suffering, but the extent to which it was functioning as it was intended to.[3] There is some overlap between happiness and order, but while we moderns tend to value order only insofar as it serves as a means to human happiness, the ancients would have valued human happiness only insofar as it occurred in the appropriate context within the ordered system. In the ancient perspective, failing to harm or destroy a people who are behaving contrary to order would be bad no matter how happy they are; likewise, harming or destroying those people would be good no matter how much they suffer. This was part of the cognitive environment of the ancient world and was what ancient writers meant when they used the word that translators render in English as *good*.

It is important to recognize that the Bible does not advocate for either of these definitions of goodness. The Bible was not written to teach the ancient Israelites how to value human happiness instead of order. Neither was it written to teach modern Westerners that they should value order instead of human happiness. But because the Bible was written in Hebrew to an ancient Near Eastern audience, its language and imagery are expressed in terms of their conceptions and their ideology, not ours. Thus, when the Bible wants to depict something as good, it describes that thing in terms, concepts, and illustrations that the ancient world associated with order, not in ways associated with human happiness. Consequently, things that the Bible portrays as good do not always correlate with the things *we* associate with human happiness. Some of the things that ancients saw as good

---

[3]For a more detailed discussion of the definition of the Hebrew word *tôb* ("good") as "properly functioning," see John Walton, *The Lost World of Genesis One* (Downers Grove, IL: InterVarsity Press, 2009), 50.

are also things that we moderns happen to also see as good, such as fidelity in marriage, respect for personal property, aversion to murder, and the need to care for the poor; others are not, such as debt slavery, blood vengeance, and respect for social hierarchy. But in *neither case* does the Bible exist to tell us what goodness is in the absolute ideal sense, or how to produce it. The Bible exists to tell us what God is doing, and it describes what God is doing in terms of the language, logic, and values of the culture to which it was originally written.

What this means is that the idea of goodness described in the text needs to be *translated*, not simply adopted. If we obeyed the particular instructions of the Old Testament text, we would become good citizens of the ancient Near East. If we obeyed the particular instructions of the New Testament text, we would become good citizens of classical Rome. But what we are supposed to be is good citizens of the modern West, for the same reasons that the Israelites (the original audience of the Old Testament) were supposed be good citizens of the ancient world, and the early Christians (the original audience of the New Testament) were supposed to be good citizens of the classical world. We will discuss what those reasons might be in propositions eleven and twenty-one, but for now the point is that obeying the text without translating can potentially lead to the opposite behavior that it intends. A good citizen of the ancient or classical world is not a good citizen of the modern world, because the modern world is different from the ancient and classical world.

THE PROBLEM OF PROGRESS

Many people today who misread the Bible do so as a result of failing to properly translate its ideas. As a result, some people view the Bible's text as containing a record of God's absolute ideals, which were dictated to ancient Israel in an effort to alter their thinking to become like modern people, or at least more like modern people than they already were. This is because we see modern ideas as being better than ancient ideas. While it is reasonable for us to *prefer* modern ideas (if for no other reason than simply because they are ours), it is *not* reasonable to project our ideas onto God and ascribe them to him simply because we prefer them. This is why, if we wish to treat the text as a source of authority, it is so important to make sure that we are careful and consistent in describing what it actually says, instead of intuitively describing what we think it should say. We must never appropriate divine authority for ourselves, and we must never assume that our ideals and perspectives correlate with God's.

The idea that modern conceptions are inherently superior to ancient conceptions is itself a product of our modern Western cognitive environment. This idea, called *progress*, assumes that all of history is moving toward a common (though ambiguous) goal, developing increasing levels of efficacy and efficiency over time. Those iterations that appear earlier are seen as inferior to those that followed, simply by virtue of having occurred earlier in time (and having been replaced). This theory of progress is applied to all spheres of human experience, from philosophy and technology to morality and religion. In Christian theology, a primary example of a progressive model is called *Heilsgeschichte*, or "salvation history." It attempts to trace the progress of God's saving work through the various inferior covenants, from Adam to Noah to Abraham to Moses, until finally Christ appears and renders all the defective prior stages obsolete.[4]

The assumption that underlies all progressive models is that every iteration throughout the historical sequence is trying to accomplish the same purpose in more or less the same way, with the only difference being the level of effectiveness. The value of each iteration is measured according to how well it compares to a (usually hypothetical) ideal. A metaphor for how a progressive system works comes from technology. The ideal desktop computer is fast and has good

---

[4]Another example is the theological system known as dispensationalism.

graphics. If my computer is slower and has worse graphics than yours, it is an inferior computer, because it deviates further from the ideal that all desktop computers are measured against. Applied to the Bible and moral theology, progressive ideology assumes three things: (1) that the ideal (that is, the definition of goodness) the Old Testament is advocating is the same as the definition we use (that is, the production of human happiness), (2) that it is the same definition that the New Testament uses, and (3) that it was inferior in its ability to produce this ideal (which is why it was replaced). Modern anti-Christians extend the same claim to the New Testament—that is, that it is inferior for today and needs to be replaced. We will examine this more thoroughly when we discuss the specific application of the Old Testament in proposition twenty. However, because the progressive model of history is a modern invention, these ideas cannot be derived from the biblical text itself.[5] In fact, the ancient people who wrote the Bible were more inclined toward the reverse; what was older and established was superior to what was innovative and novel.[6] But neither the ancient cognitive environment nor modern anachronisms are useful for constructing a way of evaluating the ideals of different periods of history and developments in culture.

Although we should understand God's actions as purposeful (that is, working toward a goal), we should not imagine that God furthers that goal by producing progress. We should not imagine that God is constantly shaping humanity to ever-higher levels of goodness or morality that will eventually achieve the ideal. Neither should we imagine that we represent the society that has actually achieved the ideal. An

---

[5]This is true even though it is possible to anachronistically read progressive ideology into some texts, as for example is commonly done in parts of Hebrews. See proposition nine for a discussion of the problems of assigning anachronistic ideas to biblical texts.

[6]"Whereas we are future-oriented, akin to change, and conditioned to move ahead—the past being left behind to the point of even ignoring it—the biblical person is past-oriented, loath of change, and akin to tradition and the people's accumulated lore." Meir Malul, *Knowledge, Control, and Sex: Studies in Biblical Thought, Culture, and Worldview* (Tel Aviv: Archeological Center Publication, 2002), 431.

alternative model to understanding a process toward achieving a goal is what we could call *procedure*, as opposed to progress. In a procedural model, every iteration serves a different purpose toward a common goal, which could not be achieved without the completion of every step. The metaphor for a procedural model is the process of baking a cake. There is a final, ideal cake at the end, and some of the steps will more closely resemble it in terms of their attributes than others, but the various stages in the recipe are evaluated not on the basis of how closely they resemble the ideal, final cake but of how necessary they are to *produce* the final product.

So, for example, some people wonder why the conquest account and similar passages are included in the text, because they do not see these passages as providing instructions or examples that are useful for producing human happiness. Other people add or remove elements from those passages until they look like they might become useful for producing human happiness. Both of these approaches are misguided; evaluating biblical texts (whose language and logic belong to an ancient cognitive environment) based on whether they match the modern ideal is like evaluating each step of a cake recipe based on whether it tastes like cake. If we skip the "mix eggs, milk, and vanilla extract" step because it does not taste like cake, or if we add sugar and pudding to the mixture until it does, we will not wind up with a functional cake at the end of the baking process. This defeats the purpose of even having a recipe in the first place. Likewise, if we change what the biblical text says so that we can use it in the way we would prefer to use it, we won't ever get the result that it was actually intended to produce, in which case we might as well not even have it at all.

On the other extreme from progress, and misguided for similar reasons, is another modern idea, called *relativism*. Where progress asserts only one single ideal, which different cognitive environments achieve with varying degrees of success, relativism asserts that there are no such things as ideals at all. In other words, for relativism, since none of the steps of the recipe taste like cake, there is no cake. For some people, cake tastes like eggs and vanilla extract; for others it tastes like flour and butter; for others it tastes like a greased baking tin; each of these is an equally valid interpretation of cake. Applied to the Bible and moral theology, relativism says that, if the Bible does not tell us what God's ideal of goodness is, then God has no ideal of goodness at all. Or, said another way, since the ideal of goodness that God presented to the Israelites is not an ideal of goodness to us (by virtue of belonging to a different cognitive environment), then God's actions to Israel have no relevance at all for us.

The relativist approach, like the progressive approach, is misguided because it misunderstands what the Bible is for. The Bible does not tell us what God's ideal of goodness is because the purpose for which the Bible was written does not require us to know that. The individual steps of a recipe do not each tell you how to make something that tastes like cake; instead, they tell you how to make something that will go through a variety of processes to eventually produce something that tastes like cake. We might imagine bakers on an assembly line, each producing one step of a recipe over and over. None of them are personally making cake, and none of them, by examining the thing they are making, will have any real understanding of what the cake that comes out of the factory at the end will be like. In this metaphor God is the factory, and the cake is the goodness that God is acting to produce. The Bible does not tell us what that final product is; the Bible tells us how to do our part on the assembly line. If we fail to translate the teaching properly, we will fail to do our part in the process; we will not produce goodness, and we will not contribute to the procedure. If we do translate properly, we will be able to contribute to the procedure, but we ourselves will still produce no goodness. This is because, once again, the Bible was not written to tell us how to produce goodness; it was written to tell us how to participate in the goodness that God is producing.

TRANSLATION VERSUS RATIONALIZATION

We believe by faith that God is good. The choice to serve God includes the recognition that God's purposes produce a higher good than we could produce ourselves. If we believe that serving God will simply serve as a means to bring about our own idea of goodness, then we aren't really serving God; instead, we are using God as a means to serve ourselves. But if God's ideal of goodness is different from ours, there will be areas where they do not overlap. Some of what is good to God will seem nonsensical to us; some of it might even seem evil. A final example illustrates how this works.

Consider a child who is forced to experience the "evil" of eating Brussels sprouts. The child's own determination of what is good and evil is based on taste, while the parent's higher determination that eating Brussels sprouts is good is based on nutrition. We can only evaluate taste, so we have to trust God that even things that taste bad (that is, that we perceive as evil, based on the definitions of our cognitive environment) are somehow nonetheless good. At the same time, we should not convince ourselves that Brussels sprouts taste good, nor should we recalibrate our definition of "tastes good" to put Brussels sprouts at the top. We can recognize that Brussels sprouts taste terrible while simultaneously not believing that our parents are evil for subjecting us to this terrible taste, because we understand that our parents have other concerns. (The metaphor breaks down at this point because, while we could theoretically gain the knowledge of nutrition that our parents have, we can never gain any knowledge of the higher good that God is working to bring about. In terms of the metaphor, we can know that it is good to be fed Brussels sprouts, but we can never understand why.)

God through the Bible does not tell us how to produce his ideal of goodness, but God through Moses did not tell Joshua how to produce it, either. The conquest account is written in such a way that the ancient audience would have understood it as good according to the metric of establishing and sustaining order (see proposition fourteen), but the ancient definition of *good* does not match God's ideal any more than the modern definition of establishing and sustaining human happiness does, for the same reasons. The text does not affirm that killing the Canaanites is good, because killing the Canaanites is not the objective of the conquest. The objective of the conquest is to fulfill the covenant, which in turn is only a part in a larger process leading up to the new covenant, which in itself is only a part of the process leading up to the new creation. The conquest account was not written in order to tell us what we should do; it was written to teach us about what the Israelite covenant is, which in turn is necessary for us to know what the new covenant is, which in turn is necessary for us to know what specifically we are supposed to do in our own cultural context to play our part in the new covenant. That is the story that we are going to explore in the remainder of this book.

But that story is written in Hebrew, and it is written according to the logic of the ancient Near Eastern cognitive environment. Therefore, if we want to understand it, we will have to translate it. But before we will be able to do that, we have to stop imagining that the purpose of the conquest account is to teach us that God's ideal of goodness involves us going out and killing Canaanites (or whomever they represent today) and then either adopting that idea or rationalizing it away by embellishing the text so that killing Canaanites seems good according to our own logic.

PART 2

THE CANAANITES ARE NOT DEPICTED AS GUILTY OF SIN

The Bible Teaches Clearly and Consistently That Affliction by God Cannot Automatically Be Attributed to Wrongdoing on the Part of the Victim

The book of Job tells the story of a man who suffers a great calamity carried out at the command of God. His friends arrive and bear witness to the devastation. They have not heard the commendation of Job to the heavenly council (Job 1:8); they see a man, perhaps not flawless, but not sufficiently worse than all other men to warrant such catastrophe. Unable to conceive of a God who would strike a person without cause, they bring coherence to their worldview and its flawed conception of deity by hypothesizing all manner of monstrous transgressions on the part of Job. Their indictment draws on all of the wisdom of their culture, on the force of logic, and even on claims of the revelation of God. But the text tells a different story: Job is blameless and upright, and God has indeed struck him without cause (Job 2:3).

When we read about the conquest of Canaan, we find ourselves in a similar position to Job's friends. We see a catastrophe of devastation carried out by the command of God. As in the case of Job, we can see no remarkable difference between the victims singled out for calamity and those living beside them who remain unscathed. Can God strike people without cause? Like Job's friends, many readers of the biblical narrative say no. Like Job's friends, they conjure up all manner of heinous indictments, with appeals to logic, tradition, or even revelation from God to support the claim. But, like Job's friends, this worldview derives from a flawed conception of deity. The text tells a different story.

THE RETRIBUTION PRINCIPLE

The retribution principle is the belief that the righteous will prosper and the wicked will suffer, both in proportion to the degree of righteousness and wickedness. This is sometimes extended to the idea that those prospering must be righteous, and those suffering must be wicked. We understand easily that the Bible denies this extended idea in terms of prosperity; we know, for example, that God's gifts, blessings, and grace are not dispensed based on merit. What we often fail to appreciate is that the reverse is also true, that suffering can also be dispensed without merit. We fail to appreciate this because we commonly conflate the idea that God is good with the idea that God's purpose is to make us happy unless we specifically do something that compels him by virtue of his moral nature to do otherwise. As discussed in proposition three, however, God's purposes are not simply to make us happy as long as we are moral.[1] God dispenses grace in absence of merit, not to make us happy but to suit his purposes. God can dispense suffering, likewise in absence of merit, for the same reasons. Jesus himself suffered without cause, but for a purpose. God's actions are not limited to responses to our behavior (or misbehavior).

---

[1] Compare the phenomenon called moralistic therapeutic deism, identified by Christian Smith in *Souls in Transition: The Religious and Spiritual Lives of Emerging Adults* (New York: Oxford University Press, 2009).

The book of Job is a thought experiment designed to examine the retribution principle and its limitations.[2] The opening scene is set in heaven, where the adversarial character (*haśśāṭān*) proposes that God's policies of blessing the righteous are misguided. After all, if righteousness invariably brings blessing, who can say whether someone is truly righteous or is selfishly pursuing personal gain? The adversary argues that, if God withdraws Job's blessings, Job will reveal that his motives have always been selfish by cursing God (Job 1:11). This in turn will demonstrate that the policy of blessing the righteous is flawed because it undermines the actual practice of righteousness, which should serve God for nothing. This emphasis deals with the more difficult side of the retribution equation, for it is much easier to discuss why the wicked prosper.

God submits his policies to the test, and Job's suffering begins. At this point, Job offers a policy criticism of his own; blessing the righteous may be ethically counterproductive, but allowing them to suffer is theologically counterintuitive. Nonetheless, if Job succeeds in forcing God to account for himself and explain his actions in terms of cause, the adversary will win the case; in doing so, God would be forced to admit that the world fundamentally operates in terms of the retribution principle and that deviations from its tenets are bad policy or poor execution on the part of God. God never gives such an account in the book of Job; if we wish to represent God properly, we should not rush to give account on his behalf, either. God's wisdom, not God's justice, forms the basis of God's activity in the world. Faith trusts that God is wise and that therefore his purposes are good, even if they don't seem that way to any system we can understand. God does not need to be defended; he wants to be trusted.

---

[2]This section adapted from John Walton, *Job*, NIV Application Commentary (Grand Rapids: Zondervan, 2012), 26-27.

THE RETRIBUTION PRINCIPLE
AS AN EXPLANATION FOR SUFFERING

The retribution principle inherently conceives of suffering (or prosperity) as a product of God's justice. However, we will never be in a position to evaluate God's justice. In order to appraise the justice of a decision, we must have all the facts, for justice can be derailed if we do not have all the information. If we try to issue a verdict on God's behalf, we only create a cosmic kangaroo court, in which evidence is admitted only when it supports a preconceived verdict; this is the *opposite* of justice. We cannot reach an affirmation about God's justice through our own limited insight or experience. The book of Job wants to transform how we think about God's work in the world and about our responses to observations of suffering.

While the Bible never affirms that those prospering must be righteous and those suffering must be wicked (and indeed takes some pains to undermine this), the retribution principle (the righteous will prosper and the wicked will suffer) itself is conditionally affirmed as representative of the functioning order of the world. Nonetheless, the world order is not a promise. The world order is not founded in the inherent nature of God (although God created it) and places no compulsion on God to act in accord with it (though it is a tool for his purposes). Accordingly, we need to recognize the tension between the retribution principle as *theodicy* (an explanation for suffering as a manifestation of the justice of God) and the retribution principle as *theology* (insight into God's nature and purposes). The affirmations of the retribution principle in the biblical text (e.g., Prov 3:33) are intended to be theological in nature; by this we mean they demonstrate that God delights in bringing blessing to his faithful ones and takes seriously the need to punish evil. Both blessing the righteous and punishing the wicked serve God's purposes. In contrast, many people in Israel and the ancient world, along with many people today, are inclined to wield the principle as *theodicy*; that is, we want to apply it to our expectations and experiences in life, and in that process to understand the reasons behind suffering. The role of the book of Job is to perform the radical surgery that separates theology from theodicy, contending that in the end God's justice (and the goodness of his purposes) must be accepted on faith rather than worked out philosophically.

An alternative approach to suffering is described in John 9. Jesus' disciples encounter a man, no worse than any other man, who has nonetheless suffered a calamity from God; he has been born blind. Like Job's friends, they seek to defend the justice of God by impugning the man with imaginary crimes: "Who sinned, this man or his parents?" Rather than offer a cause to rationalize the damage, Jesus instead offers a purpose: "This happened so that the works of God might be displayed." God can strike without cause, but God does not strike without purpose. This was true of Job; it was true of the man born blind; and, as we will see, it was also true of the people of Canaan. Job suffered terribly, but his friends were nonetheless wrong to assume that his suffering was earned through evil. The man born blind also suffered, but Jesus' disciples were wrong to assume that his suffering was earned through evil. When we see the people of Canaan suffer, therefore, we dare not assume that their suffering must have been earned through evil. Biblical theology does not allow us to automatically suppose that punishment for wrongdoing is the motivation behind God's actions.

Nonetheless, some interpreters point to a handful of passages as evidence that the text indicts the Canaanites for sin. We will examine these passages over the next few propositions to demonstrate that this is not the case.

None of the Usual Textual Indicators for Divine Retribution Occur in the Case of the Canaanites

Even though the biblical text overall is clear that retribution, and therefore wrongdoing, cannot be automatically assumed from observation of calamity, it is also undeniable that wrongdoing *can* result in divine retribution in the form of calamity. Fortunately, it is possible to tell the difference in the Bible, because the text is reasonably clear that an offense has occurred whenever it intends to depict punishment for offense. Accordingly, we will now briefly examine the elements we would expect to see if the biblical authors intended the conquest to be interpreted as an act of retribution.

WE WOULD EXPECT TO SEE A FORMAL INDICTMENT

In the case of destruction as a punishment, we would expect to see a formal statement of the crimes of the accused by the document's narrator, or in the form of an oracle if the genre is prophecy. For example, in the case of the flood, the narrator tells us, "The LORD saw how great the wickedness of the human race had become on the earth, and that every inclination of the thoughts of the human heart was only evil all the time" (Gen 6:5), and then also that "the earth was corrupt in God's sight and was full of violence. God saw how corrupt the earth had become, for all the people on earth had corrupted their ways" (Gen 6:11-12). In the case of Sodom, the narrator says, "The people of Sodom were wicked and were sinning greatly against the LORD" (Gen 13:13). In the case of the house of Jeroboam, the narrator says, "Jeroboam did not change his evil ways. . . . This was the sin of the house of Jeroboam that led to its downfall and to its destruction from the face of the earth" (1 Kings 13:33-34), and, after the family is annihilated, "This happened because of the sins Jeroboam had committed and had caused Israel to commit, and because he aroused the anger of the LORD, the God of Israel" (1 Kings 15:30). In the case of Baasha, the narrator describes how Zimri "destroyed the whole family of Baasha, in accordance with the word of the LORD . . . because of all the sins Baasha and his son Elah had committed and had caused Israel to commit, so that they aroused the anger of the LORD, the God of Israel" (1 Kings 16:12-13). The whole book of Judges is a cycle of the narrator saying "the Israelites did evil in the eyes of the LORD," after which they suffer oppression as a consequence (Judg 2:11). Finally, a full third of the canon is dedicated to prophetic oracles describing the case against Israel that leads to the exile (see also 2 Kings 17:7-23, where the narrator summarizes the case against Israel, and 2 Kings 23:26-27, where he does the same for Judah). However, there is no direct exposition from narrators or prophetic oracles describing the offense of the Canaanites.

WE WOULD EXPECT TO SEE THE MISBEHAVIOR OF THE DEFENDANT DOCUMENTED

Sometimes the text doesn't dictate an offense through expository dialogue but instead describes it through narrative. So in the case of Sodom we don't have much exposition, but an entire chapter illustrates the behavior of the citizens and shows them acting in a manner beyond the limits of propriety as understood by every ancient society (Gen 19:1-13). This is so that when a character (God) says, "The outcry against Sodom and Gomorrah is so great and their sin is so grievous that I will go down and see if what they have done is as bad as the outcry that has reached me" (Gen 18:20-21), and then a character (an angel) says, "The outcry to the LORD against its people is so great that he has sent us to destroy it" (Gen 19:13), the reader knows that the offense is something that exists in reality and not only in the minds of those depicted as performing the evaluation or those producing the outcry (whoever they were).[1] When the tribe of Benjamin is punished in Judges 20:10, a character recounts their offense (Judg 20:4-7), but the narrator also describes it as it happens in Judges 19:14-28, confirming what the character says. We see the Amalekites assault Israel in Exodus 17:8, which confirms what characters say in Deuteronomy 25:17-18 and 1 Samuel 15:2. Jeroboam's offensive behavior is recorded in detail in 1 Kings 12:25–13:34. The covenant violations of Israel and Judah are documented extensively throughout the books of Judges, Samuel, and Kings. However, while a small handful of verses appear to depict characters describing or alluding to offensive behavior on the part of the Canaanites (most notably Lev 18:11-24; Deut 9:4-7; Gen 15:16; these verses will all be addressed later), that we never see those accusations substantiated by narrative should make us at least curious, if not suspicious, and lead us to examine the issue more carefully (see propositions six and twelve).

WE WOULD EXPECT THE CANAANITES TO UNDERSTAND
WHAT IS HAPPENING TO THEM AND REACT ACCORDINGLY

The text does not always record the reaction of people to an impending destruction (for example, there is no reaction recorded in the flood account), but when the narrator records a reaction, we would expect that the reaction has been recorded for the purpose of

---

[1]Narrative as a genre can report the perspectives, opinions, and rhetoric of its characters without necessarily endorsing or affirming those stances. In practice it can be difficult to tell the difference.

helping the reader understand the event. If an event is intended to be understood as divine retribution, we would expect the reported reaction to indicate that the people understand that they are experiencing judgment. The Canaanites do give some indication that they understand what is happening, but that understanding does not consist of their thinking they are being punished for misdeeds. Rahab tells the spies, "I know that the LORD has given you this land and that a great fear of you has fallen on us" (Josh 2:9), but the source of that fear is not guilt, but rather observation of Yahweh's power (Josh 2:10-11; also Josh 5:1). Likewise, the Gibeonites are afraid of Israel's military (Josh 9:9-10) because they know about Moses' imperative to drive them out (Josh 9:24).

If the Canaanites' fear were derived from an expectation of the wrath of Israel's God, rather than an observation of the military prowess of Israel's God, we would expect them to defend themselves by offering appeasement to Israel's God. This is what the Ninevites do in Jonah 3:5-10. This is also what Saul tries in 1 Samuel 15:24-30 when he hears of the judgment on his dynasty (1 Sam 15:23), though in that case it does not work; and this is also what a prophet prescribes in Joel 2:12-17, in which case it does. Joshua works to appease Yahweh after the Israelite defeat at Ai, both with contrition before the ark (Josh 7:6) and by dealing with the perpetrator of the offense (Josh 7:26). The Israelites do not attempt appeasement to avert the exile (Josiah's reforms perhaps excepted; 2 Kings 22:19), but this is not because they don't understand that Yahweh is angry, but rather because they don't think the exile will actually occur because they believe they are protected by the temple (see, e.g., Jer 7:4-11). When the exile does occur, the diaspora is not confused about why.[2] In contrast, the Canaanites

---

[2]See for example Sara Japhet, *From the Rivers of Babylon to the Highlands of Judah* (Winona Lake, IN: Eisenbrauns, 2006), 379: "The people of the Restoration are presented as being fully aware of God's justice and having completely internalized the principles of retribution. They are permeated with a sense of guilt, take full responsibility for their actions, and repeatedly confess their sins."

fully understand that Israel's attack is imminent. However, instead of offering appeasement to Yahweh, as the Ninevites do, they negotiate for peace with (or try to defeat) Israel's army. It is interesting to note that in Joshua 7:5 the reaction of Israel to its own defeat is the same as that of Canaan in regard to Israel's army in Joshua 5:1: "Their hearts melted in fear." However, Israel responds to the fear with appeasement of Yahweh (because they have angered Yahweh by taking devoted things), whereas the Canaanites do not, because the Canaanites have not angered Yahweh. Further, Rahab, who is spared from the destruction, does not exhibit any kind of penitence at any point before, during, or after the process,[3] nor does she undertake any form of purification to cleanse the sin of the Canaanites, of which she would have supposedly been guilty. This indicates that the document's narrator is not expecting the audience to understand the Canaanites as being punished.

IF RETRIBUTION THEOLOGY IS INDEED IN PLAY, WE WOULD EXPECT THE PROPER TERMINOLOGY TO BE USED

Hebrew has several words that can mean "punish for crimes." The most notable are *dyn* (Gen 15:14, "I will *dyn* the nation they serve as slaves"), *ysr* (Lev 26:18, "I will *ysr* you for your sins seven times over"), and *pqd* (Ex 32:34, "I will *pqd* them for their sin").[4] None of these verbs ever take the people of Canaan as their object. *Dyn* refers to pronouncing a verdict, which can be positive or negative; in Genesis 15:14 it is negative

---

[3]Acknowledgment of Yahweh as a powerful cosmic deity in Josh 2:11 is not the same thing as contrition and repentance for violation of Yahweh's universal moral law or any of the particular offenses described by the modern retribution theodicy, although it does signify a desire to assume an Israelite *identity*, with all that entails (see Peka M. A. Pitkänen, *Joshua*, Apollos Old Testament Commentary [Downers Grove, IL: InterVarsity Press, 2010], 125-26). See propositions sixteen and eighteen for a discussion of Israelite community identity markers.

[4]Other potential words are *špṭ* (Ex 5:21; Ezek 23:24; 2 Chron 20:12), *ḥaṭā'ṭ* (Zech 14:19), and *ykḥ* (2 Sam 7:14; Ps 94:10). None of these words take the people of Canaan as objects or referents.

("punish"), but in Genesis 30:6 and Deuteronomy 32:36 it is positive ("vindicate"). *Ysr* means "discipline" (Deut 4:36; 8:5) and indicates a resultant improvement for the recipient, not death.[5] *Pqd* has a broad semantic range but occurs five times in Genesis–Joshua in a context indicating punishment; its objects are the Israelites in Exodus 32:34 and the land in Leviticus 18:25, and it is part of the idiomatic phrase "*pqd* the children and their children for the sin of the parents" in Exodus 20:5; 34:7; and Deuteronomy 5:9. *Pqd* in this context is best read as "determine destiny."[6] As we will discuss in proposition six, the "sin" (*ʿāwōn*) of the parents refers to a destiny of calamity or destruction. "*Pqd* the *ʿāwōn* of the parents on the children," then, means "declare that the destiny [*pqd*] decreed for the parents, which is a destiny of destruction [*ʿāwōn*], will also be the destiny of the children." *Pqd* can result in positive as well as negative destiny; see Exodus 3:16-17, "I have *pqd* ["watched over"] you in Egypt . . . and I have promised to bring you up out of your misery"; Ruth 1:6, "the LORD had *pqd* ["come to the aid of"] his people by providing food"; and Psalm 8:4, "what [are] . . . human beings that you *pqd* ["care for"] them?"[7]

In 1 Samuel 15:2 Yahweh announces an intention to punish (*pqd*) the Amalekites (called "sinners" in 1 Sam 15:18; NIV "wicked people").

---

[5]In Lev 26, the discipline falls on the nation as a whole (not only the individuals who die) for the sake of an improvement for those who survive the judgment (Lev 26:44-45; the same is true of the noun form of the root, *mûsar*, as in Is 30:32; Jer 30:14). No such remnant is ever suggested for the Hivites, Jebusites, and so on, and therefore they are not being disciplined. Their situation is different from Israel's in Lev 26 (see proposition eleven).

[6]Gunnel André, *Determining the Destiny: Pqd in the Old Testament*, Coniectanea Biblica Old Testament Series 24 (Lund: Gleerup, 1980), 241. Stuart Creason suggests that this definition is too limited and prefers instead the definition of "to assign a person or a thing to what the subject believes is its proper or appropriate status in an organizational order." "PQD Revisited," in *Studies in Semitic and Afroasiatic Linguistics Presented to Gene B. Gragg*, ed. Cynthia L. Miller, Studies in Ancient Oriental Civilizations 60 (Chicago: University of Chicago Press, 2007), 27-42, quote on 30. For our purposes, however, we are interested primarily in the usage of *pqd* with a divine subject, especially in collocation with *ʿāwōn* and *ʿal*. In this context, André's definition is suitable, especially since "assigning a place in the [world] order" is what "decreeing a destiny" essentially means.

[7]André, *Destiny*, 204-5.

Neither this word (*ḥaṭṭāʾim*) nor any version of the root (*ḥaṭṭāʾ*) is ever used to describe any of the other Canaanite nations or any of their actions. In Jeremiah 50:14-15 the verbal form (*ḥāṭāʾâ*) indicates Babylonian military violence (specifically against Israel), and Ezekiel 28:16 uses it to describe the prince of Tyre's violence, which in turn is the same word (*ḥāmās*) that is used for the indictment of the antediluvian population in Genesis 6:11. We will discuss the Amalekites more fully in proposition eighteen, but for our present purposes we will note that the offense of the Amalekites is not violation of Yahweh's universal moral law, or anything related to idolatry, or anything related to the list of offenses in Leviticus 18. Instead, they are being punished "for what they did to Israel when they waylaid them as they came up from Egypt" (1 Sam 15:2). That an indictment is offered against the Amalekites, together with a documentation of the event (Ex 17:8) and stated intent to punish, is an indicator that what is happening to the Amalekites is not the same as what is happening to all of the nations that Yahweh is driving out before Israel, even though the specific action taken against them (*ḥerem*) is the same. The action is the same, but the motivation and circumstances are different. See proposition sixteen for a discussion of *ḥerem*.

The word *nqm* ("vengeance," Ezek 25:17; also appearing in Jer 50:15) is used in reference to the Midianites in Numbers 31:2. However, this event is unique in the course of the conquest.[8] First, the Midianites are neither *grš* ("driven out") nor *ḥerem*. Second, the assault is explicitly an act of revenge for something specific Midian did against Israel (Num 25:17-18; compare Num 31:13-17), not nebulous moral offenses against Israel's God committed by people Israel has never met. This indicates that the Peor incident is not a template by which we should understand all of Israel's wars, but a unique occurrence (for further

---

[8]The word is used against the northern coalition army in Josh 10:13, but the activity that is being avenged is the attack against the Gibeonites in Josh 10:6, not violations of God's universal moral law.

discussion see excursus at the end of this proposition). Although the specific nuances of the offense are lost to us, the context indicates clearly that Israel's assault is an act of retribution. Numbers 31, like 1 Samuel 15, shows us clearly how the text describes the actions of Israel when military activity is supposed to deliver justice. None of these elements are present in any part of the actual conquest.

WE WOULD EXPECT THE REASONS OFFERED FOR THE TREATMENT OF THE CANAANITES IN THE CONQUEST NARRATIVES TO INCLUDE REFERENCES TO PUNISHMENT OF THE CANAANITES

The conquest narratives do explain explicitly why the war against the Canaanites is occurring and why the level of exhibited destruction is called for. In none of these explanations, however, is any mention made of the need to punish the crimes of the Canaanites. Two themes are described and continuously repeated:

- Yahweh is both able and willing to carry out the covenant promises made to the ancestors of Israel.

- If the Canaanite nations are allowed to remain, the Israelite nation will be unable to survive under the covenant.

The first of these is the main focus of the book of Joshua and arguably the main point of the entire Hexateuch (Genesis–Joshua). Back in Genesis 15, Yahweh promises Abram that his descendants will eventually possess the land. In Joshua that promise is fulfilled, despite the resistance of the Canaanite armies and, presumably but never explicitly, the resistance of the Canaanite gods.[9] The point is concluded in Joshua 21:44-45, where the narrator reminds us that "not one of their enemies withstood them; the LORD gave all their enemies into

---

[9]In the Old Testament, though other gods are considered powerless, inferior, and unworthy of worship, Yahweh exerts his power over them (as in the plagues) and is compared to them (though they are impotent).

their hands. Not one of all the LORD's good promises to Israel failed; every one was fulfilled." This emphasis is vital to the theology of the Deuteronomistic History (Joshua, Judges, Samuel, Kings) that is driving to the exile; the exile occurred because of failure on the part of Israel, not failure on the part of God.

The second theme is more complicated. It is described most explicitly in Numbers 33:55-56, where Moses warns that "if you do not drive out the inhabitants of the land, those you allow to remain will become barbs in your eyes and thorns in your sides. They will give you trouble in the land where you will live. And then I will do to you what I plan to do to them." Moses repeats the warning in Deuteronomy 7:4, 6 ("[the Canaanites] will turn your children away from following me to serve other gods, and the LORD's anger will burn against you and will quickly destroy you . . . for you are people holy to the LORD your God"), as does the angel of the Lord in Judges 2:3 ("they will become traps for you, and their gods will become snares to you"). The narrator confirms the danger immediately in Judges 2:11-15 and indeed traces out the expulsion of Israel over the course of the rest of the Deuteronomistic History. We will discuss Israel's status in proposition ten and offer a fuller reflection on the consequences of Canaanite syncretism (the blending of different religious systems) in proposition sixteen, but for now we will simply recognize that the emphasis of the account is not on what is happening to the Canaanites; they are little more than an aside in the account of what is happening to Israel (as would be expected in the documents of Israel, which describe the relationship of the Israelite nation to Israel's God). The point is that the conquest is conceived of in terms of the purpose for which it is performed and the consequences (positive or negative) that accompany Israel's involvement in that purpose; no real consideration is given to its consequences for anyone else.

It is also worth noting that in Deuteronomy 2:9-12, 18-23, Seir and Ar are given by Yahweh to the descendants of Esau and Lot, respectively, in the same manner that Canaan is given to Israel (Deut 2:12). There is no mention whatsoever of any sin or wickedness on the part of the Horites, Emites, or Zamzummites who are displaced by Edom, Moab, and Ammon, though the text does take special note to classify them as the Rephaim (Deut 2:11, 20; see proposition twelve).

We are not attempting to provide an exhaustive list of instances of divine retribution in the Bible. Rather, we wish to establish the kinds of textual markers that we would expect to find if divine retribution is occurring. While many such instances lack one or more of these indicators, it would be highly unusual for an instance of retribution to contain none of them, especially an event as monumental and significant as the conquest. Therefore, given the total absence of common and expected indicators of divine retribution in regard to the conquest, it appears that there is no reason to believe that the conquest is presented in the text as an act of divine retributive justice.

EXCURSUS: The Midianites in Numbers 31

What exactly the Peor incident (Num 31:16) entailed is not transparent to the modern reader, though presumably the ancient audience would have understood it. Some inferences, however, are possible.

First, the offense goes beyond simple, generic idolatry or promiscuity. We know this because the primary party involved in those activities specifically is the Moabites (Num 25:2), but no vengeance is taken against them; in fact Israel is specifically prohibited from doing anything to them whatsoever (Deut 2:9). Moreover, the offenses that exclude Moab from the assembly are identified as preventing passage and hiring Balaam to curse them (Deut 23:3); no mention is made of Peor. Therefore, whatever the Peor incident is, it involves Kozbi and the Midianites specifically (Num 25:18). This is further demonstrated by the use of the introductory word *wahinnēh* (NIV "then") in Numbers 25:6, which indicates a transition in narrative focus, with the preceding content (Num 25:1-5 in this case) providing the background and context for the pericope's main plot.[10] We see a similar construction in Numbers 20:16 (NIV "now"), where the description of the exodus provides the background and context for the request to pass through Edom, and again in Numbers 32:14 (NIV "and"), where the events of Numbers 14 are recalled to provide the background and context for the accusation of the Transjordan tribes. This indicates that the relationship with the Moabites and the Baal of Peor, and the burning wrath of God (the consequences of which are unspecified), are happening in the background and providing the context for a particular incident involving Phinehas and a Midianite woman, and it is this incident that is avenged in Numbers 31.

Second, the activity of the perpetrators is deliberate, not passive. The Midianites deceived Israel (Num 25:18), following the advice of Balaam (Num 31:16).[11] This is in contrast to something the Israelites receive passively ("Israel yoked themselves to the Baal of Peor" [Num 25:3];[12] "idols . . . became a snare," e.g., Ps 106:36).[13] What exactly the Midianite scheme was, or what it was supposed to achieve, is lost to us. In any case, the description "treated you as enemies when they deceived you" (Num 25:18) indicates that it was not friendly in intention. One possibility is that they have discovered a workaround to Balaam's inability to curse Israel. The presence of Balaam among the Midianites when he is killed in Numbers 31:8 indicates that he came

---

[10]Psalm 106:28-29 describes a sequence of four events in more or less chronological order: joined to Peor, ate sacrifices, God's wrath, plague. To assume that these four events are causally linked ("Israel became joined to Baal Peor, and therefore ate sacrifices to the dead, which was the wicked deed that provoked God's wrath, which was the plague") is to commit a post hoc fallacy ("after this, therefore because of this"). Compare Ps 106:17-18, where there is no causal relationship between the earth that swallows Dathan and Abiram and the fire that consumes (Korah); the events are simply reported in sequence.

[11]The word (nkl, piel) indicates "formulated a conspiracy or plot" (compare Gen 37:18, "they plotted [hithpael] to kill [Joseph]").

[12]Niphal of ṣmd can mean either "they became yoked" or "they yoked themselves" (e.g., Ps 106:28), but cannot mean "the Moabites yoked them."

[13]"Snare" here is a noun, so it cannot mean "[the people of the land] ensnared Israel with idols."

back at some point after returning to his home in Numbers 24:25, presumably to offer the advice mentioned in Numbers 31:16. God's instructions to Moses are not classified secrets; the Gibeonites know about them in Joshua 9:24. Perhaps Balaam has learned which Israelite behaviors will invoke the wrath of Israel's God and advised the Midianites to encourage these behaviors among the people of Israel. If this is the case, the vengeance is not only for hostile intent against Yahweh's people (a common indictment in the prophetic oracles against Israel's neighbors; see proposition eight) but also for attempting to manipulate Yahweh himself (compare perhaps to Sennacherib, who tries to incite Yahweh against Israel in 2 Kings 18:22-25 and consequently receives the wrath on himself in 2 Kings 19:7, 35-37; note that the "vengeance" in Num 31:3 is "the LORD's").

Third, the incident is clearly indicated as an indictment by elements other than the fact of the destruction. The command to *ṣrr* ("treat as enemies") in Numbers 25:17 is invoked in a talionic sense (that is, an eye for an eye, a basic principle of the ancient conception of justice) and is not repeated in regard to other nations, even though the nations *ṣrr* Israel in Numbers 10:9; 33:55; also not repeated is the command to "carry out vengeance" in Numbers 31:3. Nonetheless, some interpreters claim that the command to kill all the males, and the initiation of the act by Yahweh, indicate the act of *herem* even if the word is not used.[14] However, that the *herem* is neither commanded nor enacted (the loot is spared), and that murder is not the focus of *herem* (see proposition fifteen), and that the deaths are given a specific warrant that is not repeated elsewhere in the conquest narratives (Num 31:16), all indicate that this idea is erroneous.

---

[14]See for example Timothy R. Ashley, *The Book of Numbers*, NICOT (Grand Rapids: Eerdmans, 1993), 591-92.

Genesis 15:16 Does Not Indicate That the Canaanites Were Committing Sin

This verse is generally considered to provide the strongest support for a retributive interpretation of the conquest. On close analysis, however, it becomes clear that the Hebrew cannot possibly have the meaning it is traditionally given in English. It is therefore essential for us to turn attention to some technical matters of Hebrew word usage to sort out a better understanding. The verse reads: "The fourth generation of your descendants will come back here, for *ʿad hēnnâ* the *ʿāwōn* of the Amorites *lōʾ šālēm*."

The NIV translates the words to mean "because [yet] the [sin] of the Amorites [has not reached its full measure]." This is contestable for a variety of reasons.

ʿAD HĒNNÂ

The NIV renders *ʿad hēnnâ* as "yet," which indicates anticipation of the future with an expectation of change from the current status (in English, "my car is not fixed yet" means "my car is now broken but will not be broken in the future"). Hebrew usage of *ʿad hēnnâ*, however, indicates memory of the past with no expectation of change ("my car is *still* broken"). So we see:

- Genesis 44:28: "One of them went away from me. . . . And I have not seen him *ʿad hēnnâ*" (NIV "since"). Jacob is protesting the loss of Benjamin. He has already lost Joseph in the past and at this time has no expectation that Joseph is still alive.

- 1 Samuel 7:12: "*ʿad hēnnâ* the LORD has helped us" (NIV "thus far"). Samuel's monument is remembering Yahweh's assistance and is expecting it to continue.

- 1 Chronicles 9:18: "*ʿad hēnnâ* these were the gatekeepers" (NIV "up to the present time"). This remembers the role that the family in question had played in the past and will continue to play.

- Numbers 14:19 and Psalm 71:17: both of these use *ʿad hēnnâ* in conjunction with a *min* clause to indicate a span of time in the past ("from [then] until now"). Both passages expect a continuation of the previous behavior (forgiveness and declaration of marvelous deeds, respectively).

- Judges 16:13: "*ʿad hēnnâ* you have been making a fool of me" (NIV "all this time"). Delilah is remembering past behavior. Her imperative in the next sentence is a demand for change, but the use of *ʿad hēnnâ* does not anticipate it.

- 1 Chronicles 12:29: "from Benjamin, Saul's tribe—three thousand, most of whom had remained loyal to Saul's house *ʿad hēnnâ*." The NIV translates "until then" and indicates a transition of the three thousand from loyalty to Saul to loyalty to David, but this might not be accurate. The passage could also be read, "from Benjamin, the tribe of Saul, three thousand. Most of [the tribe of Benjamin] was still [*ʿad hēnnāh*] remaining loyal to the house of Saul." In this reading, the pronoun *whom* (as in "most of whom") refers back to "Benjamin, Saul's tribe," as opposed to "the three thousand [who came]." Sara Japhet indicates that the descriptor is an apologetic for why so few came from the tribe of Benjamin;

only three thousand, *because* most of the tribe of Benjamin was ʿad hēnnâ remaining loyal to the house of Saul.[1]

So we see that ʿad hēnnâ refers to an ongoing state, not a transition between states. If a transition between states were desired, Hebrew has a construction to indicate that, which is not ʿad hēnnâ but rather ʿad ʿātâ, as in Deuteronomy 12:9: "you have ʿad ʿātâ ["not yet"] reached the resting place and the inheritance." Israel has not crossed the Jordan yet, but they are about to. We also can look at Genesis 32:4, where Jacob says "I have been staying with Laban and remained there ʿad ʿātâ ["till now"]." Jacob says this as he is leaving Laban and preparing to meet Esau. Finally, in 2 Kings 13:23, the narrator says, "ʿad ʿātâ ["To this day"] [Yahweh] has been unwilling to destroy them." In context, the narrator is referring to the change that took place at the exile; at the time of Hazael Yahweh was unwilling, but by the time of the writing of the book of Kings, he was. In Genesis 15:16, then, the use of ʿad hēnnâ cannot mean that "in the future, the ʿāwōn of the Amorites will become šālēm." At the time of Abram's vision, the ʿāwōn of the Amorites is not šālēm, and there is no anticipation that this will change in the future.

---

[1]Sara Japhet, *1 & 2 Chronicles*, Old Testament Library (Louisville, KY: Westminster John Knox, 1993), 267-68. In contrast, Gary Knoppers tries to argue that most of the three thousand were formerly (that is, they are transitioning now) Saul's personal guards, and it is unlikely that most of the tribe of Benjamin were guards; therefore the pronoun *whom* refers back to the three thousand. He examines the construction mišmeret bêt šāʾûl and determines that mišmeret + [X], where [bayit + X] refers to a building (usually bêt yhwh, the temple), always refers to guards. See Gary N. Knoppers, *1 Chronicles 10–29*, AB (New Haven, CT: Yale University Press, 2004), 568. However, the collocation bêt šāʾûl never refers to a building but rather an abstraction (that is, his dynasty). [Mišmeret + abstraction], in turn, does not necessarily mean "guards" but more generally refers to duties or responsibilities, especially when combined with the verb šāmar (see 2 Chron 13:11; Mal 3:14). Thus šāmar + mišmeret + bêt šāʾûl means [carrying out] [duties or responsibilities] [to the dynasty of Saul], which the NIV appropriately renders as "remained loyal." Further, the Hebrew has a different word when it wants to say "bodyguard" (mišmaʿat; 1 Sam 22:14; 2 Sam 23:23; 1 Chron 11:25).

Lō° Šālēm

The root of the word *šālēm* normally connotes wholeness or completeness, but the exact form that we see in in Genesis 15:16 occurs only there. It functions as an adjective[2] and modifies *ʿāwōn*, which is a noun representing an abstraction. Whether the negation (*lō°*, "not") means "wholly not" (antithetical) or "not wholly" (partial) cannot be determined with certainty.[3] Most uses of *šālēm* as an adjective modify physical objects, usually stones in the context of construction ("uncut," that is, whole [fieldstones], or "dressed," that is, finished [ashlar masonry]). It can also refer to bodies ("healthy," "uninjured"), to weights and measures ("accurate"), or to buildings or building projects ("completed"). Alternatively, however, in Ruth 2:12, it modifies an abstract noun indicating compensation (*maśkōret*, "wages," NIV "richly rewarded") that is in the same conceptual category as *ʿāwōn*. In Ruth, however, *šālēm* is not negated, so, in order to compare this passage to Genesis 15, we have to try to guess what the negation of "full recompense" (good or bad) means conceptually.

The modification of "wages" with *šālēm* in Ruth 2:12 dictates that she (Ruth) will receive all that she is owed ("fully compensated").[4] She

---

[2]Specifically, it is a predicate adjective functioning as a stative verb. The NIV instead renders *šālēm* as "reached its full measure," with the addition of "not" indicating a process in progress involving a *transitive* verb ("reached"). The phrase "reached its full measure" is intended to convey the idea that it has not yet become full. The decision to translate *šālēm* as "full [measure]" follows the Septuagint and seems to be derived from the use of *šālēm* to describe weights (meaning "accurate," that is, "weighing what it says it does," e.g., Deut 25:15). The idea of accurate weight is then extrapolated to "entire amount of measurement," which is then further extrapolated to both sides of the balance as "fully measured amount." *Šālēm* is never used for a measured-out amount; the concept of measured punishment is found in Is 47:9 (NIV: "[two calamities] will come upon you in full measure"), where the word translated "full measure" is *kĕtummām*, not *šālēm* (*kĕtummām* lit. "according to their completeness"; John Goldingay and David Payne, *Isaiah 40–55*, International Critical Commentary [London: T&T Clark, 2014], 104).

[3]The combination with the negative particle (*lō°*) occurs only in collocation with *lēb* ("his [heart] (was) *lō° šālēm* to the LORD his God," translated "not fully devoted") in 1 Kings 11:4; 15:13. Despite the collocation, the negation of *šālēm* clearly does not indicate a process in progress; Abijah is not working toward full devotion.

[4]Ruth 2:12 combines the feminine predicate adjective *šĕlēmâ* with the verbal form of the same root (*šālēm*, piel) to indicate the process of an economic transaction: "May the Lord

will receive her accrued wages. What would it mean, then, for a wage to be not *šālēm*? Does it mean that the account is paid partially, or not at all? If not at all, is the payment deferred, never accrued, or canceled?[5] Without any information there is no way to know for certain. The Amorites do seem to have *ʿāwōn*, so the best tentative interpretation for *lōʾ šālēm* in this context of recompense would be "deferred." The balance has been tabulated and remains on the books, but it is not (*lōʾ*) being paid out (*šālēm*).

ʿĀwōn

The NIV translates *ʿāwōn* as "sin," and the word is generally interpreted to refer to spectacular sin like the kind reported at Sodom two chapters earlier in Genesis 13:13 and referenced again in Genesis 18:20. However, the word used in both of those cases is *ḥaṭāʾ*, not *ʿāwōn*. There is a reference to the *ʿāwōn* of Sodom, and it occurs in Genesis 19:15, when the angel warns Lot to get away "or you will be swept away when the city is punished" (lit. "in the *ʿāwōn* of the city"), referring to its destruction, not its offenses. Elsewhere in Genesis, Cain complains that "my *ʿāwōn* is more than I can bear" in reaction to his exile (Gen 4:13), and in Genesis 44:16 Judah laments that his *ʿāwōn* has been "uncovered," (lit. "found") by God, referring not to the theft of the cup but rather the

---

šālēm your works, and may your wages (be) *šelēmâ* from the lord." The active verb *šālēm* deals with what is owed in a situation where reciprocation (2 Sam 3:39), vow (2 Sam 15:7), or restitution (Ex 22) is involved. It is more abstract in Ruth and calls for the reciprocation of *ḥesed* for *ḥesed*. The wages pertains to that which is earned through labor (Gen 29:15; 31:7, 41).

[5]The collocation of [heart] + *lōʾ šālēm* would probably point to a full (as opposed to partial) negation, since the kings whose hearts are not *šālēm* generally do the opposite of what they are supposed to, as opposed to half of what they are supposed to (compare Asa in 1 Kings 15:14, who only does part of what he should—he fails to tear down the high places—but his heart is still *šālēm*). Likewise the use of *ʿad hēnnâ* in Gen 15 and its indication of a steady state argues against cancellation, which would be a change; therefore, the account of the Amorites being *lōʾ šālēm* would possibly refer to it either being deferred or not accrued, depending on whether the account already has a balance.

"comeuppance" that is due to them because of what they did to Joseph.[6] This indicates that in Genesis the emphasis of *ʿāwōn* is on the punishment, not the crime that incurred it. It refers to what God does, not to what the possessors of the *ʿāwōn* have done. This emphasis is fortunate because punishment here carries the concept of compensation that was represented by the *maśkōret* in Ruth 2, thus giving us a fitting comparison.

If we consider *ʿāwōn* to mean a destiny of calamity, we know that the Amorites have one because Yahweh has just decreed it; he has promised that their land will be taken from them and given to Israel at some later time. This is indicated as a true state of affairs, not speculative rhetoric delivered by a character; we saw Yahweh make the promise in Genesis 15:7 (Amorites specified in Gen 15:21), and the narrator records the displacement in Joshua. The question that must be faced by a would-be interpreter is *why* they have *ʿāwōn*; specifically, do they necessarily have *ʿāwōn* because of something they did? The word can variously refer to "something that happens to you," "something you did," or "something that happens to you because of something you did." However, these three meanings are not interchangeable in any given circumstance. Given this range of use, we have to judge by context which aspect is intended. As we have seen, Genesis has other contexts where the emphasis is on the aspect of consequence. If, for the purposes of our translation, it is important to understand the words and ideas as Abram would have understood them, the question we should ask is whether Abram would have

---

[6]First, Judah ascribes the *ʿāwōn* to all of the brothers, even though only Benjamin is considered guilty of theft (Gen 44:10). Second, God is the one who has uncovered the *ʿāwōn*, not the steward who rifles the sacks. The Hebrew terminology is themed around the word *found*, used throughout the passage, and does not pass into good English idiom, but the statement essentially says "our fateful destiny (for what we did to our brother) has finally caught up with us." See Claus Westermann, *Genesis 37–50*, trans. John J. Scullion (Minneapolis: Augsburg, 1982), 133-34; Victor P. Hamilton, *The Book of Genesis Chapters 18–50*, NICOT (Grand Rapids: Eerdmans, 1995), 566; Gordon Wenham, *Genesis 16–50*, Word Biblical Commentary (Waco, TX: Word, 1994), 425.

understood Yahweh's declaration to necessarily mean that the Amorites were experiencing calamity because of something they did. In this approach, Abram's understanding of the event would come from the ancient Near East, not from technical Israelite theology.[7] Therefore, it would be productive to see whether there are any examples from the ancient Near East where a decree of destruction is issued for some reason other than offensive behavior toward the god or gods who execute it.

One such example is found in the Lament for the Destruction of Sumer and Ur. Anu and Enlil level the city not because they perceive any wrongdoing on the part of the inhabitants, but because it is time for kingship to pass on. The patron gods of the city try to plead with and appease Enlil, but it does not work because Enlil is not angry; the destiny of Ur is part of some larger program they are following for the order of the cosmos. This is actually very similar to the conquest; Yahweh has decreed that the land will pass to Israel, not because the Canaanites deserved to lose it, but because it is part of a larger operation. Another example is the Cuthaean Legend of Naram-Suen, where the gods create an army of monstrous invincible barbarians to attack Babylonia for no specified reason.[8] Finally, a Sumerian prayer laments for "young people (who) had no sin" and later acknowledges that the god was "not motivated by" sin.[9] In the Bible itself, we also observe Psalm 40:12, where *ʿāwōn* is parallel to "trouble" in a context where the psalmist confesses no sin (and indeed asserts his righteousness,

---

[7] If for whatever reason (e.g., later redaction) an interpreter finds it necessary for this passage to reflect later Israelite theology, then for the sake of consistency the passage must also reflect later Israelite rhetoric. In that case, the *ʿāwōn* of the Amorites would be conceptually comparable to the *rešaʿ* of the nations and would thus stand as part of the trope of the invincible barbarians (see proposition twelve). Abram in his time would not have regarded the Amorites as invincible barbarians, but the redactor of Genesis may have.

[8] Joan Goodnick Westenholz, *Legends of the Kings of Akkade* (Winona Lake, IN: Eisenbrauns, 1997), 294.

[9] *No. 54: Eršema nir-ǧál lú è-NE, "Prince, appearing"* lines 11, 26; Uri Gabbay, *The Eršema Prayers of the First Millennium BC* (Wiesbaden: Harrassowitz Verlag, 2015), 181.

Ps 40:8-10) and requests deliverance from oppressors (Ps 40:14). Thus, we see that in the ancient Near Eastern worldview held by Abram, the presence of divinely decreed calamity does not necessarily indicate the presence of spectacular misdeeds. In contrast with Cain, Sodom, and Joseph's brothers, we are never shown any misdeeds of the Amorites, and we have no real basis for assuming that they did them based only on the presence of *ʿāwōn*.

WHY DOES GENESIS 15:16 COME AFTER GENESIS 15:15 AND NOT BEFORE?

If Genesis 15:16 is read according to its standard interpretation (the fourth generation will return because by that time the Amorites will have done enough sin to deserve being wiped out), its position in the discourse is somewhat incongruous. Logically we would expect the thought to run as follows:

> Your descendants will leave for four hundred years (Gen 15:13)
> They will be oppressed (Gen 15:13)
> They will be delivered (Gen 15:14)
> Their oppressors will be punished (Gen 15:14)
> They will return (Gen 15:16)
> The Canaanites will be punished (Gen 15:16)
> but you will have peace in your time and will be dead by then
> (Gen 15:15)

That Genesis 15:16 comes after Genesis 15:15 would seem to indicate that whatever Genesis 15:16 says should continue the idea of peace in Abram's time, as opposed to returning to a description of what will happen in four hundred years.

Who Is the Fourth Generation?

Most interpreters want to read "the fourth generation" in parallel with the "four hundred years" in Genesis 15:13.[10] This is problematic for several reasons.

First, in the context of the exodus, a generation usually refers to forty years. The wilderness generation wanders for forty years until they are all dead (Num 14:33-34; 32:13), and an idealized twelve generations of forty years each pass between the exodus and the construction of the temple (1 Kings 6:1). For *generation* to suddenly mean a different number is not impossible, but it would be rather odd.

Second, none of the genealogies ever cover only four generations in the allotted four hundred year timespan. When taken literally, the phrase "fourth generation" counts the patriarch plus four, as is shown in 2 Kings 10:30, when God promises Jehu that "your descendants will sit on the throne of Israel to the fourth generation." Then, in 2 Kings 15:12, the line of Jehu ends after a sequence of Jehu (the patriarch, generation zero) plus Jehoahaz, Jehoash, Jeroboam, and Zechariah. In Genesis 15:13 the count of "four hundred years" starts when the Israelites become "strangers in a country not their own." The patriarch who transitions the house of Israel to Egypt is Jacob (Gen 46:6-7), so "four generations" begins counting with the sons of Jacob as the first.[11] By this count, the closest genealogy has five and occurs in Exodus 6:16-20 (also in 1 Chron 6:1-3; 23:12-13):

---

[10]Nahum Sarna argues that *generation* refers to lifespan and, combined with the idealized 110-year lifespan of Joseph in Gen 50:22 and the fixed lifespan of 120 years in Gen 6:3, concludes that four generations is more or less four hundred years. Nahum M. Sarna, *Genesis*, JPS (Philadelphia: Jewish Publication Society, 1989), 116. This is plausible enough and certainly sufficient to defeat a claim of logical contradiction between Gen 15:13 and Gen 15:16, but is not sufficient to prove a parallel.

[11]It is also possible to read the passage in 1 Kings as saying "four generations of your descendants (as opposed to "the fourth generation of your dynasty") will sit on the throne," which excludes Jehu the patriarch and thus counts a total of four people to reach the fourth generation rather than five. In this case the first generation in Egypt would be Jacob himself, not his sons, and the shortest genealogical record would be six. But since neither count produces four generations to the conquest, the distinction is for our purposes academic.

the first generation: Levi, son of Jacob

the second generation: Kohath

the third generation: Amram

the fourth generation: Moses and the wilderness generation, which does not return

the fifth generation: the generation that returns[12]

Joshua 17:3 puts seven generations from Joseph (father of Manasseh) to the daughters of Zelophehad,[13] who enter the land with the conquest generation (also Num 27:1); 1 Chronicles 7:23-26 puts twelve generations from Joseph (father of Ephraim) to Joshua;[14] and Matthew puts seven generations from Judah to Rahab (Mt 1:2-5; also 1 Chron 2:3-10; Lk 3:32-33).[15] Genealogies as a genre can have omissions, so the fact that they do not match is of no significance, but the point is that regardless of the actual historical sequence of lineage, there is not even a *tradition* anywhere of four generations elapsing between the migration to Egypt and the conquest.

Third, the phrase "fourth generation" has idiomatic value, as in the phrase "punishing . . . to the [third and] fourth generation" (Ex 20:5, 34:7; Num 14:18; Deut 5:9). In this context it refers to the entire household, with the four generations being the patriarch, his children, his grandchildren, and his great-grandchildren, all of whom would live together as an extended family (*bêt-ʾab*, lit. "father's house"). Taken this way, it might be possible that "the fourth generation will

---

[12]There are also five generations from Judah to Achan (1 Chron 2:3-7; Josh 7:1; Judah, Zerah, Zimri, Karmi, Achan), and four from Reuben to Dathan and Abiram, who, like Moses and Aaron, belong to the generation that dies in the wilderness, so their genealogy is also five (Num 26:5-9; Reuben, Pallu, Eliab, Dathan and Abiram, [conquest generation]).

[13][Joseph], Manassah, Makir, Gilead, Hepher, Zelophehad, who died in the wilderness (Num 27:3).

[14][Joseph], Ephriam, Beriah, Rephah, Resheph, Telah, Tahan, Ladan, Ammihud, Elishama, Nun, Joshua (who is technically the only survivor of the wilderness generation, so we should probably add one more).

[15]Judah, Perez, Hezron, Ram, Amminadab, Nahshon, Salmon (father of Boaz, whose mother was Rahab).

return" means "the entire family will return," but this is highly unlikely because Genesis 15:16 lacks the "to the third and" part, and also because such a reading does nothing to continue the idea of peace in Abram's time.

We might observe, however, that the fourth generation, when they live in the patriarch's house, are very young children. By the time those children grow up and begin doing things, the patriarch will be dead. Thus the fourth generation is the first one that the patriarch is not going to see into adulthood, and anything this generation achieves will happen after the patriarch is gone, even under ideal conditions (compare Job 42:16, where Job "saw his children and their children to the fourth generation"). This idea matches perfectly with the idea of assurances to Abram of a peaceful life. "The fourth generation" does not mean "in four hundred years"; it means "after your time is over."[16]

What Is Special About the Amorites?

Genesis 15:16 mentions the *ʿāwōn* of the Amorites, but not of any of the other Canaanite nations. Commentators usually argue that the Amorites are a synecdoche for the entire list[17] (that is, they are an example intended to represent the whole), as they are, for example, in 1 Kings 21:26 and 2 Kings 21:11. This is certainly possible, but if this was the case it seems odd that the entire list would be given immediately in Genesis 15:19. Therefore, it is worth asking whether the Amorites specifically have any special significance to Abram that might indicate why they in particular are mentioned.

---

[16]"'Fourth generation,' however, may only be a stereotypical expression, conveying the idea of completeness; the duration of a father's life would not normally extend to four generations." Kenneth A. Matthews, *Genesis 11:27–50:26*, New American Commentary (Nashville: Broadman & Holman, 2005), 175.

[17]Bruce K. Waltke, *Genesis* (Grand Rapids: Zondervan, 2001), 244; see also Victor P. Hamilton, *The Book of Genesis Chapters 1–17*, NICOT (Grand Rapids: Eerdmans, 1990), 436; Sarna, *Genesis*, 117; Gordon J. Wenham, *Genesis 1–15*, Word Biblical Commentary (Waco, TX: Word, 1987), 332.

It turns out that they do. In Genesis 14, a coalition of kings attacks Sodom and carries off Lot. Abram goes to his rescue along with "Mamre the Amorite, a brother of Eshkol and Aner, all of whom were allied with Abram" (Gen 14:13; also Gen 14:24). The Amorites, then, are Abram's friends and allies. Now it becomes perfectly clear why the idea of the destiny of the Amorites is tied to the idea of peace in Abram's time; he isn't only concerned about his own fate but also that of his allies. By delaying the displacement of the Amorites until sometime in the distant future, Yahweh assures Abram that his children will not negatively affect the people to whom he has some attachment (whether sentimental, obligatory, or simply pragmatic; the exact nature of the alliance is never described).

PUTTING IT ALL TOGETHER

The preceding analysis indicates that the Hebrew text is highly unlikely to match its common English interpretation. Specifically, we have noted that ʿad hēnnâ should indicate a state that is not expected to change (whatever the ʿāwōn of the Amorites is not, it should continue to not be that), and the ʿāwōn of the Amorites should be something happening *to* them, not something they are doing, and carries no specific implications about why it is happening. Furthermore, we might also observe that if the traditional interpretation were intended, Hebrew has better words to say it:

- Given the immediate context of Sodom in Genesis 13, the expected word for "sins" in the sense of offenses or crimes would be ḥaṭṭāʾ, not ʿāwōn.

- If the "full measure" indicated by šālēm is supposed to carry a connotation of punishment, a better way to say it would be a construction involving *pqd*, as in for example Exodus 32:34 (when the time comes to punish [*pqd*], I will *pqd* their ḥaṭṭāʾ), or Exodus 34:7 and others (*pqd* the ʿāwōn of the fathers on the children to the third and fourth generation). Another, even better word is *rāṣâ* ("pay for"), used in Leviticus 26:41, 43, as a fulfillment of a destiny of destruction (they will *rāṣâ* their *ʿāwōn* because they rejected my laws and abhorred my decrees). If it is supposed to indicate that an accruing balance of offense has finally reached a critical stage and now demands attention, a better construction would be "[their sin will] come up before me" (compare to Jon 1:2), or perhaps "the outcry [will reach] me" (compare to Gen 18:21).

- The NIV's anticipation of a new future state (interpretation: "The sin of the Amorites has not yet reached its full measure, but it is going to") should be represented by *ʿad ʿātâ*, not *ʿad hēnnâ*.

It is impossible to provide a sure translation without being certain of the precise meaning of *lōʾ šālēm*. However, in light of all the evidence discussed above, we offer the translation in table 1 in contrast to the common interpretation:

Table 1. Translations of Genesis 15:16

Text	The fourth generation		the *ʿāwōn* of	the Amorites	*ʾad hēnnâ*	*lōʾ šālēm*
Traditional Translation	after four hundred years, your family	Will return here because	the evil being done by	your enemies	is at this moment but by then will no longer be	in the process of being completed
Suggested Translation	It won't be until after your lifetime is over that your family		the destiny of destruction that has been decreed for	your friends and allies	has been and will continue to be	deferred

This tentative interpretation has nothing to do with rationalizing the conquest, because the destiny of destruction in the ancient Near Eastern context that would have been familiar to Abram does not inherently imply misdeeds (unless of course those misdeeds are shown by the text's narrator, which those of Cain, Sodom, and Joseph's brothers are, but those of the Amorites are not). While we cannot identify the precise nuance of this verse because of the ambiguity of *lō' šālēm*, we will also note that it is poor methodology to base a theological position—in this case, the retributive purpose of the conquest—on a verse of which we cannot be sure of the meaning.

Neither the Israelites nor the Canaanites Are Depicted as Stealing the Other's Rightful Property

One of the accusations against the conquest by critics of the Bible is that the Israelites drove the Canaanites off their rightful land in order to steal it for themselves, much as the American government did to the Native Americans in the nineteenth century. Apologists respond with the claim that the land was the rightful property of Israel and that it was, in fact, the Canaanites who stole it: "The Canaanites are occupying land of which Israel has legal ownership—without consent of the owner."[1] Both positions (attack and defense) are untenable for several reasons.

ISRAEL'S SUPPOSED OWNERSHIP OF THE LAND

It is not uncommon for interpreters to argue that Israel has a universally binding legal ownership of the land based on the promise made to Abraham in Genesis 17:8.[2] There is no evidence, however, that the biblical author is suggesting that the Israelites believe that the land

---

[1]Paul Copan and Matthew Flannagan, *Did God Really Command Genocide? Coming to Terms with the Justice of God* (Grand Rapids: Baker Books, 2014), 62.
[2]Ibid., 63.

already belongs to them. When Rahab says, "I know that the LORD has given you this land" (Josh 2:9), it refers not to some ancient contract with Abraham, but to the (impending) future conquest; this is confirmed by the spies when they promise "we will treat you kindly and faithfully when the LORD gives us the land" (Josh 2:14, future tense). Most tellingly, in Genesis 23, Abraham has to buy a field. We should note that Abraham does not say, "Look, you know that God gave me this land and all of it belongs to me, so I'm just going to use this cave." Instead, he acknowledges Ephron's legal ownership (despite Yahweh's promise) and pays money. Even the aforementioned interpreters reverse themselves in this regard: "God cannot simply hand over [the land] at will. The rights of the citizens who presently reside upon it must be respected."[3] God's promise does not confer to Israel any kind of legal right to the land.

This distinction is actually critical for Israel's understanding of the idea of land. As we will discuss in proposition nineteen, orthodox Israel conceives of itself as a vassal of Yahweh (in the same way that other nations are a vassal of a human emperor), and as a vassal they receive custody of the land conditionally on their loyalty to the terms of their treaty, which is represented by the covenant. Part of their vassal status means that the right of ownership of the land belongs to the emperor (Yahweh), not the vassal. Thus it is important that Israel has no grounds on which to claim rights to the land for itself.[4] This ideology is the motivation for the *herem* of defeated cities, by which Israel surrenders ownership rights of the land it conquers (see proposition fifteen). The land grant, however, is only formalized after the conquest, and only after the land has been turned over to Yahweh by

---

[3]Ibid., 67; citing Gary Anderson, "What About the Canaanites?," in *Divine Evil? The Moral Character of the God of Abraham*, ed. Michael Bergmann et al. (New York: Oxford University Press, 2010), 250.

[4]This is also the reason Abraham refuses to take profits from his military victory in Gen 14; see John H. Walton, "Genesis," in *ZIBBCOT*, 1:83-84.

Joshua (via *ḥerem*). Therefore, the land grant cannot be invoked as a preexisting warrant for either the conquest or the *ḥerem*.

THE CANAANITES' SUPPOSED OWNERSHIP OF THE LAND

Gods in the ancient Near East were thought of as unaccountable and could do whatever they liked, and this is how Yahweh would have been perceived by both the Israelites and the Canaanites. The Canaanites never complain that Yahweh is failing to respect their natural rights; such a claim would be nonsense in the ancient world. If a city or nation is about to fall, the event is understood in one of three ways: either the gods are angry with the city, or the city's gods are not powerful enough to defend it, or the gods have impassively decreed that the city will fall.

If the gods of the city or nation are angry, it means they have abandoned it (or even turned on it), thus allowing it to be attacked by enemies. This condition is commonly claimed by the biblical authors about Israel, most notably in the cases of the exile and of the cycles of oppression in Judges, but also about the various civil wars and wars of the divided monarchy (against their neighbors or each other). From elsewhere in the ancient Near East, Mesha of Moab claims that the anger of his god Chemosh allowed Omri of Israel to subjugate his land,[5] and the Babylonian king Nabonidus claims that Assyria's gods abandoned it in response to Sennacherib's actions against Babylon.[6] In 2 Kings 18:25, Sennacherib claims that Yahweh is aiding him in the attack on Jerusalem, because Hezekiah has torn down all of his high places (2 Kings 18:22). The rhetoric of the conquest account, of course, does not want to contribute any element of Joshua's victory to the Canaanite gods, so it is not surprising that the text never claims that the Canaanite gods were angry with Canaan. If divine wrath were

---

[5]"The Inscription of King Mesha," trans. K. A. D. Smelik, in *COS* 2.23:137.
[6]Sellim Ferruh Adalı, *The Scourge of God: The Umman-Manda and Its Significance in the First Millennium BC*, SAAS 20 (Helsinki: The Neo-Assyrian Text Corpus Project, 2011), 144.

supposed to be emphasized by the narrative, though, we would expect to see attempted appeasements of the gods on the part of the Canaanites. The biblical text elsewhere does not mind recording attempted appeasement of foreign or enemy deities (2 Kings 3:27; 1 Kings 18:26-27), or attempted appeasement of Yahweh by enemies (Jon 3:5-9), but neither are recorded in the case of the Canaanites. Thus it does not appear that the text wishes to emphasize the anger of the gods (including Yahweh) due to any offense, including trespassing (see proposition five).

If the gods of Canaan are not angry, they are supposed to be defending the cities against attack by the enemy army and the enemy deity. In this case, the ability of the gods to protect their domains depends on their relative strength. In 2 Kings 18:33-35, Sennacherib taunts Hezekiah with the relative weakness of the gods of his neighbors as compared to the might of the gods of Assyria, and the powerlessness of the idols is mentioned frequently in the prophetic oracles against the nations (see proposition eight). While the Canaanites do fear Yahweh's power (Josh 2:9-11), the conquest narratives themselves make no mention of the helplessness of the Canaanite gods (such as was implied about the Egyptian gods, e.g., Ex 12:12). There is no record of Canaanite temples defiled, images smashed, and priests and prophets slaughtered (compare to Dagon in 1 Sam 5-7 or Baal in 1 Kings 18); there is not even a documentation of Israelites tearing down the high places and Asherah poles. This lack of emphasis indicates that the conquest is not intended to be understood simply as an exercise of divine power.

The third option is that the gods, for their own inscrutable reasons, have determined that it is time for the city to fall. This situation is recorded in Lament for Sumer and Ur, where the city is destroyed because it is time for kingship to pass on. As discussed in proposition six, this is the circumstance most closely represented by the conquest. When this happens there is very little that the humans can do about it;

the gods cannot be appeased because they are not angry, and they cannot be bribed because in decreeing the destiny of destruction they have already accepted the losses they will incur. The best that humans can do is survive as best they can until the gods change their minds, as, for example, Naram-Suen is forced to do in the Cuthaean Legend while barbarians pillage his kingdom. Eventually Yahweh does change his mind (Judg 2:21-23), though not out of recognition for anything the Canaanites do to earn it.

Yahweh's Supposed Ownership of the Land

Because gods in the ancient world are unaccountable, they are limited only by their own power, their commitment to cosmic order, and propriety toward other members of the pantheon, the group of gods in a religious system. We moderns tend to think of cosmic order in terms of natural rights (to life, liberty, and property) that even the gods (if they exist) are obligated to uphold. In the ancient world, however, cosmic order consists only of the decrees of the gods; there is nothing above the gods that they are required to conform to with their decrees.[7] If the gods decree that a city will stand, it stands; if they decree that it will fall, it falls; both are manifestations of the cosmic order. As such, whichever god or gods are able to make decrees can assign land to whomever they want.

In this regard, Yahweh is depicted similarly to other ancient Near Eastern gods. The existence of the covenant allows Israel what we might call rights to which they can hold God accountable (that is, the covenant blessings, conditional on their fidelity), but this arrangement

---

[7]This is not the same thing as saying that the gods were the absolute authority in the cosmos. The gods were forced to operate within a framework of metadivine control attributes, called MES, which (among other things) determined their function within the hierarchy of the pantheon. However, while the MES limited what the gods were *able* to do, they did not dictate what the gods *ought* to do. The metadivine structures were a limitation on the power of the gods, not a standard to measure their competence or morality. See John Walton, *Ancient Near Eastern Thought and the Old Testament* (Grand Rapids: Baker Academic, 2006), 97-99, for a discussion of MES.

is so far unattested elsewhere in the ancient world, and in the Bible does not apply to anyone outside Israel (see proposition eight). The ancient world does have a concept of sacred territory, though, so it is worth examining whether the biblical text depicts the land as the kind of delineated region on which trespass is a punishable offense against deity.

The first potential indicator is the reference to the land as a sanctuary in Exodus 15:17. In the ancient world, gods chose the sites for their temples based on where the heavenly and earthly realms touched. Jacob (accidentally) discovers such a site at Bethel in Genesis 28:12-17 (Gen 28:17, "this is the gate of heaven").[8] However, there is no indication that the entire land is like this; further, the central sanctuary is not established at Bethel, and indeed Bethel is not featured in the conquest account as a site of particular importance (it is conquered as an aside in Judg 1:22-25). The place where the Jerusalem temple is built is distinguished not as a gate of heaven, but as the place where the plague stops in 2 Samuel 24:16. Jerusalem (that is, Zion, the "holy mountain," which is paralleled to "sanctuary" in Ex 15:17) is likewise not featured in the conquest account and indeed remains in the possession of those Yahweh refuses to drive out until it is taken by David. This indicates that purging a corrupting influence from especially sacred ground is not a high priority for the conquest.

The second potential indicator is the statement that God "made [the land] for his dwelling" (Ex 15:17), that the land is the place God has "chosen as a dwelling for my Name" (Neh 1:9). We will discuss this in more detail in proposition nineteen, but for now we will note that Yahweh's name does not dwell in the land until after the conquest; the "place where I will cause my name to dwell" usually refers to the Jerusalem temple, which in Joshua's time does not exist. The Canaanite presence in the land can therefore not be giving offense to Yahweh's

---

[8]Walton, "Genesis," 1:106-7.

name. For what it means that the land is defiled in Leviticus 18:25, see proposition eleven.

The third potential indicator is Yahweh's statement in Leviticus 25:23 that "the land is mine." In context, however, this passage refers specifically to Israel's vassal status under the covenant: "The land is mine and you reside in my land as foreigners and strangers." The Canaanites were not vassals to Yahweh, so the stipulations of the covenant do not apply to them. Psalm 24:1 says "the earth is the LORD's, and everything in it," but this is clearly an appeal to divine prerogative, not a claim of special status of all that is Yahweh's; if it were, the logic would demand that the whole earth be subject to *herem* for trespassing, and not only the inhabitants of the land. There is therefore no textual indicator that the land of Israel is Yahweh's special property that the people who live there have committed a particular offense by encroaching on.

The accusation made today concerning the conquest is that Yahweh is violating the Canaanites' rights in a barbaric and immoral manner. This objection, however, has nothing to do with the text in context (where there is no such thing as either human rights or divine morality). The text in context does indicate that Yahweh distributes land to whomever he wants to because he can, but in context this is part of the definition of a god (Chemosh can do it too, in Judg 11:24) and is not especially significant; the text emphasizes that Yahweh *did* give land to Israel but does not place particular importance on the idea that Yahweh *could* give land to Israel (that is, that he had a legal right to do it).

On the other hand, the text's inscrutable divine prerogative is not normally what apologists want to refer to when they say that Yahweh is the rightful owner of the land. If argument on the subject is inevitable, an appropriate analogy is not appeal to property rights but rather eminent domain. Eminent domain is something that the government has a legal right to do, but whether exercising that right is civil service or tyranny depends on the context in which it is employed. The government is not necessarily justified merely because it possesses the legal right; neither is it necessarily vilified because observers (or victims) of the action are not happy about it. The rightness or wrongness of appropriating property for public use has nothing to do with the specific actions of appropriating property and everything to do with the purpose for which the property will be used. The conquest works the same way; the value of the action is not determined by the specifics of the action, but by the purpose that the action is intended to fulfill. Therefore, the conquest should be evaluated (positively or negatively) on the basis of the purpose for which it was done, not on the basis of the legal rights of any of the parties involved. Ownership of the land or rights to it are not at issue here, and since the text does not emphasize them, apologists should not emphasize them, either.

PART 3

THE CANAANITES ARE NOT DEPICTED AS GUILTY OF BREAKING GOD'S LAW

The People of the Land Are Not Indicted for Not Following the Stipulations of the Covenant, and Neither Is Israel Expected to Bring Them into the Covenant

One of the more notable consequences of misreading the covenant as an outline of God's universal moral law is that the purpose of the old covenant is badly misunderstood. Many interpreters believe that the whole world stood under condemnation for breaking this universal moral law, but that they could be saved if they obeyed all of the rules given by God through Moses. Consequently, the conquest is interpreted as a missionary endeavor, in which the Canaanites are offered the choice between salvation and judgment, the former exemplified by the conversion of Rahab and the latter carried out by the *ḥerem*.[1] Eventually, says this interpretation, Israel was supposed to convert (or, implicitly, destroy) all people everywhere until the whole world was brought under the covenant. As we will see, every aspect of this interpretation is erroneous. As we will discuss over the next several

---

[1]For a better understanding of what happens to Rahab, see proposition eighteen.

propositions, the conquest was indeed about establishing the covenant, and the destruction of the Canaanite nations was essentially related to their not being included in it, but the logic of how those concepts relate to each other is different from what is commonly assumed. To clarify the issue, it is essential that we turn our attention briefly to what is often referred to as the theme of mission in the Old Testament.

THE JUSTIFICATION FOR MISSION IN THE OLD TESTAMENT AND ITS FLAWS

Mission in the context of biblical theology is a rather nebulous concept that tends to be flexible in its usage as it is molded to the purposes of the interpreter. Definitions cover a range of themes from evangelism to ecumenism to multiculturalism. We, however, are interested specifically in the idea that Israel (individually or collectively) was expected to encourage, intimidate, or in some other way recruit non-Israelites into joining the covenant.

This idea of mission as the purpose of the old covenant is derived partially from the modern concept of progress discussed in proposition three. Specifically, the idea is that the old covenant, by means of laws and wars, was trying to accomplish the same goal as the new covenant's forgiveness of sins and directive to go and make disciples. Consequently, as discussed, we tend to view these old covenant methods as inferior or even contemptible. But the presumption of progress also leads us to lay the same broad, conceptual categories—such as "missionaries" or "sinners"—from the New Testament onto the Old Testament narratives, instead of examining the Old Testament's own categories on its own terms.

Once again, an alternative approach to the idea of progress is the idea of procedure, and once again we can use the metaphor of baking a cake. Although every step contributes to cake in one way or another, we do not expect every step to contribute the same things in the same way; we would not imagine that the "mix the dry ingredients" stage is trying to do by friction what the "bake for thirty minutes" stage does with an oven. Yet this is essentially what we do when we assume that all of the biblical covenants were trying to achieve the same purpose. We will discuss the purpose of the old covenant in proposition twenty; for now, it is important to recognize that the Old Testament in context does not depict the Canaanite nations as standing condemned under the law, and neither does it portray Israel's wars as a kind of primitive old covenant Great Commission. The Old Testament text in context has its own conceptual categories, which are different from those of the New Testament, and we will now examine these.

IMPRECATIONS AGAINST THE NATIONS

The idea that God has some sort of universal moral law that people have broken and therefore they need to be saved from God's wrath by obeying the Mosaic covenant is also commonly supported by looking for examples of non-Israelite people experiencing wrath. The most frequently cited occurrence of this supposed punishment is, of course, the conquest,[2] but also popular are the various judgment oracles on the nations. But are these texts really accusing the nations of violating Yahweh's laws?

The most important thing to notice about the judgment oracles on the nations is that the direct audience is not the nation in question. We should not imagine that the prophet delivered the message to the ruler and people of the nation he addresses.[3] The oracle is delivered to Israelites, in Israel.[4] The reason for this is that Israel's covenant infidelity is based on aspiring to emulate the nations. By condemning the

---

[2]See for example Christopher J. H. Wright, *The Mission of God* (Downers Grove, IL: IVP Academic, 2006), 457.

[3]"There is no evidence that [the oracles] were ever delivered to the named recipients." Philip S. Johnston, "Amos," in *ZIBBCOT*, 5:58.

[4]"Even though they are directed against the foreign nations, these oracles are primarily intended for Israelite ears." Steven Voth, "Jeremiah," in *ZIBBCOT*, 4:335.

nations that the Israelite audience admires and imitates, the prophet condemns Israel as well.

It is also worth noting that the indictments against the nations do not normally correspond with the sins that are supposedly redressed by adherence to the Israelite covenant, or even any universal principle at all. Many of the condemnations are for (usually military) actions against Israel (e.g., Jer 49:1). Further, there is a notable absence of sexual deviations of the kind described in Leviticus 18, or of child sacrifice, despite the insistence of some interpreters that these were common practices of all Levantine cultures.[5] Even more striking is the absence of condemnation for any kind of idolatry,[6] which they certainly practiced and which, in contrast, is the most common accusation against Israel. While the nations are frequently accused of failing to uphold order (as the concept was understood in the ancient Near East), these offenses would be punishable by any ancient Near Eastern god and do not represent offenses against Yahweh or Yahweh's law specifically. As discussed in proposition three, we should not conflate the ancient world's ideal of order with God's ultimate ideal of goodness. These texts are designed to depict Yahweh carrying out the proper function of a god in the context of the ancient Near East, not to describe the offenses that will earn Yahweh's wrath in any time and place.

---

[5]For example: "The worship of the Canaanite people was morally corrupt. Their religious practices were degrading and damaging to human life and experience. It was widely held that these agricultural deities demanded certain cultic acts in order to promote fertility. . . . Canaanite worship was socially destructive. Its religious acts were pornographic and sick, seriously damaging to children, creating early impressions of deities with no interest in moral behaviour. It tried to dignify, by the use of religious labels, depraved acts of bestiality and corruption." Raymond Brown, *The Message of Deuteronomy* (Downers Grove, IL: InterVarsity Press, 1993), 145-46. See also Paul Copan, *Is God a Moral Monster? Making Sense of the Old Testament God* (Grand Rapids: Baker Books, 2011), 159-60, and to a lesser extent Richard S. Hess, "Leviticus," in *Expositor's Bible Commentary*, ed. Frank E. Gaebelein (Grand Rapids: Zondervan, 1992), 1:737, where the list of offending nations includes Egypt (which is not a focus of the conquest).

[6]Especially notable in light of the assertions of many missiological interpreters who depict idolatry as the root of all evil and sin. See, for example, Wright, *Mission of God*, 164-65.

Contrary to many interpretations, Jonah is not an exception to this. While Jonah is unique in the sense of actually visiting the foreign city,[7] Jonah does not deliver a call to repentance but merely a pronouncement of doom. The Ninevites are offered no option for salvation.[8] Even when they receive a reprieve, there is no evidence that they earned their pardon by converting to Yahwism.[9] There is no example anywhere in the Old Testament of anyone being actively persuaded to join the assembly of Israel (Ruth is actually discouraged; Ruth 1:11, 15) or being punished for failing or refusing to do so.

ISRAELITE IDOLATRY AS A POLITICAL OFFENSE

Many missiological theologians invoke the condemnation of Israelite idolatry to assume that idol worship in principle is especially abhorrent to God. According to Christopher Wright, "Idolatry [is] within the realm of that which incurs the wrath of God. . . . It issues in a catalog of vice and viciousness, polluting every aspect of human life."[10] This interpretation, however, is based on an anachronistic imposition of Anselm's model of atonement (wherein blood sacrifice is demanded to appease the wrath of God, which is incurred by failing to accord him proper honors) onto the Old Testament and cannot be warranted or sustained from the content of the Old Testament itself. No nation other than Israel is ever reprimanded for serving other gods, although the inability of their gods to protect them is occasionally mentioned with scorn (e.g., Jer 48). In context, however, this should not be read as an implicit call to conversion. Sennacherib mocks the gods of his victims in a similar manner (2 Kings 18:33-35), but the

---

[7]Kevin J. Youngblood, *Jonah*, Hearing the Message of Scripture: A Commentary on the Old Testament (Grand Rapids: Zondervan, 2013), 53.

[8]Jack M. Sasson, *Jonah*, AB (New York: Doubleday, 1990), 87.

[9]John H. Walton, "Jonah," in *Expositor's Bible Commentary*, 8:452-90, especially 457-58, 479-84.

[10]Wright, *Mission of God* (2006), 179.

purpose of the taunt is not to make disciples for Aššur; the intended response is fear, despair, and surrender. Moab does not even receive the taunt against Chemosh from Jeremiah, and even if they did, they are not expected to turn to Yahweh as a consequence; Moabites are specifically forbidden from joining the Israelite assembly (Deut 23:3). The purpose of the oracles against the nations is to remind Israel that Yahweh is not failing to protect Israel because Yahweh is impotent. Yahweh is destroying Israel's neighbors for offenses against Israel (e.g., Jer 48:27),[11] and despite their diligent service, their gods will be unable to save them (Jer 48:35).[12] The purpose of the oracle is not to explain to the Moabites that Yahweh is angry with them for burning incense to Chemosh. The purpose is to explain to the *Israelites* that even though Moab burned incense to Chemosh, Chemosh could not save them. Israel likewise burns incense to Chemosh, and Chemosh will not be able to save them, either.

But if idolatry is not inherently immoral, why is Israel punished so severely for practicing it? The answer is that the wrongness of the action for Israel is not anything in the action itself, but the context in which it is performed. As an example, there is nothing inherently wrong with the practice of dating a person. But if you happen to be married, then suddenly dating becomes very wrong, even though it is still acceptable for anyone who is not married. It is worth noting that marriage is exactly the metaphor that the Bible uses for the covenant. If I sleep with my neighbor's wife, it counts as adultery, and it is wrong. But if my neighbor sleeps with his own wife, it isn't wrong, even though it is the same action with the same woman. The source of the wrongness is not anything in the nature of the action or the recipient of the action, but in the relationship between the participants. In Israel, that relationship is defined by the covenant. The crime of idolatry is

---

[11] William L. Holladay, *Jeremiah 2*, Hermeneia (Minneapolis: Fortress, 1989), 360.
[12] The impotence of foreign gods is also mentioned (often explicitly) in, e.g., Is 16:11-12; 21:9; Jer 50:38; 51:17-18, 52; Ezek 30:13; Hab 2:18-20; Nah 1:14.

not failing to give God the proper reverence that he demands from all of humanity; rather, it is breaking the covenant that God has made with Israel. Those outside the covenant cannot commit this crime because they have no covenant to break.

Gods in the ancient world do not make covenants with their worshipers; a covenant is normally made between a king and his subjects. As we will examine further in proposition nineteen, Israel's covenant takes the form of a legal treaty between a sovereign and a vassal. Thus Israel relates to Yahweh as a patron deity (as an Assyrian would relate to Aššur), but also as an emperor (as an Assyrian vassal would relate to the Assyrian king). Most interpreters assume that the offense of idolatry is theological or dogmatic in nature and therefore that the crime of idolatry concerns improper relations with a deity.[13] In fact, however, since idolatry is a covenant offense, and covenants are made by kings and not gods, it seems more logical that Israelite idolatry is not offensive to Yahweh in his role as their God but in his role as their king. When we examine ancient vassal treaties, we see such language as "you shall not desire any other power over you"[14] and "[do not] set any other king or any other lord over yourselves, nor swear an oath to any other king or any other lord."[15] Therefore, we should conclude that idolatry in Israel does not represent religious apostasy—worshiping the wrong God—but rather political rebellion. Notably, this is exactly the word that the Bible itself gives to covenant infidelity (e.g., Jer 3:13). But Yahweh has not made a vassal treaty with any nation but Israel, so other nations cannot rebel.

---

[13]Normally this assumption is made based on the idea that the Bible specifically advocates the ideology we call monotheism; see, for example, Wright, *Mission of God*, 71, 126-35. However, a more careful reading of the text in context indicates that this is not the case. For a discussion on monotheism in the context of ancient Israelite religion versus modern understandings of the word, see Mark S. Smith, *The Origins of Biblical Monotheism* (New York: Oxford University Press, 2001), 10-14; André Lemaire, *The Birth of Monotheism: The Rise and Disappearance of Yahwism* (Washington, DC: Biblical Archeological Society, 2007), 43-47.

[14]Gary Beckman, *Hittite Diplomatic Texts* (Atlanta: SBL, 1996), 72.

[15]Simo Parpola and Kazuko Watanabe, *Neo-Assyrian Treaties and Loyalty Oaths* (Winona Lake, IN: Eisenbrauns, 2014), p. 31, line 68-72; p. 34, line 129; p. 41, line 301.

A LIGHT TO THE NATIONS

Some of the more common prooftexts cited in defense of Old Testament mission are those that reference the idea of Israel being a "light for the Gentiles" (Is 49:6).[16] Paul appropriates this verse for his own purposes in Acts 13:47, but that does not tell us anything about what it meant to Isaiah's original audience. We have no reason (apart from our assumptions of progress) to assume that this was any kind of Old Testament Great Commission. Nonetheless, neither is it without meaning. The essence of what it means to be a light to the nations is summed up in Zechariah 8:23: "In those days ten men from every language of the nations shall grasp the sleeve of a Jewish man, saying, 'Let us go with you, for we have heard that God is with you'" (NKJV). Note that it is the Gentiles who are chasing after the Jews, not the other way around.[17] Israel's purpose is not to create converts; it is to create something that people might potentially be able to convert *to*, namely, a people and a nation that God is with.

Importantly, though, God is with them whether they keep the covenant and prosper or break the covenant and are destroyed. In the former case, they are the envy of the nations; in the latter they become a byword. The purpose of the covenant is not to bless Israel (or anyone else), although it *can* accomplish this. The blessing of Abraham refers specifically to ownership of the land by Abraham's family, not the Sinaitic covenant (which is never cited as the fulfillment of Yahweh's promise to Abraham). Esau (Edom), Ammon, and Moab all receive their inheritance in fulfillment of the Abrahamic blessing just as Israel does (Deut 2:9-22), even though none of them are given a covenant, none of them are declared holy, and none of the nations that Yahweh drove out before them (Deut 2:21-22) are imprecated in any way. Israel's purpose, its participation in the covenant, and its holy status

---

[16]See, for example, Walter C. Kaiser, *Mission in the Old Testament* (Grand Rapids: Baker, 2000), 57.

[17]See also Esther 8:17.

have nothing to do with appeasing the wrath of God against humanity or purging the world of things God hates. They will be a light to the nations by being the medium through which God reveals himself. We will examine this further in proposition sixteen.

The same is true of the pilgrimage motif found in Isaiah (e.g., Is 2:2-4) and several psalms. The pilgrims come *from* all nations *to* Jerusalem. Israel does not go and bring Jerusalem to the nations; not with prophets (even Jonah converts no one), not with missionaries, and certainly not with an army. Foreigners can enter the assembly of Israel if they choose to unless they are from Ammon or Moab (Deut 23:3), but the exclusion of these indicates that the covenant was not intended to be universal; neither can the case be made that the reason these people are prohibited is punishment for sin, because eunuchs are also proscribed from the assembly (Deut 23:1), and it is not sinful to be a eunuch. But the most notable evidence that Israel is not supposed to absorb other nations by converting them is the differing treatment of cities within the land (Deut 20:16-18) and those outside it (Deut 20:10-15). The nation of Israel is (supposed to be) established in the land in a way that is never intended to apply outside it. Culturally (and behaviorally) there is no difference between the nations living between Dan and Beersheba and those to the immediate north or south; however, Israel is permitted to make treaties with the latter and live happily alongside them. Those people might be envious of Israel (because of Yahweh's blessing) and thereby wish to become Israelite, but there is no indication that they were ever expected (or inclined) to do so, or that they would be in any way punished for failing to do so.

We have proposed that the so-called missiological focus of the Old Testament is typically not found in the text itself but imposed on it by a larger canonical perspective (reading the conceptual categories of the New Testament back into the Old Testament) or a presumed meta-narrative (our modern concept of history as progress). In connection with that we have shown that the Old Testament neither indicts nor condemns the nations for their idolatry. The idols are powerless, and it is a covenant violation for Israel to serve them, but the nations are not under the covenant and therefore cannot violate it. Israel's role as a light to the nations does not give them the task of going out to the nations to convert them but indicates that if they serve well as God's covenant people, the nations will come to them. Consequently, we can conclude that Israel's conquest of the Canaanites cannot be interpreted as wiping them out for either their idolatry or for their refusal to join the covenant people.

It is worth noting, however, that the normal reason for finding mission as an objective of the old covenant comes as a result of finding mission as an objective for the new covenant and assuming, based on an ideology of progress, that the two covenants are the same. Mission *is* an objective for the new covenant, and how we interpret the old covenant in context does not affect that conclusion in any way. The two covenants are not the same; the new covenant is concerned with mission, the old covenant is not. For a discussion of the relationship between New Testament teaching and the Old Testament in context, see propositions twenty and twenty-one.

EXCURSUS: Demons and Idolatry in the Old Testament

A popular rationalization for the assumption that idolatry is the root of all evil and must be eradicated by the expansion of the Israelite covenant is the belief that idols somehow represent demonic opposition to God: "The Old Testament connects idolatry with the demonic—that is with the cosmic enemies of God who rebelled against him. . . . God's commands to Israel to wipe out Canaan's idols and false, immoral worship illustrate the cosmic warfare between Yahweh and the dark powers opposed to his rule."[18] This interpretation is anachronistic and cannot be derived from anything in the Old Testament itself.

---

[18]Copan, *Is God a Moral Monster?*, 167.

The most common source of the assertion that Old Testament idols are demonic is 1 Corinthians 10:20: "The sacrifices of pagans are offered to demons, not to God." In context, however, Paul is making an observation about something Greco-Roman religion claimed for itself, not offering cosmic revelation about how idols in all times and places really work. Plutarch, a Greek philosopher contemporary with Paul, writes that "demons" served as mediators between the gods in heaven and the human religious activities that took place on earth,[19] and Plato had said much the same thing four hundred years earlier.[20] But while Greco-Roman religion incorporated demons (as that culture understood the term, which is different from the way we moderns normally understand it) into the operations of its ritual system, the ancient Near East did not.

The word *daimonion* ("demon") meant something different to a Jew than it meant to a Platonist, but which meaning Paul intends does not matter because his observation concerns co-identity with a community, not the metaphysics of idols (which is why he also says that an idol is nothing in 1 Cor 10:19-20): "You cannot drink the cup of the Lord and the cup of demons too; you cannot have a part in both the Lord's table and the table of demons" (1 Cor 10:21; see the concept of co-identity in proposition sixteen). "Having a part in the table" is an idiom for co-identification and community;[21] compare to eating with

---

[19]"Let us not imagine that the god . . . is present at these ceremonies and helps in conducting them; but let us commit these matters to those ministers of the gods to whom it is right to commit them, as to servants and clerks, and let us believe that demigods [*daimonas*, "demons"] are guardians of sacred rites of the gods and prompters in the Mysteries." *Obsolescence of Oracles* 417. In *Plutarch: Moralia V*, trans. Frank Cole Babbitt, Loeb Classical Library 306 (Cambridge, MA: Harvard University Press, 1999), 389.

[20]Plato speaks of demons "interpreting and transporting human things to the gods and divine things to men; entreaties and sacrifices from below, and ordinances and requitals from above . . . through [demons] (*to daimonion*) are conveyed all divination and priestcraft concerning sacrifice and ritual and incantations, and all soothsaying and sorcery." *Symposium* 202e. In *Plato: Lysis, Symposium, Gorgias*, trans. W. R. M. Lamb, Loeb Classical Library 166 (Cambridge, MA: Harvard University Press, 2001), 179.

[21]"Idolatry involves a participatory union which excludes one from the union of Christ. . . . Union with Christ and union with demons are mutually exclusive." E. P. Sanders, *Paul and Palestinian Judaism* (Minneapolis: Fortress, 1977), 455.

Gentiles (or not) in Galatians 2:12, and the admonition to not even eat with immoral Christians in 1 Corinthians 5:11. The threat in the next line (1 Cor 10:22, "Are we trying to arouse the Lord's jealousy?") invokes Deuteronomy 32:16-17: "They made him jealous with their foreign gods and angered him with their *tôʿēbâ* idols. They sacrificed to *šēdîm*, which are not God." Despite the translation of *šēdîm* as "demons" (*daimoniois*) in the Septuagint (the Greek translation of the Old Testament used by the New Testament writers), "demons" in the ancient Near East never received sacrifices, so it is more likely that the *šēdîm* (whatever they were) were considered by their worshipers to be gods, not demons, and thus Paul's observation would not extend to them. The emphasis, however, is not on their taxonomy, but on their status as *tôʿēbâ* (outside the order of the community; see proposition thirteen), and as not-God. Paul's point is that Christians should not co-identify with anything outside the Christian community, just as Israel was not supposed to co-identify with anything outside the covenant community, regardless of what it is. For Christians that includes idols, but it also includes a lot of other things that have nothing to do with either idols or demons (see proposition twenty-one).

Demons in the ancient Near Eastern conception that forms the context of Deuteronomy 32 were extraneous to the ritual system.[22] They had no needs that humans served to meet and did not work to bring about cosmic order, so demons and humans were useless to each other. They inhabited liminal areas on the periphery of the ordered world such as mountains and deserts and attacked humans opportunistically (when the gods aren't looking) or when ordered to by the gods. The metaphysics of the inhabitants of the liminal world is actually somewhat blurred, with demons being classified interchangeably

---

[22]There is no overarching categorical term (i.e., *demon*) for this class of creature; the category basically includes any spirit being that is neither a god nor a ghost (e.g., a deceased mortal). John H. Walton, "Demons in Mesopotamia and Israel: Exploring the Category of Nondivine but Supernatural Entities," in *Windows to the Ancient World of the Hebrew Bible*, ed. Bill T. Arnold et al. (Winona Lake, IN: Eisenbrauns, 2014), 229-45.

with wild animals, the spirits of the dead, and even living people, both outcasts from society[23] and the hordes of "invincible barbarians" (see proposition twelve). Isaiah 34:14 describes a desolate region inhabited by wild goats (NIV) and uses a normal word for "goats" (*śāʿîr*, e.g., Gen 37:31; Lev 4:23) even though the Septuagint translates it *daimonia*, "demons." Isaiah 34:13 also mentions *lîlît* (NIV "owls"), which is a cognate of the name of an Akkadian demon (*lilitu*), but the other creatures mentioned in Isaiah 34:13-15 are all ordinary animals (jackals, ostriches, snakes, and hawks). The category of liminal creatures also includes the chaos monsters (i.e., Hebrew Leviathan, Ugaritic Litan), the personified sea (Hebrew Yamm, Akkadian Tiamat), and perhaps even the personified wilderness (Hebrew Azazel).

The Second Temple period's idea of demons as an army of evil engaged in combat against God (or the gods) is unknown to the Old Testament or to anywhere else in the ancient Near East. While the gods do occasionally fight against chaos monsters to establish or preserve order (see proposition fourteen), the Old Testament does not in any way attempt to associate idolatry with the chaos monsters. Even when human enemies are depicted as chaos creatures, as Egypt is in Isaiah 30:7 and Ezekiel 29:3; 32:2, the monster is Pharaoh, not Egypt's gods. Further, even though God fights the chaos creatures, they are in no way depicted as evil or opposed to the will and purposes of God. Yahweh creates the chaos monsters in Genesis 1:21 (NIV "great creatures of the sea," Hebrew *tannîn*), the Behemoth in Job 40:15 ("which I made along with you"), and the Leviathan in Psalm 104:26 ("which you formed to frolic there"). The sea serves as Yahweh's weapon against the Egyptian army (Ex 15:10, 19) and against Jonah (Jon 1:4), and the *tĕhôm* ("deep," the cosmic waters from Gen 1:2) is his weapon against antediluvian humanity in Genesis 7:11. Other demonic beings serve as Yahweh's agents as well. An evil spirit from the Lord afflicts Saul

---

[23]Meir Malul, *Knowledge, Control, and Sex: Studies in Biblical Thought, Culture, and Worldview* (Tel Aviv: Archeological Center Publication, 2002), 274.

(1 Sam 16:14-16) and perhaps also Abimelech (Judg 9:23; NIV "animosity"); God sends a spirit to trick Ahab's prophets into sending him to his death (1 Kings 22:20-22); God takes credit for the satan's affliction of Job (Job 1:20; 2:3). The seven men in Ezekiel 9:2 who slaughter the people of Jerusalem and defile the temple (Ezek 9:5-7) are probably a reference to a group of Babylonian chthonic deities called the Sebetti,[24] and the great fish that God sends after Jonah is probably a chaos creature of some kind.[25] Even the "invincible barbarians" are summoned by God to attack Israel (Ezek 38:16-17).[26] Foreign *deities*, however, are never portrayed using chaotic or liminal imagery. Thus, in the Old Testament, idols are not associated with the demonic (that is, the liminal and chaotic), and the demonic (where it does appear) is not depicted in absolute opposition to God.

---

[24]Daniel Bodi, *The Book of Ezekiel and the Poem of Erra*, Orbis Biblicus et Orientalis 104 (Freiburg: Universitätsverlag, 1991), 100.

[25]John H. Walton, "Jonah," in *ZIBBCOT*, 5:104-5.

[26]For Ezekiel's description of Gog's hordes being based on the depiction of enemies in the Cuthaean Legend, see Daniel Bodi, "Ezekiel," in *ZIBBCOT*, 4:484-85.

Ancient Law Codes Such as the One Contained in Leviticus 18–20 Are Not Lists of Rules to Be Obeyed, and Therefore the Canaanites Cannot Be Guilty of Violating Them

The so-called holiness code that contains Leviticus 18–20 is often interpreted as a list of divine demands that constitute God's mandatory moral standards. Depending on the interpreter, these demands either represent the highest standard of human moral excellence (common in Judaism) or an unbearable burden designed to be contrasted with the future liberation by Christ (common in Christianity). Some of the imperatives (e.g., Lev 19:19) are cited by skeptics as evidence of the inherent absurdity of the Bible's moral system. These interpretations are misguided because the text in context is not intended as a litany of moral instructions. Instead, it falls into a genre of ancient Near Eastern wisdom literature called *legal wisdom*.

LAW CODES ARE NOT LISTS OF MORAL COMMANDS

One of the early mistakes when the ancient Near Eastern law documents were first found was that they were labeled codes and considered legislation. As analysis continued, however, the literary context that they were in and the fact that they were not comprehensive, combined with growing knowledge of ancient culture and literary genres, brought a gradual revision. Scholars came to recognize that the ancient tradition of circumscribing literature in a particular area of knowledge by means of lists was a means of communicating wisdom with regard to that area.[1] Lists of symptoms and treatments, for example, were gathered to give practitioners wisdom about disease (in the way it was understood in the ancient world). Likewise, lists of divinatory observations and the resulting prognoses were gathered to give divination experts wisdom regarding the messages that they believed were embedded in the signs provided by the gods. These served the utilitarian purpose of preparing experts in these fields to give competent advice to their clients. In the legal tradition, the lists of sayings in documents like Hammurabi's stele serve a similar purpose. By gathering together lists of legal situations and then identifying a judicial response, judges receive the wisdom of the king regarding being wise and just in their decisions.[2] This understanding of the genre is well established and supported by all scholars of ancient Near Eastern literature.

All of this indicates that the propositions of an ancient legal treatise are not intended to be read as rules; instead, they serve a pedagogical function. Collectively they circumscribe the bounds of civil, legal, and ritual order. The lists inform the specialists whose task it is to preserve the order (judges, priests, etc.) about the nature of what exactly they are upholding so that they can perform their duty effectively. We

---

[1]"The ancients . . . [do not] present us with what might be termed 'prescriptive' treatises. Their written specimens were mostly incidental to the points that we want to make." Meir Malul, *Knowledge, Control, and Sex: Studies in Biblical Thought, Culture, and Worldview* (Tel Aviv: Archeological Center Publication, 2002), 447.

[2]Jean Bottéro, *Mesopotamia*, trans. Zainab Bahrani and Marc Van de Mieroop (Chicago: University of Chicago Press, 1992), 161-69; Marc Van de Mieroop, *Philosophy Before the Greeks* (Princeton, NJ: Princeton University Press, 2015), 175; John H. Walton, *Ancient Near Eastern Thought in the Old Testament* (Grand Rapids: Baker, 2006), 287-88.

might imagine, for example, a medical doctor, whose task it is to preserve health and do no harm; in order to perform those duties she must first know what constitutes health and what counts as harm. Modern medical ethics describes the ideas of health and harm through elaborate definitions; the ancient Near East would have described them by compiling lists of examples of what an ideal health care specialist would and would not do in various situations (some practical, some purely hypothetical, and some intentionally absurd).

One thing that we moderns still circumscribe in this way is art. The difference between art and not-art is not normally understood by evaluating objects according to a fixed definition of art, or even by compiling a checklist of criteria that an object must meet in order to be considered art. Rather, the difference is learned by visiting museums and galleries and studying things that are known to be (or not be) art; the objective is not to formulate a definition but to train the prospective artist (or scholar of art) to know art when they see it. This intuitive recognition is what we mean when we say that ancient treatises teach wisdom. A legal treatise is not like a checklist of the properties of art that someone could either consult to evaluate art or follow to produce art. Indeed, even the *making* of such a list would defeat its purpose. Art cannot be produced by a mechanical process of following instructions, and the same is true for wisdom. Rather, the legal treatises are like a book of paintings with the title *All of This Is Art*. The laws contained in the ancient treatises are not a list of bullet points that someone can follow in order to produce justice. Instead, they instruct the potential judge as to what justice looks like so that the judge will know it when they see it.

The purpose of ancient Near Eastern lists is to illustrate the underlying principles of the subject at hand through a series of (hypothetical) examples.[3] We can see a similar concept in the way we use

---

[3]Malul, *Knowledge*, 447.

word problems to teach mathematics: "If the shadow of a building is fifteen feet, and the angle of the sun is forty-five degrees, the height of the building shall be fifteen feet." The purpose of this statement is to illustrate the underlying principle of trigonometry. It does not presume to instruct the student in the proper technique that one ought to use for measuring buildings or to dictate the height and setting of an ideal building. The student who comes away from the lesson only with the knowledge that a building is fifteen feet high has, in fact, missed the object of the lesson entirely. The truth of the exercise—where its authority is vested—is in the underlying theory, not the details of the illustration. A student who memorizes a list of solutions to math problems has not actually learned any math. He knows that a train leaving Station A at sixty miles per hour will pass a train leaving Station B, one hundred miles away, at sixty miles per hour fifty minutes after they both depart at five o'clock, or she knows that if the boy has four apples, and the girl has half as many apples as the boy, and the teacher has three times as many apples as the girl, then the teacher has six apples. So now let us imagine that he or she applies the authority of math—meaning the list of the solutions to word problems—to railway timetables and food distribution. "Math teaches that trains must pass at 5:50 and that teachers must have six apples. You aren't denying the authority of math, are you?"

We can compare this example to the list of propositions in Leviticus 19:19: "'Do not mate different kinds of animals. Do not plant your field with two kinds of seed. Do not wear clothing woven of two kinds of material." Just like the math problems, these are illustrative, not prescriptive. Reading them as somehow providing a guide to practice in the fields of textiles, agriculture, and animal husbandry is like reading a trigonometry problem as somehow providing a guide to the field of civil engineering. In Leviticus 19:19 the underlying principle being communicated involves the ancient Near Eastern idea that mixed things belong to the divine realm.[4] Divine creatures are composites of various kinds of animals, and cloth woven from two kinds of thread is used in the tabernacle and the vestment of the priests. The underlying principle in this case is that divine things should not be put to ordinary, mundane use. Although the underlying principles vary by context, all of the instructions in Leviticus should be read in this way. They are hypothetical examples designed to communicate abstract principles, not commands to be obeyed.

UNDERLYING PRINCIPLES ARE
NOT MORAL COMMANDS EITHER

Nonetheless, we should not make the mistake of thinking that the underlying principles are any more prescriptive than the laws themselves. Walter Kaiser, for example, proposes what he calls a principalizing model of hermeneutics, wherein a particular command is analyzed for its underlying (moral) principle, which is then extrapolated into a timeless moral truth, which can then be applied specifically to any given circumstance.[5] The methodology of this approach is flawed for several reasons.

First, the principalizing process requires taking the original statement out of context. For example, it is not uncommon to hear arguments that the kosher food laws were given as rules for God's ideal diet in terms of the nutritional effects of various foods on the human body (see also Ezek 4:9; Dan 1:8-16). While there is nothing inherently absurd in the idea of a divinely prescribed ideal diet, and no reason to suppose that the ancient world could not have imagined such a thing, we nonetheless

---

[4]Jacob Milgrom, *Leviticus 17–22*, AB (New York: Doubleday, 2000), 1659.
[5]The particular command he uses is Deut 25:4, "Do not muzzle an ox while it is treading out the grain"; the underlying (moral) principle is "animals are God's gift to humanity and should be treated kindly," and the timeless moral truth is "giving engenders gentleness and graciousness in those mortals who care for and can minister to those who serve them as well, whether they are animals or people." Walter C. Kaiser, "A Principalizing Model," in *Four Views on Moving Beyond the Bible to Theology*, ed. Stanley N. Gundry and Gary T. Meadors (Grand Rapids: Zondervan 2009), 25.

understand that the dietary laws of the Pentateuch are in no way concerned with the domain of health. If we did think the laws concerned health, we would continue to observe them no matter what the New Testament allows, for the same reasons that we would not eat seventeen donuts for breakfast even though nothing in the New Testament says we can't. But most of us realize instead that there is no such thing as God's ideal diet, at least not that can be derived from the Bible. It is true that God made our bodies to handle certain foods in certain ways, and that what we eat can affect our well-being in profound ways, but we are left to discover the specifics of nutrition on our own.

In the context of biblical legal treatises, morality is like nutrition. Trying to derive God's moral ideals is like trying to derive God's dietary ideals and is misguided for the same reasons.

Since the text of legal treatises in context does not address the formation of moral principles any more than it addresses the formation of dietary habits, *any* moral principle that we derive from the text is out of context. Imagine trying to derive timeless moral truths from a chocolate-chip cookie recipe. While this might theoretically be possible ("the mixing of the wet and dry ingredients teaches us that we have to work together with those who are different from us in order to accomplish goals that would be impossible to achieve by ourselves"), if that is all you use your cookie recipe for, you'll never make any cookies, which defeats the purpose of even having the recipe in the first place. The Old Testament legal texts do exist for a purpose, but that purpose is not for the formation of moral principles. The purpose might potentially have some application to the formation of moral principles, but not in the form of lifting direct quotations. (See proposition twenty-one for a discussion of applying Old Testament teaching outside its original context.)

Second, because the principalizing process inherently (and intentionally) involves expanding particulars into abstractions, the results of the process can vary widely based on which particulars are being emphasized. The (inevitable) result is that the timeless truths at the center of the process are *essentially arbitrary* and can sometimes be quite absurd. L. William Countryman, for example, argues, based on select New Testament criticisms of conservative Roman family and social conventions (the passages that advocate mutuality in marriage, for example), that the timeless moral truth involves the church fighting against *any* family or social convention in principle, which he then interprets as a moral obligation for Christians to allow (and encourage) homosexuality, promiscuity, and pornography, in order to undermine the conservative family and social convention of modern culture.[6] More to our present purposes, the various commands to *ḥerem* the people of Canaan (e.g., Deut 7:2) are commonly principalized to reveal a timeless moral truth that infidels and/or sinners ought to be slaughtered without mercy.

Often interpreters attempt to resolve these issues by proposing distinctions between occasional commands that cannot be extrapolated into timeless moral truths and universal commands that apply to everybody: "While the whole Torah does not purport to be binding on all mankind, *part of it does. . . .* A good example is seen in the contrast between laws prohibiting Israel from eating certain types of meat that are deemed unclean and the prohibitions regarding sexual immorality."[7] As we have just discussed, however, even this supposedly good example is far from clear. Biblical nutritionists still say that the food laws are binding because they reflect God's ideal of health, hygiene, or propriety. Countryman says that sexual laws are not binding for the same reasons that food laws are not binding, because the New Testament released all of the old Jewish restrictions on purity equally.[8] Ultimately, the determination of which commands

---

[6]L. William Countryman, *Dirt, Greed, and Sex* (Philadelphia: Fortress, 1988), esp. 244-45, 264-65.

[7]Paul Copan and Matthew Flannagan, *Did God Really Command Genocide? Coming to Terms with the Justice of God* (Grand Rapids: Baker Books, 2014), 54-55.

[8]Countryman, *Dirt, Greed, and Sex*, 42-44.

are universal and which are occasional is just as arbitrary as the contents of the commands themselves.

The third problem with the particularizing model is that it is inherently anachronistic. Timeless moral truths cannot be derived purely from examination of the text in context; if they could, no extrapolation or abstraction would be necessary, and we could simply take the command literally. But once we move beyond the context of the text, we have to consider what we're bringing into the process. A good example of how this works is the (similar) hermeneutic of finding *scientific* (rather than moral) truths, called concordism. Concordists look at texts that describe the way the earth was made (cosmogony) or what its structures are (cosmic geography) and try to extrapolate abstract principles that can be read to accord with the observations of modern science. So, for example, Genesis 1:7 ("God made the vault and separated the water under the vault from the water above it") is abstracted to the timeless principle of "God made the thing up in the air where the water comes from," which is then interpreted specifically to mean "God made the atmosphere." Likewise, Job 26:7 ("he suspends the earth over nothing") is abstracted to "God put the earth where nothing was holding it up" and is interpreted to mean "God put the globe of planet earth in the vacuum of space."

Concordist hermeneutics are *arbitrary* because they (deliberately) disassociate the text's interpretation from its meaning in context. They are *anachronistic* because the meaning texts are given is based on the context of the interpreter, not on the context of the text. When Christians adopted Aristotelian cosmology in the thirteenth century, all of their concordist hermeneutics identified timeless cosmological truths that supported Aristotelian geocentrism. When a steady state cosmology was popular in the nineteenth century, all of the timeless cosmological truths pointed to a static universe, until the Big Bang cosmological model replaced it, at which point all of the Bible's timeless cosmological truths suddenly supported the Big Bang. In all of this development, none of the Bible's actual content changed; what changed was *which* passages were identified as occasional or timeless and/or which principles were extrapolated from them. This change, in turn, was prompted by the demands of the times. It was *science*, not the biblical text, that determined what the Bible did or did not say. This remained true whether the interpreters were trying to defend the Bible or defame it; apologists argued that the Bible's scientific teaching supported whatever was the consensus at the time, while critics argued (often using different passages) that the Bible taught ridiculous falsehoods.

The same arbitrariness and anachronism is found in the principalizing model, which should perhaps be called moral concordism. Moral theologians (whether apologetic or critical) who practice moral concordism identify the Bible's timeless moral teaching according to what a combination of the interpreter's cognitive environment and personal biases (conscious or unconscious) indicates that it should be. In Countryman's case, he expects the New Testament to teach the supreme importance of personal happiness, individual autonomy, freedom of self-expression, and universal equality of all people, so he chooses his passages and timeless principles accordingly. Whether or not these things are valuable is not the point; the point is that these values are derived from modern humanism, not the text's first-century Hellenized Judaism. Their presence in the Bible, like the presence of the Big Bang cosmology, is derived entirely from the needs of the (modern) interpreter, and not from anything in the text at all. As we discussed in proposition three, if we want to read the text in context, we cannot do so under the assumption that it is going to affirm our values, because our values come from our (modern) cognitive environment and do not necessarily have anything to do with the concerns of the text.

CAN WE USE THE BIBLE FOR MORAL KNOWLEDGE ANYWAY?

As discussed in proposition three, the Bible as Scripture—that is, as the divinely inspired, authoritative word of God—does not provide us with moral knowledge because God's purpose in providing it for us does not include teaching us how to be moral. We have also seen that, even in context, the statements in a legal treatise would not have been understood as commands even to the original audience. However, the entire Bible is not in the genre of legal treatise. When Joshua tells the Israelites to "keep away from the devoted things, so that you will not bring about your own destruction" (Josh 6:18), he is not illustrating an abstract principle; he actually intends his audience to obey. The book of Proverbs is intended as (essentially) ethical instructions; proverbial sayings are not commands, either, but the underlying principles circumscribed by the sayings in Proverbs describe something that is similar to what we would call ethics, as opposed to the holiness described in Leviticus (see proposition ten). Finally, even though in context the law is not giving commands, the principles espoused by the various statements (especially the Ten Commandments) do in fact represent their society's basic moral knowledge. Further, even if God through Scripture is not providing us with moral knowledge, we still have moral knowledge, which in turn means we must get it from somewhere. Why should that somewhere not be the Bible?

So far in our discussion of what the Bible is, we have focused on its capacity as the divinely inspired and authoritative Word of God. That is what the Bible is, but that is not *all* the Bible is. The Bible is fully divine and fully human. The Old Testament especially is a masterpiece of literature that preserves the accumulated wisdom of two thousand years of human culture. As such, it can be—and has been—used for anything that literature can be used for. Its content has inspired great art, music, and philosophy and has provided a resource for anthropologists and historians. It has aesthetic value; the prose and poetry (especially in the Psalms) are works of art in themselves. It has symbolic value, as when it is used to swear in witnesses or inaugurate presidents. In the Eastern Orthodox Church, it can serve as an icon. It can even serve the basic functions of a book; it can be read for edification or pleasure, or it can decorate a coffee table. However, that the Bible is *also* the inspired and authoritative Word of God does not make it better in the capacity of these human functions than any of its mundane counterparts. Art that is based on scenes from the Bible is not better than art that is based on scenes from, say, Shakespeare or Homer simply because it is based on the Bible. In the same way, a moral philosophy based on sayings that happen to be found in the Bible is not better than something based on sayings found elsewhere simply because it is based on the Bible. Its value as a moral philosophy would have to be determined by whatever process is used to determine such things.

Saying that the Bible was not written in order to teach us how to be moral is not the same thing as saying that we can have no moral knowledge at all. The Bible was not written to teach us about nutrition or to teach us about science, yet we can still have perfectly functional knowledge of those things. It does not necessarily even mean that our moral knowledge does not ultimately originate from God; some proponents of the so-called divine command theory of ethics do not even make use of the Bible but rather affirm that, while God sets the standards of morality, our knowledge of specific moral principles is provided by conscience: "A divine command theorist could argue that, in principle, the rightness or wrongness of an action is identical to and constituted by God's commands and prohibitions but that we *know* what is right and wrong through our conscience and not from any purported written revelation like the Bible."[9] It may be the case that the wisdom of ancient cultures preserved through their literature is a fine source for our moral knowledge. That, however, is a determination for philosophers, not theologians; further, if it is the case, the

---

[9]Copan and Flanagan, *Did God Really Command Genocide?*, 154.

Bible would not (in that capacity) be qualitatively different from any other work of ancient literature. We must not conflate the Bible's status and function as *Scripture* with its status and function as *literature*.[10] Providing us with moral knowledge is not its purpose as *Scripture*; consequently, any moral knowledge we can derive from it does not carry the *authority* of Scripture, but rather only the authority of human wisdom. If we want to use the Bible as a source of moral knowledge, then, it will have to be either as part of a broad sample of the accumulated wisdom of human culture (as is done, for example, by C. S. Lewis in *The Abolition of Man*), or perhaps because we find ancient Israelite culture especially inspiring (as, for example, European neoclassicists in the eighteenth century found ancient Greece). A case could perhaps be made for either, but the point is that if we want to use the Bible as a source of moral knowledge, we cannot do so on the basis that it is *Scripture*, because providing us with moral knowledge is not what Scripture is for.

It may theoretically be possible to reconstruct what the principles defined by the lists of statements in the Bible's legal treatises actually were (as with the mixed things described above), but even this is not really the point of the text. The legal treatises (or any other biblical document, for that matter) were not canonized simply to preserve the record of their contents. We do not, for example, read historical narratives as merely a record of who did what, even though recording who did what is the purpose of the narrative genre. Just as the historical books were not preserved as Scripture for the purpose of allowing posterity to make accurate documentaries, so the legal wisdom of the Pentateuch was not preserved as Scripture for the purpose of allowing posterity to reconstruct the governing principles of Israelite society. We might compare the legal texts in this sense with the official

---

[10]To use metaphors from theological language, we need not be gnostic in regard to the biblical text (that is, denying that it has any human aspect), but we must not be Eutychian either (merging the human and divine aspects).

rules of a game or sport. The players read the rules and obey and apply them directly; they are the primary audience. In this analogy, the players represent the ancient Israelites. The fans and spectators of the sport also read the rules, but they read them not to follow them, and also not simply to regurgitate trivia about their content, but so that they will understand what is happening as they watch the game. In this analogy, the fans represent Christians who are interested in taking what the Bible says seriously. But we would never expect a referee to show up at a fan's house handing out penalties because the fan has failed to behave according to the rules of the game, even though penalties would be handed out to players in the context of the game. Likewise, we should not expect God to show up handing out judgments on individuals or institutions because they have not behaved according to the principles that were set down for Israel. Those principles were written to Israel, not to us. For a discussion of what significance they *do* have for us, see proposition twenty-one.

The Old Testament's legal wisdom literature in context is indeed supposed to shape Israelite society, but it is not supposed to provide a set of instructions by which anyone in any place or time can construct God's ideal society. We will discuss this further in proposition twenty. It is likewise not profitable to defend the Bible's supposed moral superiority by comparing the underlying principles from ancient Near Eastern law codes with those of the Pentateuch, as best they can be derived, and examining all the ways Israel's principles are more ideal.[11] As discussed in proposition three, the ideal in such an argument that Israel would supposedly align more with will end up being based on what the *interpreter* thinks is ideal. This kind of thinking reduces the Bible to nothing more than one book among many that is useful for defending modern ideals.

---

[11]See for example Paul Copan, "Are Old Testament Laws Evil?," in *God Is Great, God Is Good*, ed. William Lane Craig and Chad Meister (Downers Grove, IL: IVP Academic, 2009), 138-44.

The purpose of such passages as Leviticus 18 and Deuteronomy 12 is not to teach that God is punishing the evil Canaanites for criminal violations of timeless moral principles that happen to accord exactly with the sensibilities of modern humanists (Christian or otherwise). It is also not to teach that sacrifices must be made in order to produce a society that is closer to the kind that would be approved of by modern humanists. It is certainly not to teach the Israelites how to be better humanists; conversely, neither does it teach humanists how to be better Israelites. Legal treatises do not document moral commands or moral violations of any kind. Nonetheless, those passages exist for a reason, and they were documented and preserved for a reason. What that reason is, and what purpose these passages serve, we will examine in the next proposition.

Holiness Is a Status Granted by God; It Is Not Earned Through Moral Performance, and Failing to Have It Does Not Subject One to Judgment

It is not uncommon for people to read about the Canaanites and the conquest and conclude that the Canaanites are being punished because they were not holy. We have been contending in several of the previous propositions that the Canaanites are not being punished and suggesting that the Canaanites cannot be considered as having violated the moral principles of the law. Toward that end, in the previous proposition, we argued that Israel's legal literature does not contain a list of rules that dictates God's demands for how they should behave or how they should structure their society. We proposed instead that the legal treatise is a list of examples compiled to circumscribe an underlying principle. If that is true, the legal literature does not even provide moral principles for Israel, let alone for the Canaanites. When Israelites are unfaithful to the Torah, they are not breaking God's universal moral law; they are breaking the covenant. As discussed in proposition eight, Canaanites cannot break the covenant because they are not in a covenant relationship with Yahweh.

Now we are shifting our attention to the issue of holiness. Unlike anything that we find in the rest of the ancient world, in the case of the book of Leviticus, the underlying principle in this legal (primarily ritual) treatise is holiness. Israel is holy, and the Canaanites (in contrast) are not holy. But what does it mean to be holy in the context of the Old Testament cognitive environment? This is essential if we are to understand whether the Canaanites are at fault for not being holy.

We are familiar with Yahweh's famous words in Leviticus 19:2, "Be holy because I, the LORD your God, am holy" (NIV). Following Peter's appropriation in 1 Peter 1:15-16, this is often interpreted to read "be moral because I am moral" and invoked as the foundation of an ethical theory called *imitatio Dei*, in which being good consists of being the kind of person that God is and doing the things or kinds of things that God would do. The ensuing content of Leviticus 19-20, often called the holiness code, is then commonly interpreted as a list of commands that dictate God's demands, usually suggesting that meeting all of the demands will conform the person's character to God's.

This is not, however, what is actually happening in Leviticus. Humans are humans, and God is God, and what is proper and fitting for one may not be proper and fitting for the other. Humans are the image of God, but humans are not—and should not be—*like* God, that is, acting as God acts and doing as God does. This indeed is the entire point of Genesis 3. The serpent promises that Adam and Eve will be like God (Gen 3:5); they eat the fruit, and they do indeed become like God (Gen 3:22), and that is the entire problem. To be as God is and do as God does is the prerogative of God alone. It is not within our grasp.

We might compare to a situation in which parents have gone out for the evening and left their oldest child in charge. That child is given a measure of responsibility and authority—to rule the house and subdue it, as it were—but at the same time it would not be appropriate for the child to fully assume the role of the parents: taking control of bank accounts, disciplining younger siblings, and so on. It is proper (indeed, necessary) for the parents to do these things because they are the parents, but the child remains a sibling no matter how much (temporary) authority they may have, and it is the nature of those relationships and statuses that dictates proper actions, not anything inherent in the action itself.

Most interpreters are aware of the potential absurdity of full equation of divine and human action (in both directions; it is meaningless to say, "God does not sleep with his wife's sister," e.g., Lev 18:18) and on that basis extrapolate holiness to reflect a kind of essential character that motivates God's actions; in other words, they interpret the document to say, "This list describes what God would do if God were human." Holiness, in that way of thinking, becomes fundamentally a character trait, specifically designating a particular moral character. The specific interpretation of Leviticus 19:2 becomes, then, "Your moral character should be the same as my moral character," with an implicit "and if it is not you will be punished just like I am punishing the Canaanites, because their moral character does not live up to my standards" (derived from Lev 18:24).

The problem with this specific interpretation is that the word translated "holy" (Hebrew root *qdš*) cannot possibly mean "having a certain moral character."[1] The vast majority of things designated as holy are inanimate objects such as the ark, the altar, and the lampstands for the tabernacle. The word is also applied to places (Mount Sinai, the inside of the temple), to time (the sabbath), to geopolitical abstractions (land, nation), and to animals (devoted or sacrificed); none of these have character or moral agency of any kind. The only persons (potential moral agents) designated as a holy thing are the priests, but this is never interpreted to imply that the priests are more moral or have a different moral character from the rest of the assembly. (When the nation or people is identified as holy, it refers to the communal abstraction, not to all the specific individuals who participate in it. Otherwise, specifying the priests individually as holy would be redundant. This is precisely the mistake made by Korah, Dathan, and Abiram in Numbers 16:3 when they claim, "The whole community is holy, every one of them." The

---

[1]Although commonly invoked as a parallel, the word in Mt 5:48 translated "be perfect" (*telios*) is never used by the LXX to translate *qdš*.

holiness of the social abstraction does not extend to all of its members; only the priests as individual persons are holy. See proposition eleven.)

Likewise, *holy* cannot refer to a superlative state of cleanliness or ritual purity. This potential interpretation is sometimes based on the Akkadian cognate *qašdu(m)*, which refers (in its verbal form) to washing, in a sense of cleansing for ritual use but also in a mundane sense, that is, laundry.[2] This getting rid of physical dirt is sometimes abstracted to removal of impurity, with impurity being further extrapolated to account for any given context; so, for example:

> The experience of holiness calls for the human response of purity and cleanliness. Thus the priestly tradition requires the cleanness of proper ritual and the maintenance of separation: the prophetic tradition demands the cleanness of social justice; the wisdom tradition stresses the cleanness of inner integrity and individual moral acts.[3]

The problem with this is that Hebrew already has a word for "clean" (*ṭāhôr*), and it does not mean the same thing as *qdš*.[4] A clean thing does not become holy by applying a more rigorous version of the same process that transitioned it from unclean to clean. The unclean → clean transition and the common → holy transition are, in fact, separate processes, the former performed by humans and the latter by God.[5] The concept of cleanliness is connected to the idea of suitability for cultic ritual use or participation. Clean (*ṭāhôr*) cannot mean "moral" for the same reasons that "holy" (*qdš*) cannot; many unclean actions are not sinful (menstruation, attending a funeral), and many unclean things have no moral agency (animals, molds, locations). Cleanliness is tangentially related to immorality in the sense that sin (as immorality) is one possible cultic contaminant, but impurity (*ṭūmʾâ*) and immorality

---

[2]Jackie A. Naudé, "קדש," in *NIDOTTE*, 3:878.
[3]Ibid., 3:882-83.
[4]Philip Peter Jenson, *Graded Holiness: A Key to the Priestly Conception of the World*, Journal for the Study of the Old Testament: Supplement Series 106 (Sheffield, UK: JSOT Press, 1992), 44.
[5]Ibid., 47-48.

(e.g., *ḥaṭṭāʾt*) are in no way interchangeable.[6] Humans can make themselves clean or unclean, but holiness is a status that is conferred by God.[7] It cannot be earned or acquired (or lost) through behavior.

The actual wording of Leviticus 19:2 bears this out. Most English translations render the statement as an imperative ("make yourselves holy because I am holy") or at least an admonition ("you ought to be holy because I am holy"). If holiness is a conferred status, however, these translations are misleading. Fortunately, the Hebrew simply says "you will be holy because I am holy." The grammatical construction can carry an imperative mood (e.g., 2 Kings 11:8, "[you will be with] the king," NIV "stay close to") but does not necessarily do so. In Deuteronomy 7:14 the same construction is used to say "you will be blessed," which clearly does not mean "make yourself blessed."[8] The Septuagint (the Greek translation

---

[6]Technically, *ḥaṭṭāʾt* causes the individual to become *ṭāmēʾ* (requiring *thr*) and also causes the holy community in which the individual participates to become *ḥālāl* (requiring *kpr*). *Ṭūmʾâ* that is not *ḥaṭṭāʾt* (menstruation, corpse contact) does not *ḥālal* the community unless the individual continues to participate in the community (i.e., is not sent outside the camp) while unclean. There is *kpr* for both *ḥaṭṭāʾt* and *ṭūmʾâ* in Lev 16:16, which would be redundant if they meant the same thing.

[7]Readers of the Hebrew text will note that the verbal form of the root *qdš* does often take a human subject (commonly translated "consecrate"). However, the verb *qdš* does not describe the process by which a thing acquires the status represented by the adjective *qādôš*. For example, priests are consecrated and priests are also holy, but a person can be consecrated without either becoming holy or becoming a priest (e.g., 1 Sam 16:5). The act of consecrating ritual objects for use in the temple (e.g., Ex 30:29) actually describes a two-stage process, consecrate it (and) it will be holy; the NIV mistranslates the connecting particle as "so that," collapsing two processes into one. We see a similar two-stage process in Jonah 1:12, "throw me into the sea" and "[the sea] will become calm." The two events are related, but the one does not mechanically cause the other; humans do the first, and God does the second. This is similar to the way construction of sacred objects worked throughout the ancient Near East. The final image is the product of both humans and gods; the humans built the statue and "consecrated" it (Sumerian KU₃, an adjective with a similar range of objects to the Hebrew verb *qdš*; see discussion in E. Jan Wilson, *"Holiness" and "Purity" in Mesopotamia*, Alter Orient und Altes Testament 237 [Neukirchen-Vluyn: Verlag Butzon & Bercker Kevelaer, 1994], 13-35), but the process by which it becomes holy (Sumerian DINGIR), described by the metaphor of birth, is a different process, performed by the gods; see Christopher Walker and Michael B. Dick, "The Mesopotamian *mis pi* Ritual," in *Born in Heaven, Made on Earth*, ed. Michael B. Dick (Winona Lake, IN: Eisenbrauns, 1999), 55-122, esp. 114-17.

[8]Likewise in Ex 19:6 ("You will be for me a kingdom of priests"), Lev 26:12 ("You will be my people"), and 1 Sam 8:17 ("You yourselves will become his slaves"). These passages are not saying that the people ought to make themselves priests, God's people, or slaves, respectively.

of the Old Testament used by the New Testament authors) likewise uses an indicative form of the verb (*esesthe*), rather than an imperative; 1 Peter uses a different word (*ginesthe*).[9] Leviticus 19:2 is a declaration that a status is about to be conferred. Israel will, in fact, be holy.

WHAT DOES IT MEAN TO BE QDŠ?

Holiness in the context of the ancient world conceptually refers to the essence of divinity, "that which belongs to the sphere of God's being or activity."[10] There is a term from a cognate Semitic language that also refers to the essence of divinity and also significantly overlaps with the semantic range of Hebrew *qdš*: the determinative DINGIR (Akkadian *ilu*).[11] A determinative is a grammatical element that indicates a category to which the associated word belongs. For example, in English, the $ symbol can function as a determinative by indicating that the number to which it is attached belongs to the category of an amount of (American) money. In Sumerian and Akkadian, DINGIR indicates that the associated word belongs to the category of a god. "Dingirized" elements (those words that are accompanied by the DINGIR determinative) include the gods and their cultic objects, as expected, but also occasionally geographic locations, periods of time, people, and abstract concepts.

---

[9]The LXX form is future indicative of *eimi*, "to be"; the form in 1 Pet 1:15-16 ("just as he who called you is holy, so *be holy* [*ginesthe*] in all you do; for it is written: '*Be holy*, because I am holy'") is present imperative of *ginomai*, "to come into being." The use of *ginesthe* again in 1 Pet 1:16 is a common variant, although *esesthe* is better attested. However, *esesthe* cannot be translated as an imperative. In either case, Peter is modifying the Septuagint to a new purpose, not quoting it to explain what the original Hebrew text of Leviticus meant in context.

[10]Jenson, *Graded Holiness*, 48; see also Wilson, "*Holiness*" and "*Purity*" in Mesopotamia, 87.

[11]Sumerian signs often serve as logograms—signs that represent whole words. Logograms are conventionally represented in transliteration by using small caps. Some logograms are used in Akkadian as determinatives to graphically indicate the class of objects to which they belong. DINGIR is used in this way and in transliteration is represented as a superscript *d* in front of the word that it classifies, e.g., [d]Marduk. The Sumerian sign *an* can be the logogram AN, which equals the Akkadian word *šamû* = heaven, or the logogram DINGIR, which equals the Akkadian word *ilum* = god.

Table 2. Usage of DINGIR/*ilu* as compared with Hebrew *Qdš* and its cognates

Usage	DINGIR/*ilu*[12]	Hebrew *Qdš*	Ugaritic *Qdš*[13]	Akkadian *Qašdu(m)*[14]
Divine Title or Attribute	by definition	"Holy One" (e.g., Is 1:4); "a holy God" (e.g., Josh 24:19)	used for El and Athirat as a title, otherwise as a designation for gods in general	reference to gods
Cultic Sites or Objects	ziggurats, temples and parts of temples,[15] cult objects	the ark, the altar, and the holy place, etc.	the sanctuary	temples
Creatures Belonging to the Divine Realm That Are Not Worshiped as Gods	chaos creatures (Anzu, Tiamat), demons (*ᵈlemnu*) etc.[16]	the divine council (Job 5:1; 15:15; Ps 89:5-7; Dan 8:13)	unattested	unattested
Places	mountains, rivers[17]	Zion, Jerusalem	Baal's mountain	a river
Periods of Time	months dedicated to deities[18]	sabbath (Is 8:3), Jubilee (Lev 25:12)	unattested	unattested
Persons (Individual)	king[19]	priests (Lev 21:7)	cult officiants	unattested
Abstractions	professions, minerals, abstract concepts[20]	nation (Ex 19:6), land (Zech 2:12)	unattested	unattested

---

[12]*CAD* 7:91-97.

[13]Gregorio del Olmo Lete and Joaquín Sanmartín, *A Dictionary of the Ugaritic Languages in the Alphabetic Tradition* (Leiden: Brill, 2004), 695-97.

[14]*CAD* 13:146b-147a.

[15]Michael B. Hundley, "Here a God, There a God: An Examination of the Divine in Ancient Mesopotamia," *Altorientalische Forschungen* 40 (2013): 68-107; Barbara Porter, "Feeding Dinner to a Bed," *State Archives of Assyria Bulletin* 15 (2006): 320, 322.

[16]*CAD* 7:101b.

[17]Hundley, "Here a God," 73, 77.

[18]Some months are named after deities and form part of the constellation of the deity with which they are associated. See, for example, Daniel E. Fleming, *Time at Emar* (Winona Lake, IN: Eisenbrauns, 2000), 161-73.

[19]Peter Machinist, "Kingship and Divinity in Imperial Assyria," in *Text, Artifact, and Image*, ed. Gary M. Beckman and Theodore J. Lewis, BJS 346 (Providence, RI: Brown University Press, 2006), 163-64.

[20]Hundley, "Here a God," 73-77.

The Hebrew language, like English, does not use determinatives, but the concept (of category) represented by the determinative can still be represented in languages that do not use them. For example, in English, the semantic equivalent of the Sumerian determinative MI can be expressed variously by an adjective (*female*), a noun (*woman*; also, e.g., *mare* or *ewe* in nonhumans), a pronoun (*she*), a stative verb (*feminized*), or a compound noun (*congresswoman*).[21] Despite the lexical differences, then, it does not seem unreasonable to propose that the Hebrew *qdš* has considerable semantic overlap with DINGIR/*ilu*. Thus, while recognizing that Israel's overall theology differs from that of the ancient Near East generally, we can still examine the ideas represented by the dingirizing of various elements to try to better understand what idea is represented by the classification of a thing as holy.

THE CONCEPT OF DIVINITY IN THE ANCIENT WORLD

DINGIR (as a noun or a determinative) refers to the gods and the various elements that compose their individual identities. As Michael Hundley elaborates:

> Most major gods are identified with an anthropomorphically conceived divine person, a statue, a number, a semi-precious stone, a mineral, an animal, an emblem, a star, constellation or other celestial entity and various characteristic qualities. Ishtar in particular is simultaneously identified as a divine person who dwells in heaven, yet is localized in various terrestrial temples (most prominently Arbela and Nineveh), the planet Venus, the number 15, the semi-precious stone lapis-lazuli, and the mineral lead, and understood as the embodiment of such qualities as love

---

[21]Interestingly, there is no Hebrew adjective comparable to English *divine*; the adjectival form of the Hebrew word for "god" (*'elōhîm*) means "great" or "large" (Gen 30:8; perhaps also 1 Sam 14:15), not "having the essential properties of a god"; much like English *cyclopian* also (incidentally) means "large," not "having the essential properties of a cyclops" (i.e., only one eye).

and war. Each of these interconnected divine networks composed of many distinct elements may be viewed as a divine constellation, in which the various elements are connected to a more or less unified entity and share in its identity. In other words, each major god consists of a constellation of aspects, which may act and be treated (semi-)independently. Most divine constellations consist of several connected deified aspects, with an anthropomorphic core that is always deified and other occasionally deified elements like heavenly bodies, abstract qualities, and metals.[22]

Divine personalities, like most things in the ancient Near East, were not described by an essential definition but circumscribed by a list (see the discussion of lists in proposition 9). The purpose of the list—what Hundley calls the divine constellation—was to establish divine identity, specifically in distinction from separate aspects of the same deity (e.g., Ishtar of Arbela versus Ishtar of Nineveh) and from other members of the pantheon. Identity, in turn, establishes the god's place in the heavenly bureaucracy, indicating what their responsibilities are and thereby when and how their worshipers ought to relate to them.

Some Mesopotamian lesser DINGIRs (e.g., cult objects co-identified with the greater deity whose cult they serve in) were occasionally treated as gods in their own right; that is, they were the object of rituals and presented with offerings.[23] Literature documents the presentation of offerings to objects as diverse as chariots, instruments, weapons, and beds.[24] In one Assyrian letter, an official documents the transport of a bed (presumably intended as a gift to a great god) and indicates that offerings were made to it directly: "There is no suggestion that it

---

[22]Hundley, "Here a God," *Altorientalische Forschungen* 40 (2013): 68-107, quote on 80-81.

[23]"Labeling a word with the DINGIR determinative in Mesopotamia meant that it was understood to *be* a DINGIR, with all that that entailed." Barbara Porter, *What Is a God? Anthropomorphic and Non-anthropomorphic Aspects of Deity in Ancient Mesopotamia* (Winona Lake, IN: Eisenbrauns, 2009), 163-64.

[24]Ibid., 172-93.

was the divine owner of the bed whose wrath the king and his officials actually feared; it is the bed itself that is solicitously escorted and placated with its own offerings. Its presumed divine owner is never mentioned."[25] There is a similar episode that allows us a glimpse of Israelite thinking in 2 Samuel 6. David tries to transport the ark of the covenant (God's throne or footstool, a holy object/lesser DINGIR); the object is mishandled, and one of the attendants is struck dead. The narrator, who represents the voice of theological orthodoxy, takes care to note that it was God, not the ark, who struck Uzzah (2 Sam 6:6), but David himself might not have nuanced his understanding in this way, and his reaction gives insight into his conception of the event. When he tries to move the ark again, he offers sacrifices every six steps as it moves along (2 Sam 6:13). When God gives instructions for the transport of the ark in Numbers 4:4-20, no mention is made of sacrifices; this indicates that whatever David is doing, his inspiration for doing so comes from his cognitive environment, not Israelite orthopraxy.[26] To any observer, David's ritual actions would very closely resemble those of the Assyrian officials described above, who make "regular sheep offerings"[27] to the divine bed as they transport it. The form of David's sacrifices does not match any of the prescribed offerings to Yahweh, so it is quite possible that David is offering sacrifices to the ark (in the same way the Assyrians offered sacrifices to the divine bed) in order to appease it on its journey so that no one else is

---

[25]Ibid., 193.

[26]McCarter suggests that the sacrifices represent a standard ancient Near East inauguration ritual of bringing a deity's image to a new capital city: P. Kyle McCarter, "The Ritual Dedication of the City in 2 Samuel 6," in *The Word of the Lord Shall Go Forth*, ed. Carol L. Meyers and M. O'Connor (Winona Lake, IN: Eisenbrauns, 1983), 273-78. If this were the case, though, there should have been sacrifices offered all the way from Baalah to the threshing floor of Nakon (2 Sam 6:1, 5). The celebration and instruments from 2 Sam 6:4 supposedly continue, but the sacrifices are new, thereby suggesting that they are inspired by the Uzzah incident.

[27]Simo Parpola, *The Correspondence of Sargon II: Letters from Assyria and the West*, State Archives of Assyria 1 (Helsinki: Helsinki University Press, 1987), letter 55, pp. 51-52. See also Porter, *What Is a God*, 193.

struck. This in turn would support the idea that Israel's labeling something as holy means more or less the same thing as a Mesopotamian labeling an object with a DINGIR determinative. The narrator, the voice of orthodoxy, neither praises nor condemns David's ritual, which represents an act of syncretism, the mixing of religious systems, no matter what it is; the sacrifice is simply reported.[28] The narrative focus is on David's respect and deference to the divine (in contrast with Saul, explicitly in 2 Sam 6:20-23, and also implicitly with Hophni, Phinehas, and the elders of 1 Sam 4; 8),[29] not on his understanding of the nuances of the definition of divinity.

But Israelite orthodoxy is consistent with Mesopotamian definitions even while expressing theological innovations. In Mesopotamia, for example, the DINGIRs who constitute the heavenly council would be objects of worship in their own right. In Israel, Yahweh's council is holy but does not receive worship. Things in the heavenly realm possessing or participating in a divine identity (i.e., DINGIRs) that are nonetheless not worshiped is a category that also exists in Mesopotamia.[30] Orthodox Israel has expanded the category of DINGIRs/holy

---

[28]A reason for this may be that the ark is part of Yahweh's constellation and therefore technically not a different deity from Yahweh, as opposed to something like Baal or Chemosh, who have their own distinct constellations. Incidentally, the calf altars at Dan and Bethel (and also the golden calf at Sinai) are probably also intended to be aspects of Yahweh. The difference in these cases is that Yahweh, and therefore orthodox Israel, does not recognize the legitimacy of these; that is, Yahweh does not declare them holy, as he does with the ark. Similarly, the command to make no graven image (of Yahweh; Ex 20:4) is given because images fragment the divine identity into separate aspects, which, while still representing the same deity, are distinct enough that they can even fight each other. If Arbela goes to war against Nineveh, then Ištar will be fighting against Ištar. Israelite orthodoxy will not allow Yahweh's identity to be fragmented in this way; there can be no "Yahweh of Jerusalem" and "Yahweh of Samaria." This is why there is only one sanctioned temple (in Jerusalem) and one sanctioned image (the ark), and no other image or cult center can be tolerated (see Deut 12).

[29]See Jonathan H. Walton, "A King Like the Nations," *Biblica* 96 (2015): 200.

[30]*Lemnu* ("demons"), chaos creatures, etc. See John H. Walton, "Demons in Mesopotamia and Israel: Exploring the Category of Non-divine but Supernatural Entities," in *Windows to the Ancient World of the Hebrew Bible*, ed. Bill T. Arnold et al. (Winona Lake, IN: Eisenbrauns, 2014), 233.

things that are nonetheless not (to be) worshiped to include every element of the divine realm other than Yahweh,[31] but it has not changed the concept of what DINGIR/*qdš* actually means.

Likewise, Israel's holifying of locations is comparable to Mesopotamian conception. Mesopotamian dingirized geography (usually a mountain or river) is in the constellation of the divine patron of the feature, who shares its name. Physical rocks or water are sometimes dingirized and sometimes not, depending on how strongly the literary context wants to emphasize co-identification with its patron.[32] Nonetheless, even when dingirized, the rocks and water are not considered to have been physically transferred into the divine sphere; they are not holy ground where mortals must tread carefully or die. In this sense they have more in common with Israel's holy land, which involves the divinization of the abstraction of territory as opposed to the physical objects, water and rocks. We will discuss this further in proposition eleven. Mesopotamia does have a more direct counterpart to Israel's holy ground (and Ugarit's divine mountain residences) in the form of dingirized ziggurats, temples, and the architectural components of temples, such as doorways, pipes, and the pedestal on which the image stands, the last of which may well be the counterpart to Israel's holy place.[33] DINGIR/*qdš* emphasizes divine co-identification, so the designation here marks the area as divine territory because the deity is now present in it and manifested through it.[34] The identification of the space (or the building, or the ritual object) with the god incorporates it into the divine realm, much like an embassy co-identifies its buildings and the piece of property it is built on with its sponsoring country, such that it is considered an extension of its sovereign nation despite its location on another nation's physical dirt.

---

[31]See ibid., 231.

[32]Hundley, "Here a God," 77; Porter, *What Is a God*, 161-62, 169-71.

[33]See Porter, *What Is a God*, 164, 189; Hundley, "Here a God," 79.

[34]Contra Hundley and Porter, who argue that the status is contracted by close association. See Porter, *What Is a God*, 191; Hundley, "Here a God," 11-12.

The parallels continue in the idea of dingirized/holified individuals (kings in Mesopotamia, priests in Israel). These deified individuals are not elevated to the status of the pantheon; there is no record of dingirized kings receiving sacrifices.[35] "The deified professions or offices . . . do not simply reflect an intentional and willful process of sanctification invented for securing the ruling elite's position or to stabilize the structure of society. These items could only be included in the class of divinities because of an existing prototypical relation to the divine sphere."[36] In other words, the individual is the embodiment of the (sacred) office that they hold; the office sanctifies the individual, not the other way around.[37] The sacredness of the office, in turn, indicates its origin in the divine realm; "kingship was lowered from heaven to earth."[38] Beyond mere origin, however, Mesopotamian kings were actually thought to belong to the divine realm,[39] serving as mediators between the gods and the people.[40] By being co-identified with a divine office, the individual was effectively incorporated into the divine realm; as a thing co-identified with the divine realm, they then received the DINGIR determinative. Like chaos creatures, however, they do not receive worship (ritual offerings) and are therefore never considered actual members of the pantheon.

In Israel the divine office with a mediatory role was held not by the kings but by the priests. The details of the role differ, but the point of

---

[35]Peter Machinist notes that deified (images of) Assyrian kings do not receive worship or offerings; Peter Machinist, "Kingship and Divinity in Imperial Assyria," in Beckman and Lewis, *Text, Artifact, and Image*, BJS 346, 179-80.

[36]Gebhard J. Selz, "The Divine Prototypes," in *Religion and Power: Divine Kingship in the Ancient World and Beyond*, ed. Nicole Brisch, The University of Chicago Oriental Institute Seminar 4 (Chicago: University of Chicago Press, 2008), 13-31, quote on 18.

[37]Ibid., 19: "The concept of rulership is therefore primarily linked to objects like the scepter and the crown, to the 'office,' and only to a lesser degree to the person holding that office."

[38]Ibid., 18.

[39]Machinist, "Kingship," 184: "The Assyrian king . . . was not simply an exalted man, but someone with a place in the divine world." He goes on to note that the Assyrians emphasized the office over the individual by dingirizing the "image" of the king rather than the king's personal name (185).

[40]Ibid., 182.

the comparison is not to say that Israelite priests are the same as Mesopotamian kings; the point is to say that the use of DINGIR/*qdš* did not designate the individual, whether king or priest, as a god. As with the kings, the holifying of the Israelite priests indicated that the priestly office had a divine origin; it was instituted by Yahweh rather than by the people (Ex 28:1, notably in contrast to Israelite kingship, which is instituted by the people in 1 Sam 8; some Mesopotamian kings are DINGIRs, but Israelite kings are never holy). It also indicates that the priests were part of the divine realm, enabling them (among other things) to enter the sanctuary without defiling it (or dying). Thus it appears that Hebrew usage of *qdš* indicates that it means the same thing as DINGIR/*ilu*; it signifies that the element so designated was part of the divine constellation of a particular deity or a participant in a divine office.

All of the technical analysis of the last few pages helps us to gain an understanding of holiness relative to the ancient world—it is identifying something as associated with the realm of deity. It is on the basis of this informed understanding that we can now consider how holiness relates to Israel and how it does not relate to Canaanites.

DIVINITY VERSUS MORALITY

One pervasive interpretation of Leviticus 19 is that Yahweh is commanding Israel to be holy because holiness is something that God desires from all people. In this interpretation, the Canaanites failed to meet this standard of holiness and, as a consequence, are being ejected from the land. Based on the above analysis, however, we have argued that this interpretation is not tenable. First, God does not, indeed cannot, desire holiness *from* anyone; holiness is a status, not a set of behaviors. Second, it is not a moral status; most holy things have no moral agency. The altar and lampstand are not living in accord with the desires of God. Third, holy status is conferred, not earned. The Canaanites are not holy, but that is not because of anything they did or did not do; it is because of something God did not do. God did not declare them holy. The Canaanites' lack of holy status is not an indictment, is not itself a punishment (Israel explicitly does not earn the right to be declared holy by its righteousness), and does not indicate that they have *earned* their expulsion from the land.

The holy status refers to the association of the person or object with the identity of Yahweh. The significance of the status is derived not in terms of goodness (ethics and morality), but in terms of metaphysics, specifically in terms of ancient definitions of what it means to be divine, with the particulars varying depending on the nature of the divinized object. By virtue of being declared holy, the abstract communal construct "the nation of Israel" is being associated with Yahweh's divine identity through incorporation into his divine constellation.[41] What exactly that means for Israel we will examine in detail in the next proposition. Finally, in summary, since holiness refers to co-identification with deity and is not to be equated with morality or with meeting standards of cleanness, no one, neither Israelites nor Canaanites, can be guilty of not being holy. It is a status. The conquest of the land is certainly related to Israel's holy status but has nothing to do with an absence of holiness on the part of the Canaanites.

---

[41]It is worth noting, however, that these definitions do not carry over into the New Testament. The Greek *hagios* translates *qdš* in the Septuagint (and also several other words, most notably "clean," *ṭāhôr*, in Lev 10:14, and "nazirite" in Judg 13; these interpretive choices indicate that Greek *hagios* has a broader range of meaning than the more technical Hebrew *qdš*), but by the Second Temple period the definition of divinity and metaphysics in general has been reconceived in terms of essential categories. Since the purpose of the categorical system was to fix rigid boundaries between what a thing is and what it is not, some of the fluidity of the ancient, pre-Aristotelian classification system, used in the ancient Near East and the Old Testament, is lost (see Selz, "Prototypes," 16, and especially Hundley, "Here a God," 70-72). Accordingly, *qdš*/*hagios* does not describe the essential nature of divinity and divine identity (the theological *ousion*) in New Testament metaphysics. If there is any parallel to the ancient divine fluidity (described by *qdš*) inherent in the term *hagios* as used in classical and postclassical theology, it would be along the lines of *theosis* (participation in divine *energeia*, e.g., "God became man so that man might become God" (Athanasius, *On the Incarnation* 8.54), not Trinity.

The Expulsion of the Canaanites from the Land in the Conquest Cannot Be Evaluated by Comparison to the Expulsion of the Israelites from the Land in the Exile Because Israel Is Under the Covenant and the Canaanites Are Not

Passages such as Leviticus 18:28 ("if you defile the land, it will vomit you out as it vomited out the nations that were before you") are commonly interpreted to suggest that the expulsion of Israel from the land by Assyria/Babylon in the exile was more or less an exact parallel of the expulsion of the Canaanites from the land by Israel. Since Israel's offenses are well documented, consisting mostly of cultic violations and social injustice, the supposed recapitulation is invoked to apply those same offenses to the Canaanites, which in turn produces the idea that these behaviors are somehow inherently offensive to God. However, this supposed parallel fails to take into account something that by all rights should be of critical importance: the covenant. Israel has it; Canaan does not. The covenant defines Israel's relationship with God and the relationship of both to the land. Anyone without the covenant would therefore naturally be expected to relate to both Yahweh and the land differently from how Israel does.

Israelite Identity and Divine Constellation

The nation of Israel that is declared holy in Leviticus 19 refers to the communal abstraction, not the aggregate of all individuals present. Unlike the priesthood, the nation is not a sacred office; it does not originate from the divine realm (explicitly so; see Deut 26:5; Ezek 16:3). Likewise, Yahweh's declaration does not holify every individual who participates in the nation; this is the mistake made by Korah and his confederates in Numbers 16 when they misunderstand the metaphorical kingdom of priests (Ex 19:6) to mean that *any* member of the community is qualified to serve as an *actual* priest. The same is true of the abstractions "land" (Zech 2:12) and "city" (e.g., Is 52:1); the real estate does not literally become holy ground (compare Ex 3:5). The abstraction transcends the elements that make it up, and it is the abstraction, not the elements, that is holy. The recognition of abstractions treated this way in Mesopotamia (by use of DINGIR) offers us a means to understand the nature of Israel's holiness, since we have seen that dingirizing things in Mesopotamia is comparable to labeling things as holy (*qādôš*) in the Old Testament.

Dingirized abstractions, unlike dingirized objects, are not treated as gods (given offerings), even in polytheistic Mesopotamia. Nobody offers sacrifices to war or truth. Instead, the abstractions are associated with a greater divine personality and collectively serve to define that god's identity. In Israel, Yahweh is alone in the pantheon, but Yahweh still has a divine identity (circumscribed by a constellation), which, as in Mesopotamia, includes holified abstractions. The holy status of the nation of Israel, therefore, does not identify any particular qualities of the nation of Israel, for the same reasons that identifying Ishtar as goddess of love and war does not identify any particular properties of love and war. Instead, the status designates the identity of *Yahweh* by virtue of Israel's being incorporated into Yahweh's constellation, just as Ishtar's association with love and war says something about her as a goddess. This is the full meaning of the statement "you will be my people and I will be your God"; it is a statement of function, but even more so it is a declaration of identity. With the ratification of the covenant, Yahweh becomes the God of Israel. This change is monumentally significant, comparable to when God becomes human at the incarnation. With this declaration, whatever Israel is or does irrevocably reflects on what Yahweh is or what Yahweh does.

THE HOLINESS OF THE NATION

As we discussed in proposition nine, the purpose of the holiness code is to define order; more precisely, however, its purpose is to define the order that specifically defines the nation that defines Yahweh. This is the reason for the refrain repeated throughout Leviticus 19–22, "I am Yahweh." Contrary to many interpretations, this statement does not mean "do this because I am God and because I say so."[1] It is not an assertion of authority; it is a declaration of identity. In the ancient Near East, legal treatises were written by kings and presented (to the gods) as declarations of the king's identity as a wise and just ruler.[2] By appropriating the genre and casting himself as the author, Yahweh is making a similar declaration of identity for himself.[3] By incorporating

---

[1] See for example Erhard S. Gerstenberger, *Leviticus*, Old Testament Library (Louisville, KY: Westminster John Knox, 1993), 255.

[2] "Mesopotamian kings strove to present themselves as just rulers. . . . The kings regularly identified themselves in their inscriptions as promoters of justice. . . . The [Code of Hammurabi] was to make known Hammurapi's efforts to bring justice and good order to the land." Dale Launderville, *Piety and Politics: The Dynamics of Royal Authority in Homeric Greece, Biblical Israel, and Old Babylonian Mesopotamia* (Grand Rapids: Eerdmans, 2003), 280, emphasis added. See also Jack M. Sasson, "King Hammurabi of Babylon," in *Civilizations of the Ancient Near East*, ed. Jack M. Sasson (New York: Scribner's, 1995), 907.

[3] Most comparisons of the Bible's legal literature with ancient Near Eastern law codes, specifically the Code of Hammurabi, typically cast Moses as the lawgiver (Hammurabi) and Yahweh as the transcendent divine sponsor (Shamas). However, in the epilogue of the

into his constellation a nation defined by principles of wisdom and justice, Yahweh is identifying himself not only as a patron of wisdom and justice (on par with, say, the Babylonian god Shamas), but also as an executor of wisdom and justice, on par with a human monarch. Of course, this does not mean that Yahweh is modeling behaviors that, if imitated by humans, will result in justice; justice doesn't work that way. A judge can send someone away to be executed; you can't. It also does not mean that Yahweh is setting down a list of rules that, if obeyed, will result in justice; as discussed in proposition nine, the laws in legal treatises are hypothetical illustrations that circumscribe an underlying principle, not commands to be obeyed. What it does mean is that Yahweh's relationship with his people will operate according to the principles of wisdom and justice, as opposed to, say, selfishness and paranoia, which was normal in divine-human relationships throughout the rest of the ancient Near East.

The nation of Israel is a reflection on Yahweh's identity, which means that his identity will be demonstrated by the nature of his relationship with them. The nation that Yahweh patronizes will be governed by wisdom and justice; that is the identity that Yahweh has declared for himself. The specific form that this governance takes depends on Israel: "See, I set before you today life and prosperity, death and destruction" (Deut 30:15). If Israel lives according to order and justice (as their culture understands these things),[4] it will reflect

---

code, the following appears: "Laws of justice which Hammurabi, the wise king, established. A righteous law and pious statute did he teach the land. Hammurabi, the protecting king am I." In the biblical text, no such statement is ever attributed to Moses; the law is established by Yahweh, the decrees are Yahweh's, and the refrain throughout is "I am Yahweh." Yahweh is the lawgiver; Moses is merely the scribe.

[4]Since the point is divine identification, the definition of *justice* is relative to the context of the observers. God commanding Israel to some ideal form of justice, whose tenets would be unjust in their conception, would defeat the purpose. This is why the Mosaic law cannot be understood in universal terms; it represents ancient Near Eastern ideals, not absolute divine ideals. Individual components have to be evaluated on their own merits; this includes both elements we moderns dislike (debt slavery) and those we approve of (care for the poor).

favorably on its divine patron, and he in turn will demonstrate his favor and bless it. It is this favorable reflection that Yahweh requires, not care and pampering: "Shall I come before him with burnt offerings? . . . He has shown you, O mortal, what is good. And what does the LORD require of you? To act justly and to love mercy" (Mic 6:6, 8). It is worth reemphasizing, however, that since God's purposes, goals, and ideals are not based around the production of human happiness (see proposition three), this requirement is for the sake of *reflection* (that is, of Israel reflecting that its God is identified with wisdom and justice) and not for the sake of the recipients of the justice and mercy per se. God does not need or want, say, care for the poor any more than he needs or wants animal sacrifices. Although some of the prophets do employ this imagery to make their points (e.g., Hos 6:6), we should not think that God in any way requires morality (personal or social) in place of dead animals. Yahweh does not require sacrifices of any kind because he has no needs of any kind, physical or psychological. The ritual system and the justice system, both components of order, are required (equally), not to make Yahweh happy or to carry out some kind of divine ideal for creation but because in the ancient world order is an indication of divine competence. As discussed in proposition three, Yahweh is not trying to construct an ideal society; he is carrying out his purpose of self-revelation in the context of the society that happens to exist.

Israel does benefit from Yahweh's commitment to justice, which in context should be juxtaposed with capriciousness (impulsivity and unpredictability) as opposed to our common modern juxtaposition with mercy. Ancient Near Eastern gods were not just; although they valued justice (because order in the human world allowed humans to serve their function of providing for the needs of the gods), they themselves were petty, vindictive, and arbitrary in bestowing favor or disfavor. In contrast, because Yahweh's identity is vested in justice, if Israel behaves according to its culture's understanding of justice (circumscribed by the holiness code), it will be a recipient of blessing. Orthodox Israelite theology, unlike the theology of the rest of the ancient world, had no room for random or unknown offenses. But even Yahweh's mercy was motivated by representation and reflection (that is, how the action would be interpreted by observers), as opposed to what we are inclined to construe as some form of empathy.[5] Ezekiel 36:19-23, for example, says: "I judged [Israel] according to their conduct and their actions. And . . . it was said of them, 'These are the LORD's people, and yet they had to leave his land.' I had concern for my holy name. . . . It is not for your sake, people of Israel, that I am going to [restore Israel to the land], but for the sake of my holy name. . . . Then the nations will know that I am the LORD." Likewise Exodus 32:12, "Why should the Egyptians say, 'It was with evil intent that he brought them out, to kill them in the mountains and to wipe them off the face of the earth'?" The concern is about what the Egyptians will say, not about what will happen to the people of Israel. If empathy is expressed at all, it is done so in the act of revelation and the giving of the covenant, not in selectively refraining from its enforcement. Refraining from enforcement in fact defeats the purpose, unless that restraint is also an expression of revelation.

Consequently, if Israel does not live according to order and justice, then Yahweh will demonstrate his commitment to order by inflicting justice on it: "Just as it pleased the LORD to make you prosper and increase in number, so it will please him to ruin and destroy you" (Deut 28:63). This is the difference between Yahweh and the gods who stand accused in Psalm 82. These gods fail to uphold justice (Ps 82:2-4), not because they are evil and want to encourage injustice—ancient Near Eastern kings testify that their gods demanded justice—but because they are codependent; if they punish their people as they should,

---

[5]This is unrelated to the question of whether God can experience empathy (i.e., what some theologians call divine impassibility). Whether God has emotional reactions or not, those emotions are not what motivate his behavior.

they will no longer receive sacrifices to meet their needs (compare the sentiment expressed in Jer 7:9-10). In contrast, Yahweh's relationship with his people is not defined by codependence but justice. Israel's behavior would be worthy of condemnation from any god (Ezek 5:7; "You have been more unruly than the nations around you. . . . You have not even conformed to the standards of the nations around you"), but specifically what it is being punished for is its poor representation of Yahweh (Ezek 5:8, 13, "I myself am against you, Jerusalem, and I will inflict punishment on you in the sight of the nations. . . . I will be avenged"). Israel's behavior forces Yahweh to identify himself in the sight of the nations as a God who is willing and able to maintain order, not only social but also cultic, as in Jeremiah 22:8-9: "People from many nations will pass by this city and will ask one another, 'Why has the LORD done such a thing to this great city?' And the answer will be: 'Because they have forsaken the covenant of the LORD their God and have worshiped and served other gods.'" Order and justice cannot be reduced to morality.

The Pharisees can serve as an illustration of this. The problem was not that they were immoral or burdensome, because they were neither of these things; their righteousness is commended in Matthew 5:20. The problem was that they had failed to understand *why* they were supposed to be righteous; thus, instead of their righteousness representing God as wise and just, their righteousness represented him as petty, arbitrary, and susceptible to manipulation. The point was never the righteousness; the point was always the representation, which is why the Pharisees are repeatedly equated with their idolatrous ancestors. Misrepresentation by righteousness is no different than misrepresentation by unrighteousness.

All of this demonstrates that the holiness of the Israelite nation refers to its status as co-identified with God and thereby serving as a medium through which he reveals himself. It is not a status it earned through moral performance, and not a status that anyone else could be expected to earn by moral performance, either. What happened to Israel at the exile was in service of the process of God using Israel to reveal himself. God does not reveal himself through the Canaanites because the Canaanites are not holy and not co-identified with him. Therefore what happens to the Canaanites at the conquest is different from what happens to Israel at the exile.

THE HOLINESS OF THE LAND

Cities and territories in the ancient Near East were part of their patron deity's constellation and therefore informed the identity of the deity (e.g., Ishtar *of Nineveh*). If the actual names of cities and territories were ever dingirized, however, it occurs extremely rarely. Reference to the land of Israel as holy is also rare; it only occurs once (Zech 2:12, though "holy border" in Ps 78:54 comes close, as does "the LORD's land" in Hos 9:3).[6] Mesopotamian practice does attest to *occasional* DINGIRs, elements that receive the divine determinative only on certain occurrences: "Celestial bodies are at times . . . listed with the divine determinative. However, at other times, they are simply referred to as stars (MUL) with no reference to their divinity. . . . In addition, abstract qualities, like truth and justice, are only occasionally marked with the divine determinative."[7] Occasional DINGIRs would have been classified with the divine determinative in order to emphasize a particular intimacy with the deity (with the emphasis dictated by context rather than metaphysics because the divine constellation represents identity rather than taxonomy; in other words, the object does not gain and lose a divine nature). Understood this way, the occasional holification of the land is designed to express an intimate association between Yahweh and his land in a specific context in the text, an idea that is

---

[6]See, for example, Carol L. Meyers and Eric M. Meyers, *Haggai, Zechariah 1–8*, AB (New York: Doubleday, 1987), 170.

[7]Michael B. Hundley, "Here a God, There a God: An Examination of the Divine in Ancient Mesopotamia," *Altorientalische Forschungen* 40 (2013): 68-107, quote on 75.

borne out in the actual context of Zechariah 2 (and arguably Ps 78 and Hos 9 as well). This intimate association is attested in Mesopotamia by the (occasional) dingirization of geographical features to identify them with their divine patrons. If the cities and nations of Mesopotamia are never dingirized, then, it means that the gods never identify with those elements of their patronage as intimately as Yahweh does.

There is only a single reference to Israel as the Holy Land, but there are many references to Jerusalem as a holy city. Again, this is the abstract territory, not the physical ground and buildings; no one has to take off their shoes to enter Jerusalem, there is no mediated access at the city walls, and this is true even when the holy mountain (the Temple Mount, whose real estate *is* part of the divine realm) is used as a figure of speech to represent the entire city.[8] The reason for this intimate association is given explicitly; Jerusalem is the place where Yahweh has chosen to set his name (Deut 12:5; 1 Kings 11:36; 2 Chron 6:6). This idea is specifically connected to the holiness of the land in Zechariah 2:12: "The Lord will . . . again choose Jerusalem."

A perhaps clearer example of the distinction between permanent and occasional divine status comes from examining the difference between priests and prophets in Israel. Priests, as described in proposition ten, are *qādôš*; they are transplanted into the divine realm and perform their duties in a space that is likewise transplanted into the divine realm. Prophets, on the other hand, are only rarely called *qādôš* (only once, 2 Kings 4:9), and they perform their duties in the human realm, although they can enter the divine realm (sometimes only virtually) when necessary (Ex 19:20; 1 Kings 22:19; Is 6:1). However, even though they do not serve in the sanctuary, they must be symbolically prepared for divine use, as priests also must; Isaiah is unclean (Is 6:5) and has to be cleansed (by fire, Is 6:6) in order to become a suitable instrument.

---

[8]Or even perhaps the entire land; e.g., Ex 15:13, 17; contrast Ex 19:12, "Put limits . . . around the mountain [and set it apart as holy, Ex 19:23]. . . . Whoever touches the mountain is to be put to death"; also Lev 16:2.

Yahweh does not necessarily need to prepare all of his tools; his anointed servant Cyrus (Is 45:1) is not ritually cleansed, and even the Canaanites serve as instruments in Judges 2:22. Yahweh's intent for the land, however, goes beyond simple utility. A comparison to the concept of specific requirements for particular usage can be found in Genesis 23, where Abraham has to buy a tomb rather than simply make use of one. It is not enough that the field and cave (Gen 23:11) be available for use; the status of the field has to change before it is suitable to be used. In Genesis the status of the field is changed by the deeding of the property to Abraham (Gen 23:18); it ceases to be Ephron's field and becomes Abraham's field. This is not to say that Abraham is actually in any way initiating or even prefiguring the conquest (what Abraham intends to do with his field is nothing like what Yahweh intends to do with Canaan); the point is to illustrate the distinction between being able to use something that is merely available and requiring something to symbolically change its status before it can be suitable for use.[9] Abraham cannot bury Sarah until the burial plot becomes Abraham's land. Likewise, in the books of Joshua, Samuel, and Kings, Yahweh cannot do what he intends to do in the land (place his name there) until it becomes Yahweh's land. In order to use the land for the purpose he intends for it, he must make it his own. The idea of preparation for special divine appropriation allows us to understand what is happening to the land in Leviticus 18:25-28.

PREPARATION FOR DIVINE APPROPRIATION

Leviticus 18:25 reads, "The land was *ṭm'*, so I *pqd* it for its *'awōn*, and the land vomited out its inhabitants." Typically, this depiction of the land is interpreted to be a synecdoche for all the peoples who live there,

---

[9]In Abraham's case, "suitable for a burial plot" means that the site must remain in his family; it can never be legally reclaimed by Ephron's family. The issue is the relationship of the living and the dead within the family, not the relationship of the family to the land (John Walton, "Genesis," in *ZIBBCOT*, 1:99-100).

to represent all of them even though only the land itself is mentioned (i.e., "all of the people defiled themselves, so I punished their evil by making the [personified] land vomit them out"); consequently *ʿawōn* is read as a synonym for "defil[ing actions]," and *pqd* is read as punitive action on the people for both. There are, however, several difficulties with this interpretation.

First, *ṭāmēʾ* ("unclean," "defiled") does not mean "evil"; it is a ritual classification, not a moral one. Ezra 9:11 says, "The land you are entering to possess is a land polluted by the corruption [*niddâ*] of its peoples. By their detestable practices [*tôʿēbâ*] they have filled it with their impurity from one end to the other." *Impurity* is the noun form of the word that Leviticus 18:24 reads as "defile" (*ṭāmēʾ*, "to make impure"), and it refers elsewhere to discharges (Lev 15) and forbidden food (Judg 13:7). It designates ritual impurity (a form of nonorder) and only applies to what we call immorality (another form of nonorder) by metaphorical extension. Likewise, the corruption refers also to ritual impurity (usually menstruation) and never immorality. *Tôʿēbâ*, as we will see, refers specifically to practices that are outside the accepted parameters of the established order (see proposition thirteen). All of this indicates strongly that just because the land is said to have been defiled does not mean that immorality was involved; it means only that the Canaanites have not taken any special precautions to purify the land. They would not have been expected to do this, either, because purity is an unnatural state to achieve and maintain. Cleanliness is not the default state of land; ordinary usage naturally generates impurity.[10] We should not imagine that the land was clean before the Canaanites got there. In Exodus 19 the Israelite people have to purify themselves by washing all of their clothes and abstaining

---

[10]The natural state of impurity of land is demonstrated by the process of temple construction, wherein the site on which the temple is built must be made and kept pure (see, for example, 1 Kings 6:7, where "no . . . iron tool was heard at the temple site" in order ensure its sanctity).

from all sexual relations, which is not a state that can be maintained for long periods of ordinary life. Nonetheless, the land's status as *ṭāmēʾ* is an obstacle to Yahweh's intended use of it, just as the status of the field in Genesis 17 as Ephron's field was an obstacle to Abraham's intended use of it. Impurity is still present and needs to be dealt with if Yahweh is going to add the land into his constellation.

That the emphasis is on the land and not the people is most notably demonstrated by the lack of active verbs to describe the actions of the Canaanites.[11] In Leviticus 18:24-25 "the nations . . . *became* defiled . . . the land *was* defiled" (as opposed to an active construction, "they defiled themselves and defiled the land"). The emphasis is on the land and its condition, not on the actions of its inhabitants. Most significantly, the *ʿawōn of the land* is addressed in Leviticus 18:25; the verse says, "the land was defiled, so I punished it"; it does not say, "*they* defiled the land, so I punished *them*." In contrast, when Israel is the subject, it says, "if you defile the land" (Lev 18:28); the emphasis is on the actions of the (Israelite) inhabitants. The sequence of [contrary to covenant order] → [defilement] → [expulsion] is the same in both cases, but the narrative focus emphasizes first what happens to the land, then what will happen to Israel if Israel causes it to happen again. The emphasis is first on the land, second on Israel, and only tangentially on the Canaanites.

Second, the phrase "*pqd* the *ʿawōn*" does not strictly mean "punish the sin." This is the same construction that occurs in the phrase "visit [*pqd*] the iniquity [*ʿawōn*] of the fathers upon the children," for example, Exodus 20:5 (ESV). As discussed in proposition six, *pqd* more accurately means "determine destiny," and *ʿawōn* refers to "a destiny of calamity"; therefore the phrase "*pqd* the *ʿawōn*" means "set (or bring) a destiny of calamity for (or on) it/them." Significantly, as discussed in proposition six, *ʿawōn* is not something that you do, it is

---

[11]The verbs are passive and stative in Josh 18:24b-25. Israel, by contrast, is the subject of a factitive in Josh 18:24a, 28.

something that is done to you. Most occurrences of the word in Leviticus mean "something that happens to you *because of something you did*,"[12] but in this case the object is the land; even personified (as an agent that can vomit), it is difficult to understand what the land is supposed to have done. Therefore in this case it seems that the emphasis is elsewhere. Specifically, we should examine the effect of the calamity rather than the cause.

ʿAwōn (whether earned by misbehavior or not) means "a destiny of calamity." It is typically translated as "punished" (e.g., Gen 19:15) because calamity is unpleasant to experience. However, even when the ʿawōn is clearly punitive (as, for example, in the case of Sodom), it is not clear that its primary objective is the infliction of pain. In Israelite ritual literature, sin is primarily thought of in terms of impurity, rather than crime; thus, removing the impurity (the technical meaning of the term *kpr*, "atonement")[13] is at least as important as punishing the criminal; indeed, even when a criminal is punished, the actual purpose of the punishment seems to be a means to an end for the removal of impurity. In, for example, Deuteronomy 13:5; 17:7, 12 ("that [person] must be put to death. . . . You must purge the evil from among you"), the emphasis is "remove the evil," not "they deserve it." Sodom is destroyed by "fire and brimstone," but these are specifically *cleansing agents*.[14] The purpose of the ʿawōn on the land is not to punish the land; it makes no sense to punish something inanimate. Therefore we should conclude that the intent is to purify it.

---

[12]"The reference is to a burden that weighs on the perpetrators. . . . Such perdition unavoidably accompanies grievous sins." Klaus Koch, "פקד," in *TDOT*, 10:559.

[13]Michael B. Hundley, *Keeping Heaven on Earth*, Forschungen zum Alten Testament 2, Reihe 50 (Tübingen: Mohr Siebeck, 2011), 81-85: "Clearing removes (past) pollutants in one fell swoop so that the people may appropriately access YHWH" (85). Likewise, "the [sin offering] . . . successfully removes the intangible stain caused by sin from individuals and the tabernacle to the end that the individual is forgiven, the sanctuary is suitably pure, human and divine are at one, and world order is restored" (ibid., 201-2).

[14]Brimstone (sulfur) is used for fumigation and medicinal purposes in Akkadian texts (*CAD* 8:333b-34a). It is used in the *Odyssey* to purify a temple (22.480-95).

Evidence suggests that the land does not experience its purification in the same way that a person would; we might imagine the experience of a metal object "put through the fire" (e.g., Num 31:23) as compared to what a human would experience from the same process. Leviticus 26:33-35 promises that the land will be "laid waste" and "lie desolate," terms normally used to designate an undesirable state (e.g., Is 49:19; Jer 12:11; compare Lam 5:18, where the condition is cause for mourning). However, it immediately goes on to say that the land will "have rest" as it "lies desolate." Rest is a universally positive experience; what the people of the land experience as calamity (ʿawōn in Lev 18:25) seems actually to *benefit* the land ("rest" in Lev 26:35). It would seem, then, that to "*pqd* the ʿawōn of the land" does not indicate a negative experience and therefore is not semantically matched by the English word *punish* (NIV "I punished [the land]"). The land is being purified; that is to say, its status is being altered so that it becomes suitable for divine use, in the same way that the status of land on which a temple is built is changed to prepare it for its sacred service. The Canaanites are, so to speak, caught up in the ʿawōn of the land.

On the other hand, we should not imagine that the purpose of the ʿawōn is to somehow grant relief to the land from the oppression of the Canaanites' defilement. *Vomit* does not inherently imply emotional disgust or internal damage (though it can, Job 20:15); the word indicates violent expulsion. The fish vomits Jonah (Jon 2:10, same word), not because it was suffering from Jonah's presence or because it needed relief from Jonah, but because Jonah needed to be ejected from the fish for the sake of God's purpose. It is worth noting that in Leviticus 26, where the imagery of relief for the land is used, the imagery of vomit is not. The purpose of the ʿawōn, which takes the form of the conquest, is the alteration of the status of the land in preparation for God's special use of it; it is not punishment, and it is certainly not liberation. The emphasis, as always, is on the purpose, not on any attendant benefits or consequences for the persons (or personified objects) involved.

In summary, the land, like the nation of Israel, is co-identified with Yahweh and serves as a medium to reveal himself on the basis of what happens there. However, what happens there is considered not in terms of the physical boundaries or geopolitical borders, but in terms of the operation of the covenant. Consequently, what happens to the land before the covenant is established in the land is different from what happens there while the covenant is in effect. The land is being prepared for its use as the place that will contain the covenant order; it is not being corrected in accordance with the conditions of the covenant order. Therefore, what is happening to the land during the conquest is not the same thing that is happening to the land at the exile.

CONQUEST AND EXILE

Because of Israel's unique holy status, it is co-identified with Yahweh in a way that no one else on earth, including the Canaanites, is. Because of what Yahweh intends to do in the land via the people and the covenant, both Yahweh's and Israel's relationship with the land is different from that of any of its previous occupants, including even the patriarchs; Yahweh did not place his name anywhere in the territory controlled by the households of Abraham, Isaac, or Jacob. Israel's punishment in the exile was a result of its misrepresentation of Yahweh and misuse of the land (expressed in the repeated accusation "they have broken my covenant," e.g., Jer 34:18), but these specific offenses were never possible for anyone other than Israel. Or, said another way, the covenant curses can never fall on those who have no covenant to follow and no covenant to break.

The repeated phrase "I will do to you what I plan to do to them" (e.g., Num 33:56) means that the actions experienced by Israel will be superficially similar to the actions experienced by the Canaanites; they will be attacked by foreign armies and forcefully expelled from the land. The similarity of the verbs *attacked* and *expelled*, however, does not imply that these verbs are occurring *for the same reasons*. The action is the same (attack, expulsion), but what the action intends to accomplish is different. At the conquest, God is removing the Canaanites from the land in order to prepare the land for his use. At the exile, Yahweh is removing Israel from the land in order to demonstrate his commitment to enforcing the order with which he has identified himself. There is no possible parallel between the events; therefore it is not legitimate to claim that what happens to Israel at the exile is the same thing that happens to the Canaanites at the conquest. The appearance might be similar, but the nature of the event is incomparable. Consequently, it is not legitimate to assume that the Canaanites earned their expulsion by doing the same things that caused Israel to earn the covenant curses and the exile.

PART 4

THE LANGUAGE AND IMAGERY OF THE CONQUEST ACCOUNT HAS LITERARY AND THEOLOGICAL SIGNIFICANCE

The Depiction of the Canaanites in Leviticus and Deuteronomy Is a Sophisticated Appropriation of a Common Ancient Near Eastern Literary Device, Not an Indictment

A few isolated passages in Leviticus and Deuteronomy are among the most commonly cited to support the idea that the conquest is intended to punish the Canaanites, so it is important to examine those passages carefully. As discussed in proposition nine, Leviticus 18 is in the genre of an ancient legal treatise. This means that its grammatical imperatives are not commands but rather descriptions of the covenant order. The propositions of a legal treatise are not rules; they are illustrations of the principles that define order, which is a prerequisite for survival under the terms of the Israelite covenant. That means that violating the Torah (that is, doing one of the behaviors that the Torah forbids) does not equate to committing a crime. It means living or behaving in a way that is contrary to the order that the treatise describes. The statement that "all these things were done by the people who lived in the land before you" in Leviticus 18:27 means that the Canaanites did not live according to the definition of order described by Israel's decrees and statutes, that is, the covenant. It is not an indictment because the things they did are not presented as crimes. In fact it is barely more than a redundant statement: "people outside the covenant do not observe the covenant." As readers we should ask, Did the Israelites understand, or were they meant to understand, these statements as a justification for going to war (i.e., "fight these people because they behave in a nonorderly manner")? *That* is the question that needs to be answered in the affirmative in order to support an interpretation of the conquest as punishment. Examining the depiction of the Canaanites in its literary context will help us to answer this question.

LEVITICUS 18 AND THE INVINCIBLE BARBARIANS

The idea of people existing outside the bounds of order is part of the cognitive environment of the ancient world. In Assyrian and Babylonian literature, the word used to describe them is *ERÍN-man-da*, or Umman-manda. In the Babylonian Cuthaean Legend of Naram-Suen, the Umman-manda are depicted as birdlike, subhuman monsters, the offspring of the chaos monster Tiamat.[1] Besides their appearance and destructive tendencies, they also exhibit deviant behavior. Assyrian descriptions of the Umman-manda include a disdain for treaties and a habit of breaking oaths.[2] Additionally, a Sumerian document called The Marriage of Martu describes liminal peoples as follows:

> Their hands are destructive and their features are those of monkeys; he is one who eats what Nanna [a goddess] forbids and does not show reverence. They never stop roaming about . . . ; they are an abomination to the gods' dwellings. Their ideas are confused; they cause only disturbance. He is clothed in

---

[1]Sellim Ferruh Adalı, *The Scourge of God: The Umman-Manda and Its Significance in the First Millennium BC*, SAAS 20 (Helsinki: The Neo-Assyrian Text Corpus Project, 2011), 86.
[2]Ibid., 115.

sack-leather . . . , lives in a tent, exposed to wind and rain, and cannot properly recite prayers. He lives in the mountains and ignores the places of gods, digs up truffles in the foothills, does not know how to bend the knee, and eats raw flesh. He has no house during his life, and when he dies he will not be carried to a burial-place.[3]

Here we see descriptions of monstrous physical traits and penchant for destruction combined with descriptions of cultic violations and bizarre, shocking behavior outside all decency and propriety. In this particular case, the point is to demonstrate that the barbarian is unsuitable for marriage. We might compare it to Ezra 9:12, which, after describing the uncouth nature of the people of Canaan in pejorative terms, adds, "Therefore, do not give your daughters in marriage to their sons or take their daughters for your sons."

Although Hebrew does not use the word, there is some indication that the depiction of the nations of Canaan is categorically similar to the Umman-manda. In addition to the bizarre and generally taboo practices (e.g., bestiality) described in Leviticus 18, we see the peoples of the land described as unworldly beings (the Nephilim in Num 13:26 and the Rephaim in Deut 2:11, 20; 3:11; 2 Sam 21:20), which are depicted in terms befitting ogres and monsters (see also 1 Sam 17:4 in connection with 2 Sam 21:19, 22). This kind of description would be expected for those living outside the ordered world.

In most of the ancient world, the order-nonorder contrast was defined in terms of urbanites versus nomadic outsiders.[4] In the case of Israel this dichotomy is reversed (the Canaanite outsiders are urban,

---

[3]Marriage of Martu, lines 127-41. "The Marriage of Martu: Translation," in *The Electronic Text Corpus of Sumerian Literature*, Etcsl.orinst.ox.ac.uk/section1/tr171.htm (accessed June 4, 2016).

[4]Beate Pongratz-Leisten, "The Other and the Enemy in the Mesopotamian Conception of the World," in *Mythology and Mythologies: Methodological Approaches to Intercultural Influences*, ed. R. Whiting, Melammu II (Helsinki: The Neo-Assyrian Text Corpus Project 2001), 195-231.

and the Israelites are nomadic), but for the Israelites order is not defined in terms of the city but in terms of the covenant.[5] Thus "those who live outside the covenant" will be described in pejorative and dehumanizing terms. Some of these descriptions in the texts may be technically accurate; the nomads ("those who live outside the city") described in The Marriage of Martu probably do, in fact, live in tents, have no temples, and dig up (at least some of) their food. But the pejorative connotations of these activities, as well as the accusations of more extreme practices (eating raw meat, disrespecting their dead, having no concept of ritual propriety, being part monkey) are rhetorical and describe not actual observed behavior[6] but whatever qualities the author happens to dislike: "By projecting onto the proverbial 'other' those characteristics one does not desire to possess, a sense of identity emerges by way of contrast."[7] The point of the rhetoric is not to objectively describe behavior but to generate a negative profile of those who live outside the established order, for the purposes of promoting the established order as the ideal state of being: "By marginalizing certain groups a society defines its own identity, which finds its expression also in a specific conception of the world."[8] This is what most of the ancient world did for the established order of the city and what Israel does for the established order of the covenant.

The Umman-manda are depicted in ancient texts as dangerous, destructive, uncouth, and generally subhuman, but even so, this is never used as an excuse to send out an army to exterminate them. In fact, "In the narrative of the Cuthaean Legend, the divine will is such that the king has to remain passive against his fierce adversaries. . . . The story

---

[5]"The Mesopotamian visualized his or her city as being located at the center of a world that could not exist without it." Marc Van de Mieroop, The Ancient Mesopotamian City (Oxford: Oxford University Press, 1997), 42. See also Pongratz-Leisten, "Other and the Enemy," 202.
[6]Pongratz-Leisten, "Other and the Enemy," 207; Adall, Scourge of God, 109.
[7]Kimberly B. Stratton, "Identity," in the Cambridge Companion to Ancient Mediterranean Religions, ed. Barbette Stanley Spaeth (New York: Cambridge University Press, 2013), 228.
[8]Pongratz-Leisten, "Other and the Enemy," 197.

connects pacifism and piety because the former is advocated on the basis of trusting the gods. The prize is the fall of the Umman-manda."[9] This, at least, is certainly not a justification for war.[10] While other documents do depict actual conflict with the Umman-manda, the pattern for engaging them is relatively consistent and also parallels the pattern followed by Joshua when he deals with the Canaanites. The parallels fall into four broad categories, which we will now briefly examine.

The Umman-manda are more powerful than their opponents and cannot be defeated militarily. This idea is present in the Cuthaean Legend, where Naram-Suen fails to defeat the enemy on three occasions, but is also found in other texts describing encounters with the Umman-manda.[11] According to the Ehulhul Cylinder, "Nabonidus faced an enemy [the Medes, described in the text as Umman-manda] more powerful than Babylon but was assured that the gods would destroy the enemy, just as Dilbat assured Naram-Sin in the Cuthaean Legend."[12] The Gyges Narrative describes a powerful enemy (the Cimmerians), in terms reminiscent of the Umman-Manda, that cannot be defeated until Gyges becomes a vassal of Assyria.[13] The Gadd Chronicle describes the Umman-manda (the Medes) as "a formidable force that the Babylonians could not touch."[14] In Israel, we observe the same. The people of Canaan, especially the Anakites, are so powerful that Israel cannot hope to defeat them (Num 13:31-33).

The king who fights the Umman-manda is told to do so by the gods. Because the Umman-manda are destined to be destroyed by the gods, the kings require special sanction to engage them (as opposed to

---

[9]Adall, *Scourge of God*, 66. Further, this stance is advocated against the Umman-manda specifically, rather than against all enemies on principle and merely happening to include them.

[10]"The stark contrast with the traditional Mesopotamian king who slays his enemies is obvious." Ibid., 65-66. See also 154-55.

[11]Ibid., 64.

[12]Ibid., 98.

[13]Ibid., 118.

[14]Ibid., 134.

watching and waiting, as Naram-Suen is made to do). Nabonidus receives a vision from Marduk and Sin commanding him to defeat the Umman-manda under Astyges in order to recapture and rebuild the ruined temple of Ehulhul.[15] Similarly, "Gyges' initial military victory over the Cimmerians was attributed to his obedience to the command of the god Ashur who appeared in [Gyges's] dream and told him to submit to Assyria."[16] Joshua does not receive his instructions in a dream, but the initiative still comes from Yahweh, commonly in the form of the repeated "as the LORD commanded his servant Moses" (e.g., Josh 11:15), and also from the "commander of the LORD's army" in Joshua 5:13-15 (cf. Josh 6:2, "the LORD said to Joshua").

When the king becomes arrogant and trusts in his own power rather than that of the gods, he is defeated by the Umman-manda. A corollary of the invincibility of the Umman-manda and the specific sanction of the gods required to engage them is that the kings cannot defeat the Umman-manda alone without trusting in the assistance of the gods (and, consequently, doing what they say). Naram-Suen is required to remain passive and trust the gods; when he takes matters into his own hands and trusts his own strength, he is consistently defeated by the Umman-manda.[17] Gyges is allowed to actually fight the Umman-manda (Cimmerians) and is able to defeat them as long as he obeys Ashur and submits to Assyria, but later he breaks his loyalty oath and is promptly defeated by the Cimmerians after being cursed by Ashur and Ishtar.[18] In the case of Israel, Joshua's army breaks Yahweh's command regarding the devoted things and is promptly defeated by the army of Ai (Josh 7:1-5). Likewise, in Numbers 14 the people disobey Yahweh's command to take possession of the land and are promptly defeated by the Anakites. Further, the books of Judges and

---

[15]Ibid., 98.
[16]Ibid., 121.
[17]Ibid., 122.
[18]Ibid.

Samuel especially are full of accounts of Israelite defeats by the peoples of Canaan that are reversed when they begin to obey Yahweh and trust in him to fight on their behalf (see especially Gideon in Judg 7, David in 1 Sam 17, and Jonathan in 1 Sam 14).

The Umman-manda are defeated by the power of the gods, not the king. "One of the significant themes in the Cuthaean Legend is that the Umman-manda are a force that the gods will eventually destroy, regardless of how powerful they are and how incapable the Mesopotamian king is of defeating them. Their collapse is described around the massacre of their city arranged by the gods without any [Mesopotamian] interference."[19] In addition to the Cuthaean Legend, "Nabonidus' inscriptions describe Cyrus' defeat of Astyages as a manifestation of divine will to do away with Median hegemony,"[20] and the fall of the Medes (described as Umman-manda) in the Gadd Chronicle is engineered without any Babylonian assistance.[21] Gyges actually does fight the Cimmerians, but his victory is attributed to "the power of Ashur and Marduk." In Assurbanipal's *Inscription from the Ishtar Temple*, the Cimmerian king, Tugdamme, "king of the Umman-manda," is struck down by the gods without any Assyrian interference,[22] including one instance where the gods drop a meteor on his camp.[23] Israel, like Gyges, actually fights the barbarians, and like Gyges its victory is attributed to its god ("I am going to drive [them] out before you," in Lev 18:24). In Joshua 10, as in Assurbanipal's inscription, Yahweh uses the elements of the cosmos against the Amorites, including showering them with hail (Josh 10:11-14). Specifically in this instance but also throughout Joshua's entire campaign, the text explicitly claims that "the LORD was fighting for Israel" (Josh 10:14, 42).

---

[19]Ibid., 136.
[20]Ibid., 170.
[21]Ibid., 137.
[22]Ibid., 131-32.
[23]Ibid., 130.

All of this indicates that Leviticus 18 is describing the people of Canaan in terms of a well-known ancient Near Eastern trope about invincible barbarians destined to be destroyed by the gods. Despite the portrait of the barbarians, their status as living outside the ordered world, and their destiny of destruction, the trope is never used as an excuse to destroy them on behalf of the offended gods (what we would call holy war) because the gods reserve the right to deal with them themselves. It is also never used to justify attacking the barbarians and taking their resources (implied by the English word *conquest*), because attacking the barbarians militarily is suicide.[24] Normally the trope is employed to rationalize losing battles (not winning them) and avoiding enemies (not assaulting them). This means that Israel would not have used the trope to justify going to war, and if Israel would not have used it, an interpreter of Israel's actions cannot use it either. Likewise, the interpreter cannot use the reference to make any claims about actual behavior of actual Canaanites, because law treatises (and violations thereof) do not describe actions per se, and the trope of invincible barbarians does not necessarily reflect actual observations.

THE WICKEDNESS OF THE BARBARIANS
IN DEUTERONOMY 9:4-6

The main rhetorical force of Deuteronomy 9 begins in Deuteronomy 9:4 with a warning about what Israel might say to itself. The NIV translates, "Do not say to yourself, 'The LORD has brought me here to take possession of this land because of my righteousness.' No, it is on account of the wickedness of these nations that the LORD is going to drive them

---

[24]The Cyrus Cylinder does justify the king's conquest of the Umman-manda, but in this case Cyrus is not invoking the trope but only using the word. The Medes are not invincible barbarians to Cyrus; he only calls them Umman-manda because that is what Nabonidus called them (Adall, *Scourge of God*, 162). Propaganda designed to justify conquest no doubt exists, but it does not appear to take the form of painting the enemy to be conquered as invincible barbarians cursed by the gods.

out before you." A better translation, however, would be "Do not think 'it is because of our innocence that the Lord has brought us here to possess this land, and because of the wickedness of the nations that the Lord is driving them out before you,'"[25] placing both prepositional phrases in the hypothetical saying of the Israelites. But why would Israel even think to say this? The Israelites of the time of Joshua have had little opportunity to encounter any actual Canaanites, so what basis would they have for assuming wickedness?

We are told why in Deuteronomy 9:1-3, which is the reason these verses are included at the beginning of this section instead of launching straight into the warnings in Deuteronomy 9:4. These three verses are a rapid and concise summary of all the Canaanite traits that classify them according to the trope of the Umman-manda. They are greater and stronger than Israel (Deut 9:1). They are the Anakites, the monstrous Nephilim and Rephaim (Deut 9:2; Num 13:33; Deut 2:11). Yahweh is the one who will go before the army and destroy them (Deut 9:3). Deuteronomy 9:4-5 refers to the fourth component of the trope: the invincible barbarians are doomed to destruction by the gods. The purpose of this passage is to warn Israel that, even though the Canaanites are depicted this way in Israel's rhetoric, and the purpose of the rhetoric is to teach the Israelites how to think about themselves, that their self-conception should not include any delusions about their own righteousness. The fate of the invincible barbarians comes to them as a result of their divinely decreed destiny, not because their conquerors (Israel, in this case) have merited the victory.

In the Cuthaean Legend and other sources, the Umman-manda are depicted behaving "in an evil manner" (Akkadian *lemniš*, adverbial

---

[25] J. G. McConville, *Deuteronomy*, Apollos Old Testament Commentary (Downers Grove, IL: InterVarsity Press, 2002), 174. Most translations render the preposition *bə* as an adversative pronoun with a causative inflection (gloss: "no, the real cause is"), but *bə* never functions in a causative sense (ibid., 182). See also Moshe Weinfeld, *Deuteronomy 1–11*, AB (New York: Doubleday, 1991), 406.

form of *lemnutu*).[26] This evil, then, is part of the profile of the invincible barbarians, but like the other pejorative aspects of the profile, it is not necessarily based on actual, observed behavior. The Hebrew semantic equivalent of *lemnutu* is *rišʿâ*, the term translated "wickedness" in Deuteronomy 9:4-5. The term does not refer to a rap sheet of offenses; it is a status of standing under condemnation. We can see this clearly in Malachi 1:4, where Edom is classified as "the land of *rišʿâ*, a people always under the wrath of the LORD." Likewise, in Deuteronomy 25:2, if someone commits a crime that warrants flogging, they should be flogged with the number of lashes that the sentence (*rišʿâ*) demands for that crime. That the Canaanites have this status is part of their depiction as the trope of invincible barbarians. The evil of the Ummanmanda is one of the reasons why they are destroyed by the gods, as is also the case in Deuteronomy 9: "It is on account of the *rišʿâ* of these nations that the LORD is going to drive them out before you."[27] However, the evil cannot be conceived in terms of violating some universal moral law, or even as acting contrary to the will of the gods; evil (*rišʿâ/ lemnutu*) is a status, not a series of actions, and it is not earned by angering the gods, because the invincible barbarians are always controlled by the gods and serving the purposes of the gods.[28] In Babylonian texts, "Marduk was seen as the real power behind the Umman-manda,"[29] even as they devastate Babylon and knock down

---

[26] Adall, *Scourge of God*, 97. Additionally, Adall tentatively interprets a difficult section of line 54 in the Standard Babylonian version of the legend to refer to the Umman-manda as "tainted" (*lapatu*, "made unclean"; compare *tāmēʾ* in Lev 18:24). ibid., 48.

[27] The same idea is expressed in Lev 20:23 by the word translated "abhorred" (*qws*), which indicates antagonism (i.e., 1 Kings 11:25, where it is translated "hostile"). Leviticus 20:23 is the only occurrence of God as subject. The word itself does not imply any particular reason for the hostility. The context says "on account of" these things but does not specify what exactly it was about these things that produced the antagonism. The parallel to Lev 18:24 indicates that the statement is supposed to be read as a threat against Israel, not a description of the Canaanites (see proposition eleven).

[28] "The [Cuthaean Legend] concerns a devastating invasion of Babylonia by certain barbarian hordes, who are the creatures of the gods." Joan Goodnick Westenholtz, *Legends of the Kings of Akkade* (Winona Lake, IN: Eisenbrauns, 1997), 266.

[29] Adall, *Scourge of God*, 138.

the temples of the great gods, and, in the Kudur-Nahhunte Epic, Bel (Marduk) incites the king of the Umman-manda (Elamites) to "plot evil against Babylon," attack Sumer, and loot the temple of Esarra.[30] In the Cuthaean Legend, the Umman-manda are created by the gods specifically for the testing of Naram-Suen.[31] Interestingly enough, Yahweh employs the peoples of Canaan for a similar purpose in Judges 2:20-23, which is further evidence that the behavior they are practicing is not itself inherently offensive and therefore not the source of their condemned status.

The evil of the barbarians comes as a result of their nature as destructive, subhuman monsters. It is inherent to them as part of their chaotic origin, not a status that is earned through savagery. The Israelite ritual literature is not interested in sorting out which aspects of the trope correspond to actual observable behavior and which are pejorative rhetoric, because the ritual literature is not a treatise on anthropology. The Canaanites are being destroyed by Yahweh because that is always the destiny of invincible barbarians, and Israel is profiting by this because of the promise made to their ancestors (Deut 9:5). By affirming the trope in Deuteronomy 9:5, the text is not claiming that the Canaanites were actually, observably wicked, any more than it is claiming that they were actually, observably subhuman monsters, and, as we have discussed in proposition five, the narrators never actually depict any kind of wickedness in exposition. The purpose of Deuteronomy 9:5 is not to confirm for Israel (or for the modern interpreter) that Israel's pejorative rhetoric concerning the Canaanites is grounded in reality. Its purpose (somewhat ironically, given its history of interpretation) is, rather, to undermine the converse corollary of the retribution principle: Israel is prospering, but that does not mean Israel is righteous (for a discussion of the retribution principle and its illegitimate corollary, see proposition four).

---

[30]Ibid., 165, 167.
[31]Ibid., 56-57.

EXCURSUS: The Invincible Barbarians and the Rephaim

The parallels between the portrayals of the Rephaim and the portrayals of the Umman-manda are not confined to Leviticus 18 and Deuteronomy 9. In Deuteronomy 2 the Rephaim are driven out of their land by the nations of Ammon and Moab, "as Israel did in the land the LORD gave them" (Deut 2:12). Their monstrous features are noted in Deuteronomy 2:10, 21 (compare Num 13:32-33), as is their destruction at the hand of Yahweh ("the LORD destroyed them from before the Ammonites," Deut 2:21). The etymology of the words enforces the unworldly aspects of the enemy, similar to the monstrous bird-men of the Cuthaean Legend. *Emim* (Deut 2:10) putatively comes from the root *'êmâ*, which would therefore mean "terrible ones";[32] *Rephaim* refers to the shades of the dead.[33] Naram-Suen also thought that his enemies were spirits, specifically demons from the underworld, so much so that he had to test to make sure they could bleed.[34] Assyrian documents likewise refer to the Umman-manda as "offspring of Tiamat," directly referencing Naram-Suen's enemies and applying the depiction to their own enemies, the Cimmerians.[35] In addition to the underworld connotation, another feature of the Umman-manda is their nobility, denoted in the Cuthaean Legend by the word *šūpû* ("greatness"), which is "mostly used for gods, heroes, kings, cities, and even the stars."[36] This same idea carries over into the general usage of the term, which emphasizes the military and nobility of the enemy,

---

[32] Eugene E. Carpenter, "Deuteronomy," in *ZIBBCOT*, 1:432.

[33] H. Rouillard, "Rephaim," in *Dictionary of Deities and Demons in the Bible*, ed. Karel van der Toorn, Bob Becking, and Pieter W. van der Horst (Grand Rapids: Eerdmans, 1999), 695b-697a.

[34] Adalı, *Scourge of God*, 57, citing Giovanni B. Lanfranchi, "The Cimmerians at the Entrance to the Netherworld: Filtration of Assyrian Cultural and Ideological Elements into Archaic Greece," *Atti e Memorie dell'Academia Galileiana di Scienze, Lettre ed Arti Parte III: Memorie delle Classe di Scienze Morali, Lettre ed Arti* 94 (2002): 75-112, esp. 101-3. On the test for bleeding see Joan Goodnick Westenholz, *Legends of the Kings of Akkade* (Winona Lake, IN: Eisenbrauns, 1997), 315 (lines 64-71).

[35] Adalı, *Scourge of God*, 85-86.

[36] Ibid., 48.

rather than a specific ethnicity (even when it also specifies an ethnicity, such as the Medes, Cimmerians, or Elamites).[37] The Rephaim are most commonly associated with the spirits of dead kings specifically,[38] which carries similar connotations (as does the Septuagint translation of Zamzummites as "mighty ones").[39] It may therefore be tentatively possible that the Hebrew *rəpā'îm*, long-confusing to interpreters, could be considered a semantic equivalent of Akkadian *ERÍN-man-da*, a term indicating powerful, majestic demi-humans originating from the netherworld, and applied to enemies in historical documents for rhetorical purposes.[40]

The trope of the invincible barbarians is used again in Ezekiel 38–39 to describe the army of Gog.[41] Although this time the army is attacking Israel (because *Gog* is a cipher for Babylon), we should note that the restoration of Israel after the exile (described in this oracle in Ezek 39:25-29) thematically recapitulates the conquest in much of the postexilic literature, perhaps most notably in Ezekiel 47–48.[42] If this is the case, then the use of the trope of invincible barbarians to represent the enemy that is destroyed by God prior to the restoration might be at least circumstantial evidence that (at least in Ezekiel's time) the enemies of the original conquest were understood to be invincible

---

[37]Ibid., 81.

[38]Roulliard, "Rephaim," 696a.

[39]Carpenter, "Deuteronomy," 1:436.

[40]This is not to say that the Hebrew Bible has literary dependence on, or even knowledge of, the Cuthaean Legend specifically; the use of an etymologically unrelated term and lack of the document's specific themes of pacifism in the face of militant invaders would indicate that it does not. The term *Umman-manda* is known in Ugarit from letter RS 17.286 (Adall, *Scourge of God*, 80-81), which indicates that the concept represented by the word would have been present in the cognitive environment of the Levant.

[41]Daniel Bodi, "Ezekiel," in *ZIBBCOT*, 4:484-85: "This parallel [between Ezekiel 38 and the Cuthaean Legend] suggests that Ezekiel is using an ancient Near Eastern literary cliché in order to designate the invading hordes."

[42]"The picture of the Restoration . . . follows a venerable historical and literary model: the exodus from Egypt, followed by conquest and settlement in the land of Israel." Sara Japhet, *From the Rivers of Babylon to the Highlands of Judah* (Winona Lake, IN: Eisenbrauns, 2006), 426.

barbarians as well. It is further worth noting that the purpose of destroying Gog's hordes is not specifically to punish them (although that also happens to be involved; see proposition seventeen); the purpose is to "make known my holy name among my people Israel" (Ezek 39:7). This is fully in keeping with the trope of invincible barbarians, who are condemned by the gods to make a point to the servants of the gods, as is also the case in the conquest. Also recapitulating the conquest is the theme of cleansing the land (that is, changing its status; Ezek 39:14-16; compare Lev 18:25), although this time the word is *ṭhr* (though that is to be expected; the land is already ruled by God, so the *ḥerem* that occurred at the conquest is unnecessary; see proposition nineteen).

Behaviors That Are Described as Detestable Are Intended to Contrast with Ideal Behavior Under the Israelite Covenant, Not to Accuse the People Who Did Them of Crimes

As we discussed in proposition eight, we have no reason to believe that the purpose of Israel was to save the Gentiles from God's wrath by bringing them into the covenant. Consequently, we must reexamine the language that is occasionally used to describe people and practices outside the covenant, words such as *hate* (*śn*ᵓ), *evil* (*ra*ᶜ), or *detestable* (*tôᶜēbâ*). We know that such words do not indicate their objects as targets of wrath because the covenant paradigm does not follow the dichotomy of the saved and the damned. But once again, they are not meaningless, either. This is especially important for understanding the conquest because all three of these words are used to describe the people of Canaan.

TÔᶜĒBÂ IN DEUTERONOMY 18:12; 20:18

Deuteronomy 18:12 describes the practices of the Canaanites as *tôᶜēbâ* (NIV "detestable"). *Tôᶜēbâ* means "contrary to order" and is consistent with the classification of the Canaanites as liminal barbarians outside the bounds of order.[1] We see a similar sentiment in Genesis 46:34, where "all shepherds are *tôʿēbâ* to the Egyptians." The shepherds in question are called *shasu* in Egyptian documents, where they are a despised and occasionally feared group of outsiders.[2] Papyrus Anastasi I describes them in monstrous terms: four to five cubits (about seven feet) in height and unfriendly, with fierce faces.[3] This demonstrates a tendency in the period to describe a despised outgroup as *tôʿēbâ* and also establishes that the kind of vocabulary used to denigrate them is not unique to Israel. However, *tôʿēbâ*—deviation from established order—is always relative to the order in question. So, practices that are described as *tôʿēbâ* (occasionally specified "to Yahweh") in Israel's literature are unacceptable for Israel, as we would expect, because they are in violation of Israel's covenant. However, we should understand that, while the Canaanites would probably regard detestable behavior to be wrong in a sense of "doing bad things is bad," they might not classify their own behavior as *tôʿēbâ* because worshiping their own gods (the behavior that the biblical narrators depict them engaging in; see proposition five) is not contrary to the order of the world as they understand it. Yahweh cares whether Israel worships foreign gods, because Israel is under the obligations of a vassal treaty (the covenant), but as we have seen in propositions eight and eleven, that condition does not apply to those who are not subject to the covenant.

In Deuteronomy 20:10-11 instructions are given on conditions for sparing populations that live far away (in contrast to those who live in the land itself, who are called *tôʿēbâ* in Deut 20:18), even though the people far away probably engage in the same practices as the people who are to be driven out. The distinguishing factor is geography, not

---

[1] H. D. Preuss, "תּוֹעֵבָה," in *TDOT*, 15:602.

[2] James K. Hoffmeier, *Ancient Israel in Sinai: The Evidence for the Authenticity of the Wilderness Tradition* (New York: Oxford University Press, 2005), 240.

[3] Papyrus Anastasi I, in E. Wente, *Letters From Ancient Egypt*, SBL Writings from the Ancient World (Atlanta: SBL, 1990), 108.

behavior. If Canaanite cultic practice merits destruction on principle, it should merit destruction wherever it is practiced. Similarly, in Judges 2:20–3:4, Yahweh spares the populations specifically so that they will test Israel with syncretism, which would be an odd maneuver for someone who wanted to exterminate the practice on principle. Finally, we observe again (see proposition eight) that in the oracles against the nations in the prophetic literature, the nations are never indicted for worshiping foreign gods, although Israel routinely is. This indicates that the *tô'ēbâ* described in Deuteronomy is detestable behavior *if the Israelites do it*, but that does not mean it is detestable when the Canaanites do it; the rhetoric is delivered from a purely Israelite perspective. The emphasis is on what Israel is not supposed to do, not on what the Canaanites should be (or were) punished for doing.

RA' IN 2 KINGS 21:9-11

Deuteronomy 18 describes what will happen to Israel if they commit the same *tô'ēbâ*—behavior outside the order of the covenant—as the Canaanites. In 2 Kings 21:9, the narrator describes it as it happens: "They did more evil [*ra'*] than the nations the LORD had destroyed before the Israelites." A character elaborates in 2 Kings 21:11: "Manasseh king of Judah has committed *tô'ēbâ*. He has done more *ra'* than the Amorites who preceded him and has led Judah into sin with his idols." *Ra'* is not a measure on a scale of universal morality; it has a similar semantic range to English *bad* and therefore, like *tô'ēbâ*, is a relative term. God can do or sponsor *ra'*,[4] so *ra'* cannot inherently mean "things that are universally immoral" or "things that make Yahweh

---

[4] An "evil spirit" (*rûaḥ ra'*) is sent from Yahweh on several occasions (Judg 9:23; 1 Sam 16:14-16; 19:9); Yahweh sends *ra'* angels to Egypt (Ps 78:49); Yahweh threatens Israel with *ra'* in Deut 30:15 ("destruction") and Josh 23:15; Yahweh shoots Israel with "*ra'* and destructive arrows of famine" (NIV "deadly," Ezek 5:16); God brings *ra'* against Egypt (NIV "disaster," Is 31:2); God brings both prosperity and *ra'* ("disaster," Is 45:7); Yahweh sends *ra'* ("judgments") on Jerusalem (NIV "dreadful," Ezek 14:21); Micah claims that "*ra'* has come from the Lord" (NIV "disaster," Mic 1:12); and Job accepts both good and *ra'* (NIV "trouble," Job 2:10) from God (cf. Eccles 7:14).

angry," as in "Manasseh did more universally immoral things that make Yahweh angry than the Amorites had done." The value judgment "bad" (*ra*ʿ) is relative to the covenant. What it means in this case is that "Manasseh did more things that are forbidden by the covenant than the Amorites had done." We know that the Canaanite nations did things that are forbidden by the covenant, but these things are only punishable offenses to those accountable to the covenant, which the Canaanites are not. We know this because, again, the Canaanites are specifically sanctioned by Yahweh to test Israel by their (countercovenant) influence (Judg 2:22). *Tôʿēbâ* practices are used by Yahweh on other occasions as well: his last message to Saul is given through a forbidden medium (1 Sam 28:7-19); he causes Balaam to bless Israel through a forbidden oracle (Num 23–24); and he directs Nebuchadnezzar to attack Jerusalem through forbidden divination (Ezek 21:21-23). Ammon and Moab are given their land (Deut 2:9, 19) even though they worship Milchom and Chemosh, respectively (compare 1 Kings 11:13), and again, the oracles against them do not include cultic practices in the indictment. When the narrator of Kings indicts Manasseh for something that is also included in the condemnation of the nations—the shedding of innocent blood (e.g., Joel 3:19-21)—he takes care to distinguish this act from the cultic practices that constitute "more evil than the nations" (2 Kings 21:9). Likewise, Manasseh and Judah commit *ḥāṭāʾ* (sin) in 2 Kings 21:11, 16, but the nations and the Amorites only do *raʿ*, not *ḥāṭāʾ*.[5]

"*TÔʿĒBÂ* THE LORD HATES" IN DEUTERONOMY 12:31

Deuteronomy 12:31 says, "You must not worship the LORD your God in their way, because in worshiping their gods, [the Canaanites] do all

---

[5]Compare to the common phrase "doing *raʿ* in the eyes of the LORD and following the *ḥāṭāʾ* of Jeroboam" (1 Kings 16:19, 31; 2 Kings 13:2, 6, 11; 14:2; 15:9, 18, 24, 28), and note that the narrator does not say that Manasseh "[did] *raʿ* in the eyes of the Lord and [did] the *ḥāṭāʾ* of the nations the Lord drove out before Israel," although this would have been easy to say if an indictment of the Amorites and others were intended.

kinds of detestable things [*tôʿēbâ*] the LORD hates [*śnʾ*]." However, this passage does not offer God's hatred as a reason why the nations are being driven out before Israel (that is, it does not say "I will destroy them before you because they did the things I hate"). The Hebrew word *śnʾ* does not necessarily carry the visceral emotional disgust connoted by the English *hate*; it can indicate any level of aversion.[6] Most significantly for our purposes, however, the language of love and hate is used throughout the ancient Near East in regard to (political) covenants.[7] Hate from one party to another "is a metaphor for and communicates an unstable or broken covenant."[8] The Canaanites, of course, broke no covenant because they had no covenant to break; like *raʿ* and *tôʿēbâ*, *śnʾ* indicates practices that will violate the covenant *if Israel does them*, but they carry no implications for those who are outside the covenant. In Deuteronomy 12 the forbidden practice is specifically the worship of Yahweh using the same cultic practices the Canaanites use to worship their gods (Deut 12:2-4, 31). Why Yahweh accepts certain cultic practices for himself and rejects others is never explained; any theory, including the idea that Canaanite methods are inherently immoral[9] (by either ancient or modern standards; sacrificing children in Deut 12:31 might be, but sacrificing outside the sanctuary in Deut 12:13 is not), is purely speculative.

---

[6]A. H. Konkel, "שׂנא," in *NIDOTTE*, 3:1257.

[7]Andrew J. Riley, "*Zêru*, 'to Hate' as a Metaphor for Covenant Instability," in *Windows to the Ancient World of the Hebrew Bible*, ed. Bill T. Arnold et al. (Winona Lake, IN: Eisenbrauns, 2014), 175-85.

[8]Ibid., 184. Consistent with the theme of covenant fidelity, in the Pentateuch the object of God's hatred is always cultic (Deut 12:31; 16:22). In Deut 1:27; 9:28 God's (hypothetical) hatred is paralleled with his desire to destroy in context of a fear that Egypt will think that Yahweh himself is evil (Ex 32:12, "with evil intent" paralleled to "because he hated them" in Deut 9:28; both Deut 1:27 and Deut 9:28 assume Yahweh has secretly planned to kill them from the start and has just been stringing them along). Moses is not worried that the Egyptians will think that Israel is immoral and has acted in such a way that the people incurred the wrath of their God (cf. Deut 29:25-27); rather, they will think that Yahweh has broken his covenant.

[9]See, for example, Jeffrey H. Tigay, *Deuteronomy*, JPS (Philadelphia: Jewish Publication Society, 1996), 127, 464-65.

The biblical narrator in 1 Kings 18 confirms that the Canaanites engaged in behaviors that are contrary to the stipulations of the covenant. They really did those behaviors, and those behaviors really are contrary to the covenant. But the behaviors are never classified as punishable offenses (ḥāṭāʾ) unless the Israelites are doing them (see proposition five). If one wanted to prove that the raʿ and tôʿēbâ are punishable offenses when the Canaanites do them, one would have to demonstrate (outside the mere event of the conquest, since that would be circular) that the covenant is universally binding, even to people who have never accepted or even heard of it, and there is no indication anywhere in the Hebrew Bible that this is the case. Neither the covenant nor the law was revealed to the Canaanites; the covenant never applied to them, either in its blessings or its curses. Therefore they cannot be indicted on the basis of not obeying it. They can, however, be held up as a negative example and a foil of the ideal of the covenant order. The language used to describe the Canaanites in Leviticus and Deuteronomy is not an accusation and is not a rationale for war. It is a brilliant appropriation of literary tropes and typology designed to simultaneously emphasize Israel's dependence on Yahweh, extol the covenant order as the ideal state of being, and warn the Israelites of the consequences of covenant infidelity.

The Imagery of the Conquest Account
Recapitulates Creation

As discussed in proposition twelve, the condemnation of the practices of the people of Canaan in Leviticus 18 is not intended to describe the actual behavior of actual Canaanites. Neither is it simply negative stereotyping fabricated in order to justify going to war and exterminating them;[1] the ancient Near Eastern literary trope used to describe the Canaanites is normally applied to an enemy as an excuse *not* to fight them or as a rationalization for failure to defeat them. The stereotype of disorderly behavior is offered as a warning to Israel, but that is not its only purpose. The imagery of the enemy as invincible barbarians also establishes an ideological framework for understanding the significance of the event that is accomplished by means of the conquest.

Israel, co-identified with Yahweh through its holy status as the people of the covenant, is the embodiment of cosmic order. In contrast, the Canaanites are agents of chaos by virtue of their position outside the covenant (see proposition twelve); they are not in conformity with Yahweh's covenant order, though they are also not

---

[1]Contra, i.e., Philip D. Stern, *The Biblical* Herem, BJS 211 (Providence, RI: Brown University Press, 1991), 83; Susan Niditch, *War in the Hebrew Bible: A Study in the Ethics of Violence* (New York: Oxford University Press, 1993), 24.

expected to be. This status is emphasized for rhetorical purposes by their profile in Israel's literature as subhuman barbarians. The Israelite nation is holy, co-identified with Yahweh and the cosmic order. The Canaanite nations are thematically related to cosmic chaos. The persistent emphasis of the conquest is to *drive out* the people of the land; thus the conquest thrusts chaos aside in order to make a space in which order will be established. When stated in this way, it becomes very apparent what the conquest is: a thematic recapitulation of the creation account in Genesis 1, where chaos was driven away to establish order.

Chaos and Creation

In the earliest occurrences of the ancient Near Eastern trope, the invincible barbarians are the "offspring of Tiamat," the personified cosmic ocean; this is one of the persistent identifiers of the Umman-manda in ancient Near Eastern literature.[2] In the Israelite cosmogony in Genesis 1 the cosmic ocean (*təhôm*, cognate of Akkadian "Tiamat"; NIV "deep") is not personified,[3] but nonetheless the concept retains its thematic significance. The barbarians also retain their thematic significance through the use of the trope, so the thematic interrelationship between barbarians = chaos = cosmic ocean is preserved in Israel.

In the ancient Near East, stories of creation are accounts of the triumph of order, instituted and maintained by the gods, over the nonordered precosmic condition (often called *chaos*, taken from the Greek word used to describe the precosmic condition in Hesiod's *Theogony*). The principle of chaos is commonly represented in ancient Near Eastern literature by the personified ocean (Ugaritic Yamm, Hebrew Yam) or by monstrous serpentine or draconic creatures

---

[2]Sellim Ferruh Adalı, *The Scourge of God: The Umman-Manda and Its Significance in the First Millennium BC*, SAAS 20 (Helsinki: The Neo-Assyrian Text Corpus Project, 2011), 60-61.
[3]See, for example, John Day, *God's Conflict with the Dragon and the Sea* (London: Cambridge University Press, 1985), 49-51; David Tsumura, *Creation and Destruction* (Winona Lake, IN: Eisenbrauns, 2005), 38.

(Ugaritic Litan, Hebrew Leviathan), or both at once (Akkadian Tiamat). Occasionally the triumph of order over chaos is depicted in terms of combat, as in the famous Babylonian cosmogony Enuma Elish. The thematic motif of order battling chaos (literally or figuratively) is referred to by scholars as *Chaoskampf*. The theme can occur in cosmogony (the initial establishment of creation), but it can also be seen to occur in seasonal or daily cycles (Baal versus Mot in Ugarit, or Ra versus Apophis in Egypt, respectively) as creation is perpetually renewed.[4] The theme can also be situationally repeated in microcosm in, for example, the building of temples[5] or, in the case of the Ugaritic Baal cycle, enthronement and royal legitimation.[6] In the Hebrew Bible, *Chaoskampf* imagery is occasionally employed to describe Yahweh's defeat of Israel's political enemies (e.g., Is 51:9), but we should be careful not to read too much into the symbolism. Egypt/Pharaoh is not literally a chaos monster, no matter how explicitly it is depicted as one (Is 30:7, Ezek 29:3), so we are not intended to read some macrocosmic subtext over and behind the event (in Is 51, the parting of the Red Sea), imagining that God is doing battle with supernatural powers who seek to influence events in the earthly realm.[7] Neither are we to assume that these passages in the Bible are derivatives from ancient Near Eastern mythology. Rather, the imagery is supposed to provide a thematic context in order to understand the nature of what is happening and what God's actions signify. The emphasis is on literary typology, not cosmic metaphysics. The same is true of the

---

[4] John H. Walton, *Genesis 1 as Ancient Cosmology* (Winona Lake, IN: Eisenbrauns, 2011), 70-72.

[5] Baruch Halpern, "The Ritual Background of Zechariah's Temple Song," *CBQ* 40 (1978): 167-90.

[6] Wayne T. Pitard, "The Combat Myth as a Succession Story at Ugarit," in *Creation and Chaos: A Reconsideration of Hermann Gunkel's Chaoskampf Hypothesis*, ed. JoAnn Scurlock and Richard H. Beal (Winona Lake, IN: Eisenbrauns, 2013), 199-205.

[7] As in, for example, Tremper Longman and Daniel G. Reid, *God Is a Warrior* (Grand Rapids: Zondervan, 1995), 82: "God's conflict with the forces of chaos on the suprahistorical plane are parallel with the conflict that occurs in human history."

conquest and the representation of the people of Canaan as agents of chaos.

In Genesis 1, the cosmic waters are divided not to punish the waters or destroy the waters but in order to make room for God's activity (creation; compare to Is 51:9-10 and Ex 14:21-31, where the [inert] sea is divided to make room for Yahweh's rescue of Israel). While the combat element of the *Chaoskampf* is more clearly evident in the conquest than in Israel's actual creation story (though the Canaanite armies still offer no real resistance), the point of both accounts is not on the combat or on the enemy, but on the results following the victory, that is, what the deity *does* after the obstacle of chaos has been removed.[8] In Genesis 1 the objective is rest (sabbath), which does not mean relaxation but rather signifies God's ongoing action of maintaining and sustaining the cosmic order.[9] In the Deuteronomistic History (Joshua, Judges, Samuel, and Kings), the objective is "placing the name" (see proposition nineteen). To further cement the parallel, the conquest is completed when its objective of preparation is finished and God finally does place his name in the temple of Jerusalem (1 Kings 9:3), a building explicitly full of Edenic imagery[10] that in turn symbolizes the cosmic order:[11] "The temple and the world stand in an intimate and intrinsic connection. The two projects cannot ultimately be distinguished or disengaged. . . . Sabbath and sanctuary partake of

---

[8]The debate over whether Yahweh's dividing the *təhôm* constitutes combat imagery generally concerns the extent to which Genesis 1 is or is not literarily dependent on the Enuma Elish. It is not normally extended to a theological discussion of whether Israel perceives the *təhôm* to have the ability to resist Yahweh's activity. Every identifiable instance of the *Chaoskampf* (e.g., Ps 74:14) in the Hebrew Bible agrees: personified monster or not, resistance is futile. As for the monsters, so for the Canaanites. Therefore, for our purposes, it does not matter whether the *təhôm* in Genesis 1 is active or inert, or whether dividing implies combat.

[9]John H. Walton, *Ancient Near Eastern Thought in the Old Testament* (Grand Rapids: Baker Academic, 2006), 114.

[10]For similarities in symbolism between Eden and Solomon's temple, see Gordon J. Wenham, "Sanctuary Symbolism in the Garden of Eden Story," in *I Studied Inscriptions from Before the Flood: Ancient Near Eastern, Literary, and Linguistic Approaches to Genesis 1–11* (Winona Lake, IN: Eisenbrauns, 1994), 399-404.

[11]Walton, *Genesis 1 as Ancient Cosmology*, 109.

the same reality."[12] The establishment of the original *cosmic order* in Genesis, and the establishment of the *covenant order* in a process that spans Moses to Solomon, are both part of Yahweh's ongoing project of creation.

ORDER IN THE ANCIENT NEAR EAST: TEMPLE AND CITY

In proposition eleven we asserted that the preparation of the land for Yahweh's use is comparable to the purification of a site in preparation for the building of a temple. Temple building in the ancient Near East also invokes the thematic imagery of *Chaoskampf* to signify the order that the structure represents. Baruch Halpern argues that the visions in Zechariah 1–6 are inspired by ancient Near Eastern imagery that associates the temple construction with the *Chaoskampf*: "The ancient mind, then, associated a temple fallen into disrepair or desuetude with the absence of cosmic order. The combat myth, as the paradigm of the restoration of that order, would provide the most convenient framework for the ritual of restoration."[13]

Temples in the ancient world were the residences of the gods. The temple was where people went to perform their ritual duties (to the gods) and to experience divine presence. The temple was a point of contact between heaven and earth. It was the place where the gods took their rest and sustained the order of the cosmos, which was often represented in terms of life and fertility. Because of the deity's residence in the temple, it was considered the center of order in the cosmos.[14] Different cultures had different ways of portraying the temple as cosmic nexus. Notably in Egypt, each temple claimed to house the primeval hillock from which creation emerged. Because of

---

[12]Jon D. Levinson, "The Temple and the World," *Journal of Religion* 64 (1984): 275-98, quote on 288.

[13]Halpern, "Ritual Background of Zechariah's Temple Song," 183.

[14]For temples as a center of order, see, for example, Byron E. Shafer, "Temples, Priests, and Rituals: an Overview," in *Temples of Ancient Egypt*, ed. Byron E. Shafer (Ithaca, NY: Cornell University Press, 1997), 1-30, esp. 1.

this view of the temple, if the temple was not maintained and its god sustained, the cosmos would be in jeopardy and subject to collapse.[15] In this way the idea of temple dissolution would be considered similar today to nuclear devastation, radical climate change, or the worst imaginable effects of pollution (that is, the apocalypse).

In Israel, the land likewise served as a locus of order. While it was a place of divine residence and therefore presence, and in that sense comparable to a temple, it was not *literally* a temple; the land was not sacred space (that is, divine real estate), was not a place for ritual (ritual activity outside the physical temple is discouraged), and did not recapitulate the heavenly abode of the gods as a temple building did. Perhaps, then, a better parallel might be to the more mundane locus of order in the ancient Near East that is represented by the city.[16] The city has a temple in it, but the actual business of administrating order in the human world comes from the palaces and other official complexes that surround the temple. But more than simply administering order, the city itself is the embodiment of the cosmic order in microcosm. A properly functioning city represents the ideal state of being in the earthly realm: "The Mesopotamian visualized his or her city as being located at the center of a world that could not exist without it, both in mundane and cosmic terms. . . . When a city and its god were in harmony, its inhabitants prospered and were happy."[17] Harmony in the city represented to the rest of the ancient Near East what covenant fidelity in the land represented to Israel.

The founding of cities in Mesopotamia was much rarer than the building of temples, but the Cylinder Inscription of Sargon describes the construction of his new capital city in terms that, while less explicit, still invoke the imagery of establishing order in place of nonorder:

---

[15]Michael B. Hundley, *Gods in Dwellings* (Atlanta: SBL, 2013), 48.

[16]For cities as a center of order, see Marc Van de Mieroop, *The Ancient Mesopotamian City* (Oxford: Oxford University Press, 1997), 61.

[17]Ibid., 42.

"The site . . . [no one before me] knew how to make habitable, whose canal none thought to dig."[18] It is worth noting that, despite the fact that the area is described as not habitable, a settlement ("the town of Magganubba") already existed on the site. Sargon had to first appropriate the existing settlement on the site (by eminent domain)[19] before he could use the land to build the city. It is possible that the site was also ritually purified; Sargon makes no mention of doing so, but the founding of new cities was virtually unknown in Mesopotamia. The Romans would purify the sites of new cities, and it is not unreasonable to assume that the Mesopotamians were equally conscientious.[20] Whether literally purified or not, however, Sargon still had to alter the status of the land one way or another (in this case, by purchasing it) before he could make use of it.[21] After describing the construction of the bricks, the temples, the palace, the walls, and the gates, Sargon goes on to describe how "peoples of the four regions of the world" were brought to the city and placed in the care of Assyrian officials who would "teach them how to fear god and king."[22] The inscription ends with an imprecation: "Whoever . . . brings to naught the law which I have established or blots out the record of my honors, may Assur, Shamash, Adad, and the great gods . . . destroy his name and his seed from the land."[23]

The land of Israel was not literally a city any more than it was literally a temple, but the imagery of the locus of cosmic order is strikingly similar to the ideology that the ancient Near East associated with (capital) cities. Specifically, we observe the idea that all nations are brought to receive instruction on the nature of the world order

---

[18]ARAB 2:119. See Van de Mieroop, *Ancient Mesopotamian City*, 55, 60-61.
[19]"The price of the fields of that town I paid back to their owners. . . . I gave those who did not want to take silver for their fields, field for field." ARAB 2:119.
[20]Van de Mieroop, *Ancient Mesopotamian City*, 59.
[21]His stated reason for the necessity is "to maintain justice and right" "in accordance with the name which the great gods have given me." ARAB 2:120.
[22]ARAB 2:120-22.
[23]ARAB 2:123.

(compare Is 2:2-4; Mic 1:1-3), and also the nature of the price for disrupting that order (compare Deut 4:26; 6:15). Unlike a city, Israel was not supposed to be an administrative center for an expanding empire; as discussed in proposition eight, Israel's order was not imperialistic and was not intended to expand.[24] What it was supposed to be was a microcosm of the ideal condition of the created order, as the ideal of the created order was understood in the ancient Near East.

In order to set up a new center of order, the existing nonorder must be cleared, not to punish the existing residents but to prepare the space in which the new system will function. This was true of the land in the conquest, and it was true for Sargon's city as well. But to fully understand the distinction between preexistent nonorder and active disruption of existing order, we might note the difference between the original citizens of Magganubba, who were removed to make way for the construction, and the subjects of Sargon's imprecation, who were destroyed and had their seed removed from the land. This difference represents the same essential distinction between what happened to the Canaanites and what ultimately happened to Israel. What happened to the Canaanites is like what happened to the displaced citizens; they were cleared away in order to make room for the center of order that, at the time of their occupation, did not exist. What happened to Israel is like what happens to the recipients of Sargon's curse: retribution for the disruption of the order that has been established.

COVENANT, CHAOS, AND THE FATE OF THE ISRAELITES

If the conquest is a recapitulation of creation, then the exile is a recapitulation of the flood. The flood is a *reversal* of creation, not a repetition of it; the cosmic waters are released and wipe out creation,

---

[24]Although the Israelite nation at the height of its power was, in fact, an empire, the covenant order and the rules for "those who live in the land" were not extended to every corner of Israelite hegemony. This is, again, the difference between those who live outside the land, with whom Israel can make treaties, and those within the land, with whom they cannot, in Deut 20.

restoring the cosmos to its nonordered, precreation state.[25] Similarly, the exile is a reversal of the conquest; God's presence departs from the temple (Ezek 10), and the nations (the thematic representations of chaos) crash in and wipe out the people of the covenant (the thematic representations of the created order), except for the faithful remnant who are preserved. The essential difference between the cosmic waters in Genesis 1 and antediluvian humanity in Genesis 6 is their inherent relationship to the cosmic order, and this difference also exists between the Canaanites at the conquest and the Israelites at the exile. The Canaanites and the cosmic waters have no relationship with cosmic order at all. They exist outside it and are indifferent to it, and so when order is established they are brushed aside with neither malice nor regret. But Israel and antediluvian humanity are part of their respective constructions of order; they were established in the order to conserve it, and by living within it they enjoy its benefits. Failure to conserve the order brings a consequence of its destruction. The flood undid the created order with the return of the cosmic waters; the exile undid the covenant order with the loss of Israel's land, leadership, temple, and everything that had defined the identity of its community.[26]

The offense described by Sargon's imprecation, and also committed by both preexilic Israel and antediluvian humanity, is a corruption or perversion of an existing established order; this is the essence of what we call *sin*.[27] Chaos, on the other hand, is merely the absence of order; it cannot pervert or corrupt order because it has no order to corrupt.

---

[25]See for example Ellen Van Wolde, *Stories of the Beginning* (Ridgefield, CT: Morehouse, 1997), 121-32.

[26]See Zech 14:11, where Jerusalem (understood to mean the whole nation of Israel) is said to have been *ḥerem*; compare to the *ḥerem* of community identities discussed in proposition sixteen.

[27]Technically, antediluvian humanity in Gen 6 is not accused of sin; neither does the text say that they are being punished, nor that God is manifesting wrath. The comparison still stands, though, because the text indicates that the destiny of antediluvian humanity is a consequence of their own "violence" (a word signifying a disorderly condition), whereas the destiny of the Canaanites is a consequence of God's promise to Abraham and not of anything the Canaanites did or did not do.

Agents of nonorder *literally cannot sin* and therefore cannot ever be said to be punished for sin; this is why, as discussed in propositions five and thirteen, the Canaanites, in accordance with their depiction as agents of nonorder, are frequently accused of *rāʿâ* (badness) and *tôʿēbâ* (behavior outside the bounds of order) but never *ḥāṭāʾâ*, which is sin: the twisting, bending, perverting, distorting, or corrupting of order. Only agents of order are capable of sin and therefore able to be punished for sin.[28]

Of course, this does not mean that the actual historical people of Canaan were incapable of sin because they were outside the covenant. Sodom (accused of sin in Gen 13:13) was outside the covenant too (see also the argument of Rom 5:13-19), but the conquest account is not a technical theological treatise on how sin works (what systematic theologians call hamartiology). The historical people of Canaan were not *actually* subhuman chaos monsters any more than they were *actually* incestuous bestiophiles. The purpose of the conquest narrative is not to describe the literal nature of the literal people but to describe what is happening to them in such a way that the nature of the *event* can be properly understood. They were sinners (as all humanity is), but that is not the reason why the conquest was happening to them. They were being *treated like* chaos creatures, not *treated like* sinners, so the text *depicts them as if they were* chaos creatures (by means of the trope of invincible barbarians) to make clear what is actually going on.[29]

---

[28]Although ultimately making a different point, Paul notes this essential relationship between order ("law," *nomos*, LXX for *tôrâ*, the covenant order) and sin in Rom 7:8 ("apart from the law, sin was dead"; also Rom 5:20).

[29]Therefore, we should think of the conquest as bringing order out of nonorder, rather than bringing order out of disorder. Nonorder (the Canaanites) are being cleared away just as *tohu wabohu* is in Gen 1, so that order may be established. The Canaanites are not indicted as agents of disorder and are not punished or judged in that regard. But their presence would instigate disorder among the Israelites. See the discussion in John H. Walton, *The Lost World of Adam and Eve* (Downers Grove, IL: IVP Academic, 2015), 149-52.

PART 5

WHAT GOD AND THE ISRAELITES ARE DOING IS OFTEN MISUNDERSTOOD BECAUSE THE HEBREW WORD *ḤEREM* IS COMMONLY MISTRANSLATED

Ḥerem Does Not Mean "Utterly Destroy"

As discussed in proposition fourteen, the land is thematically represented variously as a temple or a city. What the land literally is, however, is neither of these things: literally, the land is a geopolitical domain. Likewise, Joshua's wars are recounted in terms of the typology of macrocosmic order and ongoing creation, but because of the literal nature of the land their actual actions take the form of military conquest. Yahweh's broader objective is revelation through identification (see proposition eleven), but his immediate purpose is to "place his name" in the land. Symbolism, metaphor, imagery, and typology are all important for properly interpreting the motives behind the actions, but in order to truly understand what is going on we need to also consider the literal significance of the literal actions themselves. Specifically, we need to understand what is the meaning of placing a name in a geopolitical domain and also what is the purpose of *ḥerem*.

The Meaning and Purpose of Ḥerem

The common English translations of the Hebrew word *ḥerem* (ASV "utterly destroy"; NIV "destroy totally"; CEB "place under the ban";

NET "utterly annihilate"; ESV "devote to destruction") are misleading because they imply that the word specifies something that happens to the object (that is, it is destroyed). Alternatively, we suggest that the word actually refers to the *removal of something from human use.*[1] The emphasis is not on the object but on everyone around the object; "no one shall make use of this."[2] When *herem* objects are destroyed, the purpose of the destruction is to make sure that nobody can use it, but not all *herem* objects are destroyed. Most notably, Joshua 11:12-13 reports that all of the northern cities were *herem*, yet Joshua destroys only one of them (Hazor). Likewise, a field that is *herem* is not destroyed but becomes the property of the priests (Lev 27:21). Destruction, when it occurs, is a means to an end.

A Hittite document describes the devotion of a city in terms comparable to the Hebrew *herem*, complete with imprecations against rebuilders reminiscent of Joshua 6:26:[3]

> Tešub [a storm god] my lord . . . handed it over to me and I have desolated it and [made it sacred]. As long as heaven and earth and mankind will be, in future no son of man may inhabit it! [I have offered] it to Tešub my lord, together with fields, farmyards, vineyards. . . . [Let] your bulls Šeri and Hurri [make it] their own grazing-land. . . . He who nevertheless will inhabit it and will take the grazing-land away from the bulls of Tešub . . . let him be averse party to Tešub my lord.[4]

---

[1] Jacob Milgrom, *Leviticus 23–27*, AB (New York: Doubleday, 2001), 2418. See also Giuseppe F. Del Monte, "The Hittite Ḥerem," in *Memorie Igor M. Diakonoff*, Babel und Bibel 2 (Winona Lake, IN: Eisenbrauns, 2005), 21-45.

[2] Or, to say it more precisely, the perlocution of the act of *herem* applies to those who interact with the object and not the object itself. Notably, both Milgrom (*Leviticus*, 2391) and Baruch Levine, *Leviticus*, JPS (Philadelphia: Jewish Publication Society, 1989), 196, choose the word *proscription* to translate *herem* (as opposed to *destruction*), which likewise has a perlocution aimed at those who interact with the object rather than at the object itself.

[3] Del Monte, "Ḥerem," 22.

[4] Ibid., 41-42.

Ḥerem may often involve destruction, but "destruction" is not the essential *meaning* of *ḥerem* because not everything that is *ḥerem* is destroyed. *Ḥerem* occurs first, and *because* the thing is *ḥerem, therefore* the thing must be [blank], where [blank] is typically (but not always) some variant of "destroyed." The comparison with the Hittite document here demonstrates what *ḥerem* signifies (removal from human use) and why therefore the destruction is necessary. The Hittite king Mursili levels a rebellious city and offers the site to the god Tešub as a pasture for his bulls. Because the god is using the site as a pasture, nobody else can use it for anything; this is the thrust of the imprecation directed at "[whoever] . . . will take the grazing-land away from the bulls":

> An area is granted in absolute ownership to the God but in it no temple was permitted to be build [*sic*], no economic activity was allowed to be carried on; on the contrary, the exploitation of the banned area was deemed as an "abomination" (*natta ara*) to the deity, the perpetrator of such an abomination was handed over to the divine judgment and put to death.[5]

Compare this judgment with the accusation in Joshua 7:15, where violating the ban is "an outrageous thing in Israel,"[6] and also Joshua 7:25, where Yahweh brings trouble on Achan.[7]

The imprecation of the Hittite document is aimed at anyone who makes use of the site that has been set aside for the use of the deity. It

---

[5]Ibid., 22.

[6]Hittite *na-at-ta a-a-ra* appears to have an approximate meaning of "forbidden." *CHD* L-N.440 translates "not allowed." The semantic range seems to have some overlap with Hebrew *nbl* ("outrageous"); compare especially the sample "If the deity is male, it is *natta ara* for a woman to go in to him" (*CHD* L-N.440a) with the common use of *nbl* for gross sexual impropriety (Gen 34:7; Judg 19:23; 20:6; 2 Sam 13:12; Jer 29:23). Compare also the improper treatment of the rightful possessions of royalty ("to give away even the wood and chaff of princes is *natta ara*") with the improper treatment of the rightful possessions of deity in Josh 7:15.

[7]Comparison to Achan also noted by Del Monte, "Ḥerem," 23.

is not aimed at the citizens of the town. Thus we see the following sequence of events:

1. The necessity of the town's military defeat is determined. In the Hittite document, the reason is rebellion; in the case of Israel it is so the residents will not "become barbs in [Israel's] eyes and thorns in [Israel's] side" (Num 33:55).

2. The town is attacked by the army, and the defenders are defeated. The battle is not a consequence of the *herem*; *herem* happens after the battle is over.

3. The site is declared *herem* (forbidden from human use).

4. Violators of the ban (actual or hypothetical) are punished.

Of course, *herem* in the Old Testament is not limited to cities. There are four distinct categories of things that can be *herem*: inanimate objects, including plots of land; living individuals (people or animals); abstractions representing communities of people; and cities. What specifically happens to these varies depending on how they might be used and therefore on how that use might be prevented.

ḤEREM OF INANIMATE OBJECTS

In Joshua the objects that are *herem* refer to the plunder taken from certain cities, most notably Jericho. In Joshua 6:17 everything in the city (except Rahab and her family) is *herem*. The metal objects in Joshua 6:19, 24, cannot be destroyed by burning (they could be melted, but the technology to destroy metal does not exist in the Bronze Age, and the metal itself is *herem*), so they are removed from use by consigning them to the divine realm through donation to the sanctuary. Likewise, the field in Leviticus 27:21 is assigned to the divine realm, beyond the ability of humans to make use of it. The metal objects taken by Achan are burned along with him (Josh 7:24-26), but the metal cannot be destroyed by fire, and there is no mention of giving it to the sanctuary; presumably it is buried under rocks with the rest

(Josh 7:26). The end result is the same; the objects have been removed from human use.

Ḥerem of Living Individuals

This is the rarest category. It is implied in Joshua 6:17 regarding the citizens of Jericho, since if the ban excluded people there would be no reason to specify the exemption of Rahab. It is also implied in Joshua 8:25; although the people of Ai are not explicitly *ḥerem*, Joshua 8:2 says that Israel is to "do to Ai as [they] did to Jericho," with only the "plunder and livestock" exempted. "Plunder" (*šālāl*) is nonspecific and can include people, as in Numbers 31:11 ("They took all the plunder and spoils, including the people and animals"), but since Joshua 8:2 adds "livestock" (which are included in the generic in Numbers), the plunder probably refers to material objects and food, not captives. However, since the *ḥerem* takes place after the battle, the people have already been captured. "Putting them to the sword" is an alternative to their normal expected fate, which was slavery. They are being killed not for the purpose of making them dead but to remove them from use as slaves.

This is consistent with the *ḥerem* of persons in Leviticus 27:28, which discusses the treatment of things "a person owns and devotes to the lord"—whether human or animal. A human that a person owns is a slave. The (slave) who is *ḥerem* in Leviticus 27:29 is subsequently put to death, both so that they cannot be redeemed and so that they can no longer be used as a slave. It is worth remembering, however, that Leviticus is not a list of instructions that people are expected to follow but a circumscription of the logic of general principles (see proposition nine). The purpose of Leviticus 27:28-29 is not, therefore, to give instructions on how to do certain things with one's slaves, or even what is permissible to do to one's slaves (that is, you can *ḥerem* them if you want). Leviticus 27 as a whole is describing the internal logic of redeeming various things that have been dedicated to the Lord in various ways. Leviticus 27:28 explains the conceptual difference between dedication and devotion (*herem*): "nothing *herem* . . . may be sold or redeemed; everything so devoted is most holy to the LORD." *Herem* things cannot be redeemed because they are off-limits for human use, and this is not a status that can ever be revoked.

The clarification in Leviticus 27:29, therefore, is not intended to give instructions on how to properly carry out the *herem*; note that no specification is given about what to do with devoted objects or animals. The purpose of Leviticus 27:28-29 is to explain the logic of what *herem* is, relative to what "dedication" is.[8] Exodus 13:12-13 describes how the firstborn males of humans and both clean and unclean animals belong to Yahweh, a status that is invoked in Leviticus 27:27 at the beginning of the argument that continues through Leviticus 27:29. Both Exodus 13:13 and Leviticus 27:27 describe the redemption of unclean animals (in Exodus the price is a lamb, and unredeemed animals are killed, in Leviticus the price is 120 percent of the market value, and unredeemed animals are sold; since the point of both statements is illustrating internal logic rather than instructing, the difference is irrelevant). Leviticus 27:27 says nothing about clean animals or humans, but Numbers 18:15-17 describes the price for redeeming a human (five shekels) and also unclean animals (this time also five shekels, with no option not to redeem them), and also specifies that the clean animals cannot be redeemed but must be sacrificed.

Taken together, these three passages—Leviticus 27:27; Exodus 13:12-13; Numbers 18:15-17—describe the logic of dealing with things that belong to Yahweh. Clean animals cannot be redeemed; humans must be redeemed; unclean animals have some options. Both Numbers 18 and Leviticus 27 also note that there is some similarity between the firstborn claimed by Yahweh and things that are *herem*; they both belong to Yahweh. In Numbers 18, Yahweh gives those things that belong to him to the priests, both what is *herem* (Num 18:14) and the

---

[8]See also Philip D. Stern, *The Biblical* Herem, BJS 211 (Providence, RI: Brown University Press, 1991), 131: "Lev 27:29 fits well into a chapter dedicated to separation oaths dealing with human life, which ordinarily is to be redeemed."

firstborn (Num 18:15). But the issue addressed in Leviticus 27 concerns a different aspect of the logic: the dedication of the firstborn works a certain way; does the *herem* work the same way? Must a *herem* human be redeemed, as a firstborn human must? *Can* a *herem* human even be redeemed? Leviticus 27:29 specifically answers both of those questions: no, they must not, and no, they cannot. *Herem* works differently from other forms of dedication. The differing treatments of the unclean animals in the three passages indicate that the actual *handling* of the object is not really the point; it is possible that a *herem* human (slave) could be given to the sanctuary in the same manner as a field or other indestructible object. It is worth noting that this is exactly what they do to the Gibeonites in Joshua 9:27, whom they are supposed to *herem* but whom they are not allowed to kill (Josh 9:26).[9] It is also likely that this is what happens to Samuel in 1 Samuel 1:28 (where the unique word *hišʾiltihû* [hiphil stem of *šʾl*] is used; *herem* would not be appropriate since Hebrew children are not owned and cannot be said to be used). See proposition eighteen for a further discussion of the Gibeonites.

Herem of Communal Abstractions

In proposition eleven we argued that the nation of Israel refers to the abstract identity of the community, not to each and every individual Israelite. The same is true of the nations who inhabit the land. Hivites, Perizzites, Girgashites, and so on, does not refer to each and every person of those particular ethnicities individually; it refers to the community in which they participate and from which they draw their identity. So what does it mean to *herem* an identity?

If *herem* means "remove from use," then removing an identity from use depends on what identity is used for. We suggest that the action is

---

[9]That doesn't mean they *wouldn't* kill them, though. In Josh 6:21 it specifies that everything that was *herem* was put to the sword. However, since "devoted and put to the sword" is not redundant, this indicates that the killing is not the essence of what is meant by *herem*.

comparable to what we might try to accomplish by disbanding an organization. Doing so does not typically entail disposing of all the members, but it means that nobody is able to say "I am a member of X" anymore. After World War II, when the Allies destroyed the Third Reich, they did not kill every individual German soldier and citizen; they killed the leaders specifically and deliberately (compare to the litany of kings put to the sword in Josh 10–13) and also burned the flags, toppled the monuments, dismantled the government and chain of command, disarmed the military, occupied the cities, banned the symbols, vilified the ideology, and persecuted any attempt to resurrect it—but most of the people were left alone, and most of those who weren't were casualties of war. This is what it means to *herem* an identity. We will discuss this in more detail in proposition sixteen.

ḤEREM OF CITIES

The *herem* of cities is the most direct parallel to the Hittite text and refers to the practice of prohibiting all human activity at the site. It is also, however, the clearest indication that *herem* does not mean "destroy," because apart from Jericho, Ai, and Hazor, no *herem* city is destroyed. This has led many interpreters to assume that references to "the city" actually refer to "all of the people in the city," despite the distinction normally made between "the city" and "all who are in it" (Josh 6:17; 8:25); note that in Joshua 11:12 the royal cities are *herem* but not destroyed, while in Joshua 11:14 the people are *šmd* (NIV "completely destroyed") but not *herem*. The difference comes from the fact that *herem* does not mean "destroy"; it means "remove from use." The *city* needs to be "removed from use" (*herem*), which in turn means that everyone currently using it needs to go away.

The most common word throughout Genesis–Joshua for what God intends to do to the Canaanites is *grš*, NIV "drive out." Like *herem*, the emphasis of this word concerns everyone around the object, not the object itself. It doesn't matter where they go or what happens to them as long as they are gone. Killing them is one way to make them go away, of course, but it is not the only way and probably not the preferred way (especially if they are fighting back). The terror that goes before the Israelite army (e.g., Ex 23:27; also Deut 2:25; 11:25) is probably intended to encourage them to flee rather than fight, or at least run away earlier than they otherwise might. Nowhere in the conquest account does the army systematically hunt down fleeing refugees; nowhere are urban citizens trapped in protracted sieges. Words like *šmd* ("annihilated") are rhetorical; this kind of language is ubiquitous in ancient conquest accounts and serves to indicate decisive victory (compare to modern sports, where one team is said to annihilate their opponents even though nobody actually dies), but regardless of the exact method, the emptying of the city is literal. The combination of the hyperbolic rhetoric with the successful *ḥerem* of the city does not mean "they didn't really kill all of them, but they left some of them in the city." Rather, it means "they decisively cleared them all out of the city, one way or another." The *ḥerem* is on the city, and so it is the city that must be removed from use, as was done in the event described in the Hittite document.

The most important parallel to the Hittite document, however, is what happens to the city as a result of the *ḥerem*. Mursili gives the site of the city to his god Tešub to be used as a pasture for his bulls. Joshua likewise gives the cities to Yahweh for Yahweh to use, but Yahweh has a different use in mind. Mursili destroyed his city, but Joshua leaves most of them intact, because Yahweh's intended use of them requires them intact: Yahweh is going to lease the land back to Israel. Because the land is *ḥerem*, Israel cannot make use of it for itself, but it belongs to Yahweh, and so Yahweh can do whatever he wants with it. What Yahweh chooses do with his land is to allow Israel to use it, provisionally on Israel's fidelity to the covenant.

EXCURSUS: Hyperbole in Conquest Accounts

If we want to understand the message that the conquest account is supposed to convey, it is useful to understand how the genre of conquest account operates and what it is used for. Ancient narratives are not what we would call historiography; they do not attempt to provide the audience with information to reconstruct what a video camera observing the event would have recorded. This understanding of the genre, in turn, allows for some fluidity in the documentation in regard to such things as the circumstances of the battle (including the date) and even the identity of the participants, but most notably these accounts tend to exaggerate the magnitude of the victory and the scale of the slaughter inflicted on the enemies. This does not mean that the accounts are lies in the sense that we mean when we call them propaganda; both author and audience understand the genre, so there is no intention to deceive. But the accounts are primarily interested in *interpreting* the event and only secondarily interested in documenting the phenomena that accompanied it.

Normally, in order to serve whatever purpose the interpretation is employed for (typically in the ancient Near East, the legitimation of the ruler who commissioned it) the event had to actually occur more or less as described; a king would not defend his right to rule based on a battle that never took place. The same is true of Israelite literature, including the conquest in Joshua.[10] We should assume that a military campaign of some kind occurred, and since the record is inspired we should assume that the writer's interpretation of the event is accurate, at least insofar as it claims to represent the purposes of God. But the actual details of the totality of the destruction or the quantity of victims is likely couched in rhetorical hyperbole, in accordance with the expectations of the genre.

---

[10]See K. Lawson Younger, *Ancient Conquest Accounts*, Journal for the Study of the Old Testament Supplement Series 98 (Sheffield, UK: Sheffield Academic, 1990), 242-66. Consult this work for many examples that document hyperbole in ancient conquest accounts.

Proposition 16

Ḥerem Against Communities Focuses on Destroying Identity, Not Killing People of Certain Ethnicities

The idea that the conquest is an act of genocide is based on the assumption that the *ḥerem* of the Canaanite nations is a command to kill people of a particular ethnicity (derived from Deut 7:2). The idea that the *ḥerem* is divine punishment for offenses against God is based on the assumption that the *ḥerem* of Israelite idolaters in Deuteronomy 13:15 (also Ex 22:20) is a command to carry out a death sentence in consequence for a particular crime. Both of these assumptions are false. *Ḥerem* does not mean "destroy"; it means "remove from use." Individual people who are not slaves (as enemies and idolaters are not) cannot be removed from use because they are not used. What is being removed from use (via subsequent destruction) is not people but rather the identity that those people use to define themselves. This is true in the case of the larger Canaanite national identities and also of smaller subcommunities within Israel.

COMMUNITY IDENTITY IN THE ANCIENT WORLD

Identity essentially refers to the words one chooses to use when describing oneself. When we think of identity today, we normally think in terms of an individual's own personal branding. We identify ourselves in terms of our appearance, our possessions, our education, our subculture, the place where we live, the sports teams we support, the political party we vote for, and so on. All of these things combine into our own personal constellation that sets us apart as unique individuals, distinct and separate from all others. We might refer to this idea of separation and distinction as individual identity. The purpose of individual identity is to conceptually distinguish the individual apart from other individuals around them.

In contrast, the ancient world thought in terms of what we might call community identity. We still use this idea today as well, normally when we talk of demographics. Individuals who identify themselves with a demographic (race, gender, nationality, etc.) feel a sense of solidarity with other members of the same demographic and can experience vicarious achievement (or disappointment, or outrage) when another individual within the same demographic succeeds (or fails, or is slighted). When an athlete wins a medal in the Olympics, it is normal for the citizens of that country to feel a sense of pride in the achievement, although they personally contributed nothing to it, and neither do they benefit from it in any way. When America was attacked in September 2001, many Americans felt somehow victimized, whether or not they had individually been in a building hit by a plane, or even knew anyone who had, or even lived in New York. Community identity involves thinking of oneself in terms of participating in something that transcends individuals. This is the only kind of identity that mattered for people in the ancient world.

A metaphor for community identity might be the cells that make up complex biological organisms such as humans. Each one of our cells is an individual living organism, but at the same time we do not think of our cells as distinct from ourselves. If I catch on fire, I don't think, "My skin cells are on fire, but they are only cells, so what does it have to do with me?" Instead I realize that if my cells are on fire, it means *I* am on fire. Note that this has nothing to do with anything inherent in the cells; if the hospital incinerates a skin sample, I *do* think that they are only cells. The difference is whether they are participating in the larger macroidentity that constitutes *me* at the time they are set on fire.

Community identities do not exist independently of the people who participate in them; the qualities that define a community's identity are the sum of all qualities of all those who are allowed to claim its identity for themselves. This is most clearly and commonly demonstrated by political parties (and religious denominations), whose ideology (that is, identity) changes based on the representatives they appoint and the platforms they adopt. In 1870 the American Democratic Party represented the interests of the upper classes of the (newly repatriated) Southern states. By 1980 the party's platform and constituency had changed, and it no longer did so. There was no true Democratic Party that the 1980 Democrats had deviated from; the changes in the party changed what a Democrat *was*. The Southerners who were disenfranchised by the change had to go somewhere else; where they went was the Republican Party (originally founded by the nemesis of the Southern aristocracy, Abraham Lincoln), which had also changed from its original form. As another example, Harvard University was originally founded to train ministers. Harvard still has a divinity school, but the mission of Harvard (and, consequently, the qualities associated with teaching at or graduating from there) has changed, such that even the ministers who come out of Harvard are branded in other ways. Consequently, communities that wish to retain their original identities are forced to vigorously self-censor in order to ensure that their membership and leadership remain true to the original community. This is the purpose, for example, of statements of faith at Christian colleges that do not wish to become like Harvard. In Israel, this process of self-censoring the community identity of the covenant people was carried out by the *ḥerem* against Israelite idolaters.

ḤEREM OF ISRAELITES

All Israelites—individuals possessing a certain ethnic identity marker—were part of the community of the covenant people by default, just as all faculty of Harvard are part of the community of Harvard, and all the cells of your body are part of the community of you. Possessing the identity marker of the community automatically makes you part of the definition of the community, whether you choose to reflect the preferred identity of the community or not. Self-censorship of the community involves making sure that everyone who possesses the marker of the community represents the desired identity of the community. If the marker is something that is conditional and can be revoked, such as membership in an organization or employment at an institution, the administrators of the community can revoke it. If the marker is something inherent (such as ethnicity), removing the marker is harder, but still possible; for example, it happened to (at least some of) the population of the land over the course of the exilic period, whose ethnic identity eventually disappeared after generations of inter-marriage and whose assistance in rebuilding the temple was refused in Ezra 4:2 (incidentally, this loss of the identity marker is what the prohibitions against exogamy [marrying outside the tribe], e.g., Gen 24:3-4; Deut 7:4; and Ezra 10, were intended to prevent).[1]

Israel's receipt of the covenant blessings (and avoidance of the covenant curses) is contingent on the integrity of Israel's identity. Because Israel as a community is holy and co-identified with God (as described in propositions ten and eleven), it will be blessed as long as its community identity matches the identity that Yahweh wishes to demonstrate

---

[1] Although this group is commonly assumed to be the Samaritans, this connection cannot be made with any certainty (R. J. Coggins, *Samaritans and Jews: The Origins of Samaritanism Reconsidered* [Atlanta: John Knox, 1975], 66-67).

through it. Like a human body, however, the larger community of Israel is made up of smaller units of tribes, clans, families, and cities, which we might compare to separate organs or limbs. All of them are part of the overarching community of Israel, but all of them have their own distinct microidentity as well. Your arm and your liver are both part of you, but they are distinct from each other. Nonetheless, if the cells in your liver die, the cells in your arm suffer the consequences, because when you are sick it affects every part of you, no matter what other relationship those individual parts may or may not have with each other. Likewise, what one city, or family, or even individual does in Israel affects the identity of everyone in Israel and therefore affects whether everyone in Israel receives blessings or curses.

It is not sufficient to simply disavow deviant individuals who possess community identity markers as somehow separate from the true community. Community identities do not possess qualities separately from the qualities of the people who constitute them and possess their markers; there is no true community apart from the membership of the community. If the cells in, say, your eye have cancer, then *you* have cancer. The entire corporate entity of you is sick as long as your eye remains both cancerous and attached to you. What any part of the community is determines what the entire community is. If your eye is sick, *you* are sick, and it doesn't matter how many of your other cells are healthy. In order to make you healthy, it is necessary to kill or remove the cancerous cells, or, if the cancer has spread widely enough, the entire organ. "If your right eye causes you to stumble, gouge it out and throw it away. It is better for you to lose one part of your body than for your whole body to be thrown into hell" (Mt 5:29). This warning is commonly interpreted as hyperbole, but in fact it is a metaphor. If your eye is contaminated, it's going into the fire of hell either way (whatever that represents). The question of whether the rest of the community of you is going in with it depends on whether the eye remains part of the community (that is, attached).

The objective of removing your eye is not to destroy your eye or to punish the cells; it is to make the community identity of you healthy again. This is exactly the same objective as the *ḥerem* enacted against Israelites. *Ḥerem* is not enacted in order to destroy the microcommunity (family, city, etc.) against which it is performed, although the family or city is in fact destroyed; it is also not enacted in order to kill individuals, although individuals are in fact killed. The objective of the *ḥerem* is to restore the entire community of Israel to health.

Many commentators on the topic of community identity talk about ideas of corporate responsibility, corporate guilt, and corporate punishment. These ideas may or may not be accurate, but they do not apply in the case of the *ḥerem* because *ḥerem* is not a punishment. *Ḥerem* by definition carries implications for those who interact with the object but not for the object itself. Achan's family is not destroyed along with him in Joshua 7 because they are corporately accountable for his personal guilt; they are destroyed because the microidentity of Achan's family has changed and no longer reflects favorably on the identity of Yahweh (by virtue of disregard for order). As long as Achan's family remains part of the community of Israel, *all of Israel* no longer reflects favorably on Yahweh, because what a community *is* is nothing more than the sum of its parts. Therefore all of Israel is subject to divine displeasure and abandonment, which is what happens to it in Joshua 7:12. In order to repair the larger community's identity (that is, restore it to health), the microidentity that is contaminating it needs to be excised, in the same way that surgery is required to remove cancerous cells to restore a body to health.

This idea is also represented by a common phrase used elsewhere: "cut off from the people."[2] Offenses that entail someone being cut off

---

[2] The idiomatic phrases "blot out [the name] [from under heaven/from Israel, etc.]" and "cut off [from the people/from Israel]," in addition to the word *ḥerem* when applied to a community identity, all mean more or less the same thing. "Blot out" indicates what happens to the referent itself and can also be represented by hyperbolic words such as *destroy* or *annihilate*. "Cut off" is relational and also indicates what the object is separated *from* (either

are always essentially cultic in nature[3] (as opposed to social offenses such as adultery, theft, and murder) because the offense is not a crime to be punished but rather is a signifier that the individual (or micro-community) has adopted an identity distinct from the people who reflect the covenant order. The offenses are neither accidental nor incidental but rather represent a deliberate disregard for the parameters of the covenant order, and such deliberate disregard would not be possible for someone who has chosen to identify themselves with that order. In order to preserve the integrity of the identity of the entire community, however, those who carry the identity marker of the community but do not embody the identity that the community wishes to possess need to be expelled. This process is described in detail in Deuteronomy 13. If an individual from a family changes their identity to non-Israelite (by going to worship other gods, Deut 13:6), the family has to expel them or else the entire microidentity of the family will be contaminated ("Your hand must be the first in putting them to death," Deut 13:9). If the microcommunity fails to do this (represented by the town in Deut 13:12), then the entire community is expelled. Since the identity marker of Israelite is inherent in the persons, the only way to expel them (remove the identity marker that ties them to the larger community) is to kill them, but as is the case with all instances of *ḥerem*, the destruction is incidental to the broader objective, which is

a microcommunity from the Israelite nation or the entire nation from the covenant), though it is less specific about what exactly happens to the referent. *Ḥerem*, as always, does not indicate anything about the referent at all except that those around it are not to make use of it.

[3]Failing to be circumcised (Gen 17:14); anointing anyone other than a priest (Ex 30:33); making incense for noncultic use (Ex 30:38); approaching or eating consecrated things or sacrifices in an improper manner or while unclean (Lev 7:20-21; 19:8; 22:3); eating fat or blood (Lev 7:25, 27; 17:10, 14); sacrificing outside the sanctuary (Lev 17:4, 9); failing to honor sacred time such as the Day of Atonement (Lev 23:29), the Passover (Ex 12:15-19; Num 9:13), or the sabbath (Ex 31:14); deliberately incurring uncleanliness by sex during menstruation (Lev 20:18), by touching a corpse (Num 19:20), or by flagrant disregard of propriety (Lev 18:29; Num 15:30-31); practicing divination or sacrificing to Molech (Lev 20:3, 5, 6).

to remove (the contaminated microidentity) from use by the larger community of Israel.

The community of the people of the covenant order has an ethnic identity marker, but it is nonetheless not an ethnically *defined* community whose integrity is maintained by some form of eugenics. Individuals with the Israelite ethnic identity marker *must* participate, but individuals without it are also *allowed* to participate. This continues to demonstrate that the emphasis is on identity, not ethnicity, as we will now examine further.

IDENTITY MARKERS OF THE COVENANT ORDER

All ethnic Israelites are part of the community identity of the people of the covenant order inherently, but it is possible for nonethnic Israelites to join the community as well. Since it is not possible to change one's ethnicity, a second identity marker is established in the form of circumcision. Any Israelite (male) who is not circumcised rejects the identity of the community, but because he also possess the ethnic identity marker of the community he must be cut off (Gen 17:14). Any non-Israelite (male) who is not circumcised also rejects the identity of the community of Israel, but because he possesses none of the identity markers of the people of the covenant order, he does nothing to define the community, and therefore there is nothing to cut him off *from*. If a non-Israelite wishes to enter the community, however, he must irrevocably mark himself with the identity marker of the covenant order, at which point he will be considered a full member of the community (e.g., Ex 12:48).

Circumcision is required only of males, but this does not mean that only males participate in the community of the covenant order. Circumcision is a marker of identity, and in the ancient Near East identity was patrilineal. Males possessed their ethnic and family identity within them inherently, but females inherited the identity of their closest male proxy, usually the husband or father. Since ethnic identity

was inherent in a male's person, in order to change that identity it had
to be (literally) carved out of them. Females, on the other hand, derived their group identity from their circumstances and so could
change their identity legally (through marriage [or divorce]) or symbolically (by renunciation), as demonstrated by both Rahab and Ruth,
with no physical mutilation required. Ruth is an important example
because she was (genetically) a Moabite, and no Moabite was permitted to enter the assembly of the Lord (Deut 23:3). Commentators
like to trumpet Ruth as an example of God's grace in saving Ruth from
the punishment of exclusion that is placed on Moab for its corporate
sin, but, as we discussed in proposition eight, the covenant was not
salvation and, while Moab's exclusion was punitive, it was not in consequence of generic moral violations and cannot be conceptually paralleled to damnation. Ruth is not, in fact, an exception to the prohibition at all; the prohibition was based on identity, not genetics, and
since Ruth was a (unmarried) female, she had no inherent community
identity of any kind. Like Rahab, she could join the Israelite assembly
simply by renouncing her former affiliation, which she does in Ruth
1:16-17. A Moabite *male*, who possessed the Moabite identity inherently,
would not be permitted to enter the assembly even by circumcision;
this is the intent of the prohibition in Deuteronomy 23:3. Of course,
because of the value the ancient world placed on maintaining community identity—a significant responsibility for males—they would
also be far less likely to even *want* to convert, as for example the
Gibeonites notably do not; note also that Naaman renounces his gods
in favor of Yahweh in 2 Kings 5:17, but even he does not abandon his
Aramaean identity by circumcision. We should also note that sole
worship of Yahweh was part of the covenant order (as not eating pig
and not trimming beards or sideburns also were), but we should not
think that it was somehow more significant than any other element
would have been by itself. The covenant order was tied to membership

in the community, not to incidental compliance with any of its particular characteristics.

The lack of inherent identity in (unmarried) women meant that it was not necessary to kill them in order to destroy a microidentity; indeed, the fact that they could be spared is some of the best evidence that the purpose of *ḥerem* was not to eliminate genetic material. In Judges 21:11 the command is given to *ḥrm* (the verbal form of the noun *ḥerem*, NIV "kill") the microidentity of the "people of Jabesh-Gilead" (Judg 21:9), ostensibly because they rejected their identity within the community by failing to answer the summons to the assembly that convenes in Judges 20:1-2.[4] The men and married women are killed, but the unmarried women are spared because they do not carry the identity, even though they do carry the genetics.

In fact, the entire pericope of Judges 20–21 illustrates that the emphasis of the *ḥerem* is identity destruction, not eugenics; that is, what it removes from use is a community, not a gene pool. The assembly initially asks for the microidentity of Gibeah to be destroyed (Judg 20:10-13), but the larger community of Benjamin refuses to allow this (Judg 20:13-15), thus identifying themselves with the city of Gibeah and against the covenant order. As a result, the entire Israelite microidentity of the tribe of Benjamin becomes subject to *ḥerem*, which is carried out in Judges 20:48 (although the word is not used; compare Deut 13:15). Some individuals survive (Judg 20:47; 21:7), yet the assembly still mourns the destruction of the microidentity: "Today one tribe is cut off from Israel" (Judg 21:6). If the emphasis were on eliminating a genetic legacy, even a single survivor would result in the community not being cut off; however, because the emphasis is identity, not genetics, and because no Israelite woman can marry them

---

[4]The context explains that the real motives are more utilitarian, but our present concern is for what exactly the *ḥerem* is, which is different from the underlying motives for any particular occasion of its use. Compare to the difference between explaining how a gun works mechanically versus speculating about the various reasons why people might be shot.

(Judg 21:1), their children will lose the Israelite ethnic identity marker and so vanish from the community of Israel. The solution to this problem is to find them Israelite women to marry so that their children will carry the ethnic identity marker of Israelite and thereby preserve the microidentity of Benjamin *within* Israel. If the issue were simply preserving the genetic line, the surviving Benjaminites could have married anybody, and it would have made no difference.

The *ḥerem* of Benjamin was intended to destroy its identity as a microcommunity within Israel, which it effectively did (except for some creative last-minute loopholes). It was not intended to destroy the Benjaminite bloodline, because it did not do so (and therefore no creativity should have been necessary to spare them). Likewise, the *ḥerem* against the Canaanite nations was intended to destroy their community identities, not purge their genetics. Since, however, Canaanite nations did not participate in the identity of the people of the covenant order in the same way that Israelite microcommunities did, the *ḥerem* of the Canaanite identities served a different purpose, which we will now examine.

Ḥerem of Canaanite National Identities

The Israelite community had an ethnic identity marker, but the community of the people of the covenant order was nonetheless not an ethnocracy. Foreigners were permitted to live among the people of Israel, and Israel was not commanded to annihilate them. In fact, they are told exactly the opposite: "When a foreigner resides among you in your land, do not mistreat them. The foreigner residing among you must be treated as your native-born. Love them as yourself, for you were foreigners in Egypt" (Lev 19:33-34). Further, "foreigner . . . in your land" does not merely refer to slaves (as in Ex 12:44) or those inducted into the community (circumcised); otherwise the prohibition in Exodus 12:48 ("A foreigner residing among you who wants to celebrate the Lord's Passover must have all the males in his household circumcised") would be redundant. Thus we can see that simply being a non-Israelite living in the land did not make one subject to *ḥerem*. This is because, once again, the purpose of the *ḥerem* is to remove a community identity from use, not to kill individual people.

As discussed in proposition eight, the text does not depict anything wrong with non-Israelite people using non-Israelite identities in principle. The people living outside the land are allowed to keep using their identities, along with any cultic prostitution, child sacrifice, or idol worship that participation in those communities might entail. Even those within the land are allowed (by God) to keep their identities in order to test Israel in Judges 2:22. There is nothing inherently wrong with using a non-Israelite identity, just as there is nothing inherently wrong with using a city; the reason for a city being removed from use is not because cities ought not to be used in principle. Unlike a city, however, the Canaanite identities are not given to Yahweh for Yahweh to use; the phrase "*ḥerem* to/for Yahweh" is never used of abstractions, only individuals or objects,[5] and it is hard to imagine what Yahweh would do with a human community identity in any case. The idea of "changed in status as preparation for divine use" (see proposition eleven) does not therefore seem to apply to the Canaanite community identities. Further, the purpose cannot be to preserve the integrity of a larger community, because the Canaanites have no participation whatsoever in the Israelite community. Therefore we should assume that the *ḥerem* entails its most basic definition: the identity is removed from use *so that it cannot be used*.

In one sense, the identity needs to be removed so that the Canaanite nations cannot make use of it. This is not because it is *inherently* wrong (in a moral sense) for them to do so, but it would nonetheless have negative consequences for the Israelite occupiers. When Assyria or

---

[5]Leviticus 27:28 ("nothing that a person owns"); Josh 6:17, 21 (the spoils of Jericho); Mic 4:13 (unspecified wealth).

Babylon conquered a territory, they would destroy the national identity of the conquered nation by killing or deporting the king and planting a puppet regent on the throne, deporting the cultic and community leaders, destroying cities and temples, carrying away or destroying the images of the gods, and levying a heavy tribute to depress the economy. The purpose of this was to strip away anything the conquered people could rally around in order to stage a rebellion. In 2 Kings 19:11 Sennacherib brags to Hezekiah that he has *ḥrm* all of the previous enemies of Assyria (NIV "destroying them completely"). The Canaanite armies are annihilated (or at least soundly defeated) during the conquest, but if the national identity that deployed the army is not destroyed, they will eventually raise another one (as Midian does in Judg 6:1-6, despite being defeated in Num 31:7-11).[6] Removing the identity of a conquered people is therefore a pragmatic activity that was a standard procedure of ancient warfare (see proposition seventeen).

More importantly, however, the identity needs to be removed so that *Israel* cannot make use of it. This is the essence of the threat that "they will become snares and traps for you" (Josh 23:13; Judg 2:3). With non-Israelite identities coexisting alongside the Israelite identity, syncretism, appropriating foreign religious customs and beliefs, becomes a distinct possibility, bordering on inevitable. With a non-Israelite community identity nearby, it is possible that Israelites will marry outside their community and thus lose the Israelite identity marker and vanish. More seriously, microcommunities within Israel might compromise their Israelite identity (either through exogamy or syncretism) and therefore either subject themselves to *ḥerem* or, if left alone, subject the entire community to the covenant curses.

---

[6]Note that Midian in Num 31 is not *ḥerem*; *ḥerem* and destruction are two separate processes. Midian is destroyed as talionic justice, that is, justice in accordance with the offense committed, not in order to remove their national identity from use. See excursus in proposition five. Note also that the unmarried women in Num 31:18 are spared from the vendetta because they are not inherently part of the Midianite community identity against which the vengeance is carried out.

Communities of foreigners are allowed to remain among Israel (see, for example, the [Philistine] Kerethites and Pelethites that form David's personal guards), but even if they are not inducted into the Israelite community they are still required to observe the covenant order (Ex 20:10; Lev 17:8; 18:26; and especially Lev 24:22). They are not permitted to eat the Passover and, with the exception of Caleb and his family, are not given an inheritance in the land (that is, they cannot own property), but they are allowed to exist as microcommunities just as Israelite microcommunities do. Still, even if they do not themselves identify with the people of the covenant order they are not allowed to do anything that those who are under the identity of the covenant order would not be allowed to do. What is forbidden in the land of Israel is *tôʿēbâ* (to Yahweh), that which is outside the covenant order. If foreigners observe the covenant order, they will not be *tôʿēbâ* and will not be a snare for the Israelites, and therefore there is no reason to *ḥerem* them.

The issue at stake does not concern morality versus immorality, purity versus impurity, or innocence versus crime. The dichotomy is between *within* the covenant order and *outside* the covenant order. We might possibly imagine Israel as being a patient undergoing surgery. The procedure carries benefits for them (covenant blessing and relationship with deity in this case), but meanwhile it also carries certain vulnerabilities. The conquest is equivalent to sterilizing the operating room. We don't have anything in particular against ordinary hospital staff, visitors, pets, food, or even common bacteria, but when the time comes for surgery we clear them all out of the operating room, not because we are angered or offended by anything they are or do but because it is necessary for the patient that the environment be sterile. Contaminants are *tôʿēbâ* to the operating room; visitors may be allowed inside, but if they are, they must be as sterile as the rest of the environment.

EXCURSUS: What Is Happening in Deuteronomy 7

As discussed in proposition thirteen, the word commonly used to designate something outside the covenant order is *tôʿēbâ* (specifically "*tôʿēbâ* to Yahweh," e.g., Deut 7:25). The Canaanite nations are *tôʿēbâ* by default, since the covenant was not made with them, and everything in the land that is *tôʿēbâ* is to be *ḥerem* ("removed from use"). This is expressed most clearly in Deuteronomy 7. The (infamous) command to "*ḥerem* them . . . show them no mercy" in Deuteronomy 7:2 refers, as we have demonstrated, to destroying identities, not people, as is indicated by the destruction of identity markers (that is, cult objects) in Deuteronomy 7:5. The list of things Israelites are to do to them consists of breaking down their altars, smashing their sacred stones, cutting down their Asherah poles, and burning their idols in the fire; it does not include killing every last one of them. Indeed, if every last one of them were killed, the prohibition in Deuteronomy 7:3 against intermarriage would be unnecessary. The references to nations (Deut 7:2, 17, 22), peoples (Deut 7:16, 19), and even survivors (Deut 7:20) all refer to community identities, not individuals (compare to Judg 1:25-26, where the survivor preserves the identity of his community by building a city). This is especially the case with the kings (Deut 7:24), who are the embodiment of the identity of the community they lead (which is why they are specifically killed throughout Joshua's campaigns) and whose names (identity) are "wipe[d] out . . . from under heaven" (Deut 7:24). We should also note that God's threat in Deuteronomy 7:4 is not against the Canaanites (that is, it does not say "My anger burns against them and I wish for them to be destroyed") but rather against Israel: "The LORD's anger will burn against you and will quickly destroy you."

Deuteronomy 7:25 repeats the command to destroy the cult objects, this time specifying that they are *tôʿēbâ*, that is, contrary to covenant order. Deuteronomy 7:26 warns not to "bring a *tôʿēbâ* thing into your house," which generally refers to a household (that is, a family microidentity) rather than a building,[7] in which case "bring into" does not mean "carry into a space" but rather more idiomatically "adopt as your own." The penalty for doing so is "you, like it, will be *ḥerem*" (Deut 7:26). Note that the *you* refers to the entire community, not only the building where the idol was brought or even the household that adopted it.[8] The opposite of "bring in" that they are told to do instead is *tʿb* (NIV "detest"). This is the verbal form of the same root from which *tôʿēbâ* is derived, and it means "isolate apart from the identity of the community." In Deuteronomy 23:7 the same word (translated "despise" in the NIV) is contrasted with integrating into the community. Thus Deuteronomy 7 is about preserving the integrity of the Israelite community by making sure that *tôʿēbâ* things stay outside it, where "stay outside" means "are not made use of," which is designated by *ḥerem*. If Israel associates with *tôʿēbâ*, Israel itself will became *tôʿēbâ*, at which point Israel will be destroyed by the covenant curses. But, as discussed in proposition eleven, this is not a penalty for *tôʿēbâ* in principle; only in Israel is *tôʿēbâ* a punishable offense, because only Israel is accountable to the covenant. The crime of Israel is not uncouth behavior but covenant infidelity. The people of Canaan cannot be punished for covenant infidelity because they had no covenant to break.

---

[7]Compare Deut 22:8, where the concern of "blood on your house" does not refer to splatters on the building but rather guilt for the family (i.e., NIV "guilt of bloodshed on your house"). See also 1 Sam 21:15, where Achish does not want to bring David into his house, meaning into his service (cf. 1 Sam 28:2). This would be the equivalent of the modern distinction between bringing something into your house and bringing it into your home.

[8]Although *you* in Hebrew is singular, it has been used of the entire community throughout the entire chapter (Deut 7:1; see especially Deut 7:17, 24, where the NIV translates them as plurals).

The Wars of Israelite Conquest Were Fought in the Same Manner as All Ancient Wars

Because we are not citizens of the ancient Near East, many of the actions that Joshua and his army are either commanded to perform or depicted as carrying out seem bizarre and nonsensical to us. Consequently, many interpreters assume that they would have seemed equally bizarre and nonsensical to Joshua's enemies. This results in the idea that the Bible is describing a new and innovative process for waging war. Sometimes this innovation is seen as a brutal and barbaric development from the more civilized warfare of Israel's neighbors; other times it is seen as a step toward making war more humane, as if God's commands through Moses were a prototype of the Geneva Convention. However, both of these interpretations are misguided, because Joshua's wars are conducted more or less in the same way that all war was conducted in the ancient Near East.

Old Testament interpreters (such as Gerhard von Rad) dubbed the ideology found in the conquest "holy war" (or sometimes "YHWH war") and considered it a combination of ritual and war that embodied the purest essence of Israelite orthodoxy.[1] Depending on personal biases, interpreters either contrast this (hypothetical) barbarism with a more humane and cosmopolitan (by modern standards) religious ideal supposedly dredged out of the New Testament, or they argue that the same (hypothetical) barbarism forms the essence of the orthodoxy of the New Testament as well and therefore of Christianity. Both of these approaches are misguided because the premises are false. Israelite warfare, at least in regard to the integration of war and religion, operates almost exactly like warfare ideology everywhere else in the ancient Near East. Specifically, we will examine the ritual/cultic elements most commonly invoked to symbolize a Yahweh war: oracles to determine divine favor; the consecration of soldiers and weapons; the presence of the battle palladium; the divine vanguard, which is the belief that the deity accompanies the army; and the *ḥerem*. All of these are comparable to the standard practices of ancient Near Eastern warfare. We will also discuss some significant differences between Israelite and other ideologies of war.

ORACLES TO DETERMINE DIVINE FAVOR

In the ancient Near East, nobody wanted to go into battle without the support of the gods. Therefore, before departing for battle, kings and generals would read omens and consult various forms of divination to ensure that the gods were indeed favorable toward the endeavor.[2] "The first action before battle as seen in the Mesopotamian context is to seek the divine will. . . . It is expected to avoid defeat or remove any conditions offensive to the gods."[3] The Bible records Nebuchadnezzar

---

[1]See, for example, Ben C. Ollenburger, "Gerhard von Rad's Theory of Holy War," introduction to Gerhard von Rad, *Holy War in Ancient Israel*, trans. Marva J. Dawn (Grand Rapids: Eerdmans, 1991), 1.

[2]See Peter C. Craigie, *The Problem of War in the Old Testament* (Grand Rapids: Eerdmans, 1978), 118; see also Sa-Moon Kang, *Divine War in the Old Testament and in the Ancient Near East* (Berlin: de Gruyter, 1989), 56-63.

[3]Kang, *Divine War*, 56.

seeking omens on his way to attack Jerusalem (Ezek 21:21), and Saul seeks an omen from a medium before his final battle (1 Sam 28:8, after conventional methods fail, 1 Sam 28:6). If the omen was unfavorable, the army would try to appease the deity before going to battle (as Joshua does in Josh 7, as the assembly does in Judg 20:26, and as Saul tries [unsuccessfully] to do in 1 Sam 13:12,[4] and again in 1 Sam 14:37-44). In Israel prebattle omens were normally sought by inquiring of Yahweh (e.g., Judg 20:27) by means of the Urim and Thummim (a form of divination, Ex 21:30; see Num 27:21; 1 Sam 28:6), although in 2 Kings 3:11 a prophet is consulted instead.

CONSECRATION OF SOLDIERS AND/OR WEAPONS

The Israelite army is told to consecrate themselves before crossing the Jordan to attack Jericho (Josh 3:5). Hittite soldiers also ritually purified themselves before battle to ensure that they were prepared to fight alongside their gods: "Not only the king himself, but also the army had to be ritually clean."[5] One Sumerian text describes the army as being made holy using a word that is normally used to describe the consecration of temples.[6] Joel 3:9 and Micah 3:5 also refer to the

---

[4]The word for what Saul claims he has done (*ḥlh*, piel; NIV "sought favor") can refer to appeasing wrath and restoring (divine) favor, as it does in, e.g., Ex 32:11 and especially in 1 Kings 13:6, where it reverses a sign of disfavor. The failure of Samuel to appear (1 Sam 13:8; compare Elisha's disdain for Joram in 2 Kings 3:14) and the fear and desertion of the army (1 Sam 13:7, 11) are arguably indications of divine disfavor (perhaps incurred by failing to keep whatever command Samuel refers to 1 Sam 13:13); Saul therefore attempts to appease Yahweh (by "the burnt offerings and the fellowship offerings" in 1 Sam 13:9; compare Judg 20:26, where the same process is successful), as any ancient Near Eastern military commander would do. It is the appeasement mentality, and not the technical violation of a king exercising priestly prerogatives, that earns Samuel's rebuke (note that David commits a similar violation by eating consecrated bread in 1 Sam 21:6, and this does not bring a curse on his dynasty).

[5]Kang, *Divine War*, 62.

[6]See E. Jan Wilson, *"Holiness" and "Purity" in Mesopotamia*, Alter Orient und Altes Testament 237 (Neukirchen-Vluyn: Verlag Butzon & Bercker Kevelaer, 1994), 31. See also J. van Dijk, "Un ritual de purification des armes et de l'armée, Essai de traduction de YBC 4184," in *Symbolae biblicae et mesopotamicae Francisco Mario Theodoro Böhl dedicatae*, ed. M. Beek, A. Kampman, C. Nijland, and J. Ryckmans (Leiden: Brill, 1972), 107-17.

consecration of an Israelite army, while Jeremiah 6:4; 22:7; 51:27-28; and perhaps also Zephaniah 1:7 refer to the consecration of non-Israelite armies.

In 1 Samuel 21:5 David claims that his soldiers are holy. This is a rare use of the adjective *qādôš* to refer to persons other than priests and can be compared to Korah's claim in Numbers 16:3. Like Korah, David is trying to illegitimately access a privilege (eating consecrated bread, in this case) that is normally only allowed to the Aaronic priests (Lev 24:8). Also like Korah, David is misunderstanding the technical differences between the ways in which different kinds of things are holy (see proposition ten), but the fact that his soldiers have "kept themselves from women" (1 Sam 21:4) and that he thinks of them as holy in *any* sense indicates that consecration of the army is standard procedure under any circumstances, not only in the extreme case of the hypothetical acts of holy war (note that the mission David claims to be on does not involve the accompaniment of the ark, for example).

THE BATTLE PALLADIUM AND THE DIVINE VANGUARD

The role of divine warriors is well attested in the ancient world.[7] One of the aspects of ancient Near Eastern religion was that the god would maintain order for his people, a task that included dealing with disruptive parties either coming against them or causing problems for them. In this way of thinking, war conducted by the gods was not the opposite of peace but the response to encroaching disorder. The gods gave permission to fight and not only joined in the battle but were the ones who actually achieved victory. Israelites understood Yahweh as

---

[7]Steven W. Holloway, *Aššur Is King! Aššur Is King!* (Leiden: Brill, 2002); Kang, *Divine War*; Martin Klingbeil, *Yahweh Fighting from Heaven: God as Warrior and God of Heaven in the Hebrew Psalter and Ancient Near Eastern Iconography*, Orbis Biblicus et Orientalis 169 (Göttingen: Vandenhoeck & Ruprecht, 1999); Tremper Longman and Daniel Reid, *God Is a Warrior* (Grand Rapids: Zondervan, 1995); Patrick D. Miller, *The Divine Warrior in Early Israel* (Atlanta: SBL, 2006); Charlie Trimm, *YHWH Fights for Them! The Divine Warrior in the Exodus Narrative* (Piscataway, NJ: Gorgias, 2014).

a divine warrior just as Canaanites, Assyrians, or Egyptians would have thought about some of their gods.

All ancient Near Eastern armies marched into battle beside their gods. This did not mean that war represented the essence of their religion, or that proper exercise of religion demanded war; it simply meant that the favor of the gods and the harmony with national and cosmic order that divine favor represented was important enough to the ancients (including Israel) that they wanted it to be present in anything they did.[8] The ancient world assigned a value to divinely approved order similar to the value we assign to human rights. It was important to them that this order be preserved and acknowledged, even (or perhaps especially) in war.

The presence of the divine warriors alongside the army—which modern scholars call the divine vanguard—was commonly represented by symbols or images of the gods carried into battle alongside the army. Egyptian armies carried divine effigies as battle standards as well as an image of the king's patron god.[9] In Assyria, "the presence of the gods in battle was symbolized visually by the standards and flags carried by the armies, and also by the presence of priests and diviners who represented the gods physically."[10] In Israel the presence of the divine warrior could be symbolized by the ark of the covenant (Josh 6:6; 1 Sam 4:3) but also by the presence of a priest (perhaps 1 Sam 13:8; 23:6) or a prophet (perhaps 2 Kings 3:12; Judg 4:8[11]). In Exodus 17:15,

---

[8]"While war was religious by association, it was no more a cultic and holy act than was sheep shearing." Craigie, *Problem of War in the Old Testament*, 49, cited in Georg Fohrer, *Geschichte der israelitischen Religion* (Berlin: de Gruyter, 1969) 109.

[9]Kang, *Divine War*, 101.

[10]Craigie, *Problem of War in the Old Testament*, 119.

[11]Many interpreters (along with the NIV) assume that Barak wishing for Deborah's company is a sign of weakness and cowardice, for which he is punished by being denied the glory of killing Sisera in Judg 4:9 (gloss: "If you had gone by yourself you would have had victory *and* glory, but now the glory will go to someone else"). However, the construction translated "but . . . not" is not an admonition; it is used to soften the implications of a preceding statement. In Deut 15:3 God commands the canceling of debts (a financially catastrophic event for the lender) but then softens it in Deut 15:4 by promising that the Lord's blessing

the presence of Yahweh is symbolized by Moses raising the staff of God (Ex 17:8-11), and immediately following the battle Yahweh is commended as a battle standard (Ex 17:15; NIV "The LORD is my Banner").[12] The king himself can also serve as a divine representative, either as a living image[13] or a living standard (compare Is 11:10-14).[14]

Divine warriors were thought to wield the elements of the cosmos as weapons against enemy armies, which is also reflected in biblical passages such as Psalm 18:8-14; Exodus 14:19-26; Judges 5:20-22; Joshua 10:11; and 1 Samuel 7:10. Images such as thunder, earthquake, and panic; combat by stars, water, fire, and cloud; hail and lightning wielded as weapons; and divine warriors soaring on clouds or cherubim are all well attested throughout the ancient Near East.[15]

THE ḤEREM

The entire hypothesis of holy war revolves around the *ḥerem*[16] and the (circular) argument that *ḥerem* (therefore) represents a particularly

---

will make everyone wealthy enough that it won't matter. More explicitly, in Amos 9:8 God threatens to "destroy [Israel] from the face of the earth" but then immediately softens it by adding "yet . . . not totally destroy." The construction translated "but," "yet," or "however" (*'epes* + *kî*), when *not* combined with a negation, *hardens* the previous statement, as in 2 Sam 12:13-14: "You are not going to die, but . . . the son born to you will die." In Judg 4, the phrase "I [Deborah] will go with you" means "Yahweh will go with you [as you go on your way]" (which the NIV mistranslates as "because of the course [of action] you are taking"). The full implications of divine assistance (normally victory and glory) are softened by the qualification "but the honor will not be yours." This is simply a condition of divine favor. If Barak had gone alone, he would have had neither glory nor victory.

[12]Hebrew *nēs*, translated "battle standard" in Jer 4:21; see also Is 5:26; Jer 51:12, 27.

[13]Peter Machinist, "Kingship and Divinity in Imperial Assyria," in *Text, Artifact, and Image*, ed. Gary M. Beckman and Theodore J. Lewis, BJS 346 (Providence, RI: Brown University Press, 2006), 171-72.

[14]This is part of what the elders of Israel want when they ask for a king "such as all the other nations have" in 1 Sam 8; they want something that can compel Yahweh to battle in the same way that the ark failed to do in 1 Sam 4, which is why Yahweh becomes angry with the request (Jonathan H. Walton, "A King Like the Nations," *Biblica* 96 [2015]: 196-99).

[15]Moshe Weinfeld, "Divine Intervention and War in the Ancient Near East," in *History, Historiography, and Interpretation: Studies in Biblical and Cuneiform literatures*, ed. H. Tadmor and M. Weinfeld (Leiden: Brill, 1984), 121-47. See also Kang, *Divine War*, 24-42.

[16]Von Rad, *Holy War*, 49: "The high point and the conclusion of the holy war is formed by the *ḥerem*."

primitive and barbaric form of sacrifice,[17] which flows naturally and necessarily from monotheism[18] and (therefore) requires the (otherwise unnecessary) sacralization of war in order to rationalize its execution.[19] However, we can observe that *herem* can occur independently of war,[20] or that many instances of divine war do not end in *herem*, whether in Israel[21] or elsewhere in the ancient Near East.[22] The discrepancy exists because the entire "holy war" hypothesis is flawed. The gods fought beside the armies because in the ancient world the gods were involved in everything; the idea of war as either holy or secular would have been meaningless in an ancient context. Likewise, *herem* is not a sacrifice, at least not in the sense of "giving the deity something the deity has rightfully earned by combat."[23] Finally, *herem* has nothing to do with monotheism as a religious ideology, since

---

[17]"The bloodthirsty character of the deity . . . is a projection of the bloodlust of the human beings who desire revenge on their enemies." Philip D. Stern, *The Biblical* Herem, BJS 211 (Providence, RI: Brown University Press, 1991), 40.

[18]Ibid., 222: "*Ḥrm* is an important concept for the understanding of monotheism or its historical development."

[19]"A practice like *ḥrm* reflects a certain mythicization . . . which helped justify the massacre of large populations" (ibid., 224).

[20]Stern rationalizes this on the assumption that *ḥrm* represents nothing more than rationalized bloodlust, which of course is not limited to military objects: "The fury a society may vent on its external foes is likely to be a pale thing compared to the rage it hurls at its own members" (ibid).

[21]"Other episodes are difficult to harmonize perfectly with what appears to be a principle that the war booty was turned over to the Lord" (Longman and Reid, *God Is a Warrior*, 46).

[22]"In all the ancient Near Eastern cultures we have encountered, the idea of divine intervention in war on behalf of the 'good' side is present. The idea of consecration to the god through destruction . . . leaves no trace in these reliefs" (Stern, *Biblical* Herem, 81). Likewise, "the mythological justification of annihilating one's enemies works by placing them on a non-human plane . . . [and] mythological justifications for killing were traditional. The question may then be asked . . . why was [*ḥrm*] not 'traditional' in Egypt as it was in Israel? There is no absolute answer to this question" (ibid., 83).

[23]Contra, for example, "The alliance had its price. The spoils which in the normal course of events would accrue to the victors become inviolably attached to the deity" (ibid., 221). Likewise "God won the victory, so the spoils of war belonged to him" (Longman and Reid, *God Is a Warrior*, 45).

comparable practices were carried out by polytheistic ancient Near Eastern cultures as well.

In addition to the Hittite inscription described in proposition fifteen, the most significant ancient Near Eastern documentation of *herem* is the Mesha Inscription, a commemorative inscription written in Hebrew that describes the military and building achievements of Mesha, king of Moab in the mid-ninth century. The text records that the Moabite national patron, Chemosh, was angry with Moab and allowed Omri, king of Israel, to take Moabite territory. The inscription describes how Mesha, with the aid of Chemosh, was able to repatriate some of the conquered territory.[24] In one account, all of the people of the city are killed (*hrg*) and the city "was to/for [*hyh* + *l*] Chemosh and Moab"; in another account Mesha kills (*hrg*) a much more detailed list of people, and the city is "*hrm* for Ashtar-Chemosh." Some interpreters think that these actions are essentially the same and that they represent a kind of sacrifice offered to the victorious deity, either in repayment for assistance in battle or as propitiation for the original anger. The first instance, however, is probably not *herem*; Mesha has taken possession of the city, and it now belongs to Moab, and therefore also to Chemosh, the patron of Moab.[25]

---

[24]"All four [narrative sections] treat the recovery of the land from Israel. . . . What Mesha conquered was Moab's originally." Simon B. Parker, *Stories in Scripture and Inscriptions* (New York: Oxford University Press, 1997), 55-58; see also J. Maxwell Miller, "Moab," in *Anchor Bible Dictionary*, ed. David Noel Freedman (New York: Doubleday, 1992), 4:886; Stern, *Biblical Herem*, 36. Contra Nadav Na'aman, *Ancient Israel's History and Historiography: The First Temple Period* (Winona Lake, IN: Eisenbrauns, 2006), 3:189.

[25]K. A. D. Smelik translates *hyh l* as "sacrifice to" ("The Inscription of King Mesha," in *COS* 2.23, p. 137), but Shmuel Ahituv renders it "property of" (*Echoes from the Past: Hebrew and Cognate Inscriptions from the Biblical Period* [Jerusalem: Carta, 2008], 394, line 12), and the latter is more defensible. First, it would be odd to say that the city was sacrificed to both Chemosh and Moab (see Ahituv, *Echoes from the Past*, 405); nations do not normally receive sacrifices. Second, the collocation [city] + [*hyh* + *l*] + [political entity] is attested in the Bible and refers to occupation and possession. In Josh 14:14 Caleb "drives out" the Anakites from Hebron, which then (*hyh l*) "belonged to" Caleb and his descendants. In Josh 17:6 the land of Gilead *hyh l* the descendants of Manassah, and in 1 Sam 27:6 the city of Ziklag *hyh l* the kings of Judah. Most tellingly, however, in Ezek 44:29, that which is *herem hyh l* the priests (as opposed to Yahweh, which would be expected if the collocation

Killing (*hrg*) can occur in contexts that do not involve *ḥerem*. In Genesis 34:25 Simeon and Levi *hrg* every male in Shechem in retribution for the rape of Dinah, but they keep all of the plunder (Gen 34:29) and do not prohibit the city from use; Jacob bequeaths it to Joseph in Genesis 48:22. Similarly, in Numbers 31:17 the Israelites *hrg* the males and married women of Midian but likewise keep the plunder (Num 31:18-23). Even when the *ḥerem* is also enacted, the *hrg* is a separate process; in Joshua 8:24, the Israelites *hrg* the men of Ai (referring to the army, which came out and fell into their ambush) but then return to the city and enact the *ḥerem* (Josh 8:26), which entails killing captives to ensure that they cannot be used as slaves (Josh 8:24; see proposition fifteen). Like Joshua at Ai, Mesha kills captives ("men and boys and women and girls and maidens"),[26] presumably for the same reasons (to prevent their use as slaves), which means that their deaths should not be considered human sacrifice.[27]

There is no direct parallel between the circumstances of Mesha's *ḥerem* and any instance of *ḥerem* in the Hebrew Bible. Nonetheless, the word and practice are the same. We should therefore assume that *ḥerem* is a purposeful action that can be selectively applied and not a mechanistic component of any larger sociopolitical or religious process.[28] To understand what that purpose is, we once again turn to the

---

meant "sacrifice"). *Hyh l* is clearly therefore not interchangeable with *ḥerem* and is also clearly not a "sacrifice."

[26] Ahituv, *Echoes from the Past*, 394, lines 16-17.

[27] Contra ibid., 409.

[28] Bruce Routledge, alternatively, tries to argue that the purpose of *ḥerem* in general, and specifically the *ḥerem* of Nebo by Mesha, is "to prevent exchange [and thereby prevent] the formation of a mutually recognized relationship" (Bruce Routledge, "The Politics of Mesha: Segmented Identities and State Formation in Iron Age Moab," *Journal of the Economic and Social History of the Orient* 43, no. 3 [2000]: 221-56, quote on 237-38), specifically as an alternative to making a treaty (with reference to Deut 20:16-18). This definition does not work for a number of reasons. First, there is the distinction (discussed in proposition fifteen) between the *ḥerem* of a city and the *ḥerem* of a community. Routledge cites 1 Kings 20:42, where Ahab is denounced for failing to *hrm* Ben-Hadad. We should note, however, that while the king does embody the identity of the community he leads (compare Agag in 1 Sam 15; see proposition eighteen), at no point is Ahab commanded to *ḥerem* the

cognitive environment of the ancient Near East. Unlike the Hittite *ḥerem* parallel, the Mesha Inscription's rhetoric does not depict Mesha's enemies as rebellious vassals, and likewise the inscription's instigation of military action by a god is rare in the ancient Near East (though of course it also occurs in the case of the conquest); however, when divine command to take action does occur, the parallels are enlightening. The anger and subsequent restored favor of a god, the latter demonstrated by a command to take military action, has some thematic parallels to the Basalt Stele of Nabonidus, a Babylonian inscription commemorating the restoration of the temple of Ehulhul in Harran. This inscription describes the anger of the Babylonian patron deity Marduk as manifested by the destruction of the temple by the Medes in the time of Nabopolassar, Nabodinus's predecessor,[29] and records Marduk's command to Nabonidus to defeat the Medes and rebuild the temple.[30] There is no *ḥerem* involved in Nabonidus's inscription, but nonetheless there are similarities as shown in table 3.

Aramaeans as Saul is commanded to *ḥerem* Amalek (1 Sam 15:3). Such a command cannot be inferred from Deut. 20:17 because Damascus and its cities lie outside the boundaries of the land and therefore are normally a legitimate treaty partner (Deut 20:10). So when does God inform Ahab that he has "determined [that Ben-Hadad] should be *ḥerem*"? Presumably it comes in 1 Kings 20:28, where Yahweh promises to "deliver this vast army into your hands" (perhaps implied, perhaps not recorded). The ban apparently applies only to Ben-Hadad himself and by extension his dynasty (compare Deut 7:24, where the names of kings are "blotted out from under heaven"). In 1 Kings 20:42 the talionic curse on Ahab ("your people for his people") does not apparently refer to the Israelites as "Ahab's people," but rather his house, the destruction of which is promised explicitly in the next chapter (1 Kings 21:21, 29). There is no indication that the ban was placed on Aphek or on any of the cities returned to Ahab in 1 Kings 20:34, or on the nation of Aram. Like Ahab in 1 Kings 20:42, Mesha's *ḥerem* is not carried out against a community; Ahab does not *ḥerem* Aram, and Mesha does not *ḥerem* Israel. Unlike Ahab, however, Mesha's *ḥerem* is on a city, not on a community via a royal house, and in this he more resembles Joshua at Ai. Joshua, however, is not repatriating stolen territory (see proposition fifteen) and enacts *ḥerem* on every defeated city, whereas Mesha bans only Nebo. Ahab does repatriate territory but bans no city at all.

[29] Sellim Ferruh Adalı, *The Scourge of God: The Umman-Manda and Its Significance in the First Millennium BC*, SAAS 20 (Helsinki: The Neo-Assyrian Text Corpus Project, 2011), 144-45.

[30] Ibid., 144.

Table 3. The Mesha Inscription compared with the Stele of Nabonidus

Element	Mesha	Nabonidus
Anger of patron in previous generation	Chemosh, reason unspecified (lines 2-5)	Marduk, against Assyria for Sennacherib's destruction of Babylon (column i)
Anger leads to loss of something valuable to the patron	territory taken by Omri (lines 7-8)	temples destroyed by Cyaxares (column ii)
Condition continues under oppressor's successor	unspecified (line 6)	temples continue to lie in ruins as Harran is occupied by Astyges (column x, lines 12-14)
Patron commands current ruler to relieve condition and restore valued item	"Take Nebo from Israel" (line 14)	ordered to defeat Astyges and rebuild the temples (column x, lines 4-31)
Ruler's attack is successful	city defeated and *ḥerem* (lines 15-18)	Astyges defeated, temple restored (unrecorded but implied by existence of commemorative inscription)

The comparison is relevant because Nabonidus portrays his enemies as Umman-manda, invoking the same typological rhetoric used by Israel in the context of Joshua's *ḥerem* of Canaanite cities (see proposition twelve). On closer examination, however, we see no thematic overlap between Mesha's rhetoric and that of the Pentateuch; Mesha does not in any way portray Israel as invincible barbarians. Therefore, the rhetoric of the Mesha Inscription does not appear to match the rhetoric of Israelite *ḥerem* texts, either (since these also use the imagery of the invincible barbarians). What is clear from the comparison to Nabonidus, however, is that *ḥerem* is not inherently part of the process that results from claiming divine command as a motive for war, since Nabonidus receives such a command but does not *ḥerem* the Medes in any way. (It is also clear that *ḥerem* is also not inherently a product of labeling enemies as invincible barbarians, for the same reason.)

Despite the lack of rebellion in the Mesha Inscription, however, the context more closely matches the Hittite inscription than it does anything in the Hebrew Bible. Like Mursili from the Hittite text, Mesha only puts one city to *herem*, while Joshua bans all the cities in the land. In ordinary ancient Near Eastern understanding, the *herem* of a territory is counterproductive to the acquisition of that territory, because *herem* territory is proscribed from human use. Putting an entire province to *herem* does not create a province for one's realm; it creates an empty demilitarized zone. Joshua can *herem* his entire country because of the understanding, so far unattested outside Israel, that the deity will allow his chosen humans to occupy the banned space. Outside Israel, therefore, *herem* is only enacted against token cities as a pious gesture of gratitude to the patron deity (see discussion in proposition fifteen and the excursus in proposition eighteen) and perhaps also as a means to intimidate surrounding enemies (compare Sennacherib's threat to Hezekiah in 2 Kings 19:11). It is also worth noting, however, that the lack of *herem* does not necessarily correspond to what we would consider a more humane treatment of enemies; all of Mesha's enemies are killed (*hrg*), even if the city they formerly occupied is not *herem*.

Nonetheless, while the *form* of Israel's war is the same as the form of all ancient Near Eastern warfare, the motivation for Joshua's war and the purpose that the war serves are not the same as most ancient Near Eastern wars. We can demonstrate this by examining some of the differences between the conquest account and typical ancient Near Eastern warfare ideology.

THE PURPOSE OF ISRAEL'S WARS CANNOT BE EXTRAPOLATED FROM A BROADER ANCIENT NEAR EASTERN IDEOLOGY OF WAR

Israel's divine warfare was essentially identical to the ideology and practice of war as war was understood throughout the ancient Near East. Nonetheless, Israelite warfare ideology, at least in the case of the conquest, did depart from convention in several areas. This indicates that, while the method of warfare was essentially the same, the objective of this particular war was different. The notable common elements of ancient Near Eastern warfare ideology that were absent from the conquest are the idea of war as a lawsuit and war as achieving the desires of the king.

Since the gods acted as witnesses and certifiers of political treaties, when a treaty was broken the offended party would call on the gods to judge the case and aid in the punishment of the offenders.[31] As discussed in propositions eight and nineteen, Deuteronomy (especially Deut 4; 32) is in the genre of a political treaty, with heaven and earth invoked as witnesses (Deut 4:26; 32:1). In Isaiah 1, heaven and earth are called on to observe Israel's covenant infidelity; although Yahweh is not requesting the aid of heaven and earth in a military attack on Israel, the judgment oracle is carried out by an army, which indicates that the concept of war as lawsuit was known in Israel. Likewise, sometimes irreconcilable disputes were decided by war as a kind of ordeal, with the understanding that the case would be decided in favor of the victor.[32] This may be what Jephthah has in mind in Judges 11:24, 27: "Will you not take what your god Chemosh gives you? Likewise, whatever the LORD our God has given us, we will possess. . . . I have not wronged you, but you are doing me wrong by waging war against me. Let the LORD, the Judge, decide the dispute this day between the Israelites and the Ammonites" (NIV).[33]

Even the invincible barbarians can be the objects of a lawsuit. The Assyrian king Assurbanipal records that the king of the Cimmerians, described as "king of the Umman-Manda, offspring of Tiamat, image of a [*gallû*-demon],"[34] broke a loyalty oath to Assyria, in consequence

---

[31] Kang, *Divine War*, 14.

[32] Ibid., 51.

[33] Ibid., 195.

[34] Daniel David Luckenbill, *Ancient Records of Assyria and Babylonia* (Chicago: University of Chicago Press, 1927), 385. *Copy of a Dedicatory Text from Isagila 8.1001.* See also Adall, *Scourge of God*, 128.

of which his army was destroyed by fire from heaven and he himself died from a horrible disease.[35] Similar imagery is found in Ezekiel 38–39, where the hordes of Gog, described in the imagery of the trope of invincible barbarians (see excursus in proposition twelve), receive "judgment" (Ezek 39:21, *mšpt*, NIV "punishment") for their "evil scheme" (Ezek 38:10). We might especially note the similarity between Ezekiel 38:21, 23 ("Every man's sword will be against his brother. . . . Then they will know that I am the LORD"), and the curse against the Cimmerians: "Slaughtering each other with weapons, they praised the glory of Aššur the great lord, my lord."[36] Likewise, there is similarity between Ezekiel 38:22 ("I will execute judgment on him with plague and bloodshed; I will pour down torrents of rain, hailstones and burning sulfur on him and on his troops and on the many nations with him") and the fate of the Cimmerian army: "He became ill. . . . Fire from heaven fell and it burnt him, his army, his camp."[37] Ezekiel is not quoting Assurbanipal; he is invoking standard rhetoric to describe the invocation of divine action against invincible barbarians.[38] The same imagery appears in Joshua 10:11, in response to the barbarians (the coalition of northern Canaanite kings) attacking Joshua's allies: "The LORD hurled large hailstones down on them, and more of them died from the hail than were killed by the swords of the Israelites."

What is most notable for our purposes is that lawsuit language against the invincible barbarians is very rare. In the Cuthaean Legend, Naram-Suen consults oracles as to whether he should engage the Umman-manda[39] (or, later, execute captives) but does not call out to the gods to avenge or judge the barbarians for the destruction of his

---

[35]Adall, *Scourge of God*, 130-32.

[36]Ibid., 132.

[37]Ibid., 130.

[38]In this case, even against the same enemy; "Gomer" in Ezek 38:6 refers to the Cimmerians. Daniel Bodi, "Ezekiel," in *ZIBBCOT*, 4:484.

[39]Cuthaean Legend of Naram-Suen, Standard Babylonian version, lines 72-78, in Joan Goodnick Westenholz, *Legends of the Kings of Akkade* (Winona Lake, IN: Eisenbrauns, 1997), 317.

land.[40] Likewise, Nabonidus acknowledges the destruction and defilement of the Ehulhul temple by the barbarians but does not call on the gods to render judgment on them. In no circumstances are law and judgment invoked against the barbarians simply *because* they are barbarians. The Cimmerian king is arrogant and has no respect for the gods, but the gods do not render judgment against him because he is arrogant and has no respect for the gods; they destroy him because he violates a treaty.[41] Similarly, in Joshua 10 the nation "avenged itself" (Josh 10:13) on the barbarians, not simply because they are barbarians but because they attacked Israel's allies (Josh 10:6). Conversely, this implies that when the barbarians *are* attacked simply because they are barbarians (Lev 18:24; Deut 9:4), there is no law or judgment motivating the attack.[42] In general, the lawsuit model of war is found in the Israelite prophets (invoking the imagery of a broken treaty by a rebellious vassal) and to some extent in the Davidic period (usually in reference to Yahweh fulfilling his covenant to preserve the Davidic dynasty)[43] but is otherwise absent from the Hebrew Bible. Apart from enforcement of the Sinaitic and Davidic covenants, warfare in Israel generally emphasizes the idea of carrying out a divine will and plan (as is also seen in Egypt), rather than emphasizing divine judgment on lawbreakers.[44]

The other area in which Israelite war ideology demonstrated in the conquest differed from normal Mesopotamian conception was in the idea that the gods go to war in order to assist the king in achieving his desires. Pious ancient Near Eastern kings understood that if they were attentive to the needs of the gods, which included maintaining social

---

[40]Cuthaean Legend of Naram-Suen, Standard Babylonian version, lines 125-30, in Westenholz, *Legends*, 323.

[41]Adalı, *Scourge of God*, 129.

[42]If the barbarians are attacked as judgment, then they have done something besides simply being barbarians. Therefore, if they have not done something besides simply being barbarians, *modus tollens* they are not attacked as judgment.

[43]Kang, *Divine War*, 195.

[44]Ibid., 196.

order, they would be able to rely on the support of the gods in achieving their personal ambitions, which could include war and conquest, as in this example from the correspondence of Esarhaddon:[45]

> Marduk, the king of gods, is reconciled with the king my lord. He does whatever the king my lord says. Sitting on your throne, you will vanquish your enemies, conquer your foes and plunder the enemy. Bel has said, "May Esarhaddon, king of Assyria, be seated on his throne. . . . I will deliver the countries into his hands!" The king may happily do as he deems best.[46]

Similar language is found in the writings of Tikulti-Ninurta and Ashurnasirpal:

> Tukulti-Ninurta, king of the universe, king of Assyria . . . the king whom the gods have helped to obtain his desired victories.[47]

> At that time Ashurnasirpal . . . whose desires the God Enlil helped him obtain so that his great hand conquered all princes insubmissive to him.[48]

The language is also found in the Hittite document that concludes with the *ḥerem* of the conquered city: "Tešub, my Lord, has done my soul's desire and has fulfilled my soul's desire: he handed it [the rebellious city] over to me and I have desolated it and made it sacred."[49]

In the Bible, this same language in terms of the king ruling over whatever his heart desires is found in 2 Samuel 3:21, where Abner

---

[45]For *biblu* ("desire") as political motives for war, see *CAD* B 220-21.

[46]Excerpted from "Bel-ušezib to Esarhaddon," in M. Nissinen, *Prophets and Prophecy in the Ancient Near East*, SBL Writings from the Ancient World (Atlanta: SBL, 2003), 157.

[47]Tukulti-Ninurta 1 A.0.78.5 1-10, in A. K. Grayson, *Assyrian Rulers of the Third and Second Millennium*, Royal Inscriptions of Mesopotamia, Assyrian Periods 1 (Toronto, 1987), 244.

[48]Ashurnasirpal II A.0.101.1 38-40, in Grayson, *Assyrian Rulers*, 196.

[49]Giuseppe F. Del Monte, "The Hittite Ḥerem," in *Memorie Igor M. Diakonoff*, Babel und Bibel 2 (Winona Lake, IN: Eisenbrauns, 2005), 21-45, quote on 41; see also Ada Taggar-Cohen, "Between Herem, Ownership, and Ritual: Biblical and Hittite Perspectives," in *Current Issues in Priestly and Related Literature: The Legacy of Jacob Milgrom and Beyond*, ed. Roy E. Gane and Ada Taggar-Cohen (Atlanta: SBL, 2015), 419-34 (quote on 424-25).

promises conquest to David. More significantly, it is found in 1 Kings 11:37, where God, through Ahijah the prophet, promises conquest to Jeroboam. Otherwise, the concept of deity granting a king's desires in war is unattested in the Old Testament. While the Israelites seem to have been familiar with the idea of divinely aided conquest according to the desires of a king, the idea does not feature prominently in the Israelite ideology of war and is completely absent from the wars of conquest in Canaan.[50]

---

[50]In Josh 10 Yahweh listens to Joshua, but Joshua's desire is vengeance for aggression against vassals, not for the possession of new territory.

Rahab and the Gibeonites Are Not Exceptions to the *Ḥerem*, and the Use of *Ḥerem* Against the Amalekites Does Not Indicate That *Ḥerem* Is Punishment

As discussed in proposition sixteen, the *ḥerem* of communities is based on problems posed by identity, not genetics, although there is some overlap insofar as genetics are sometimes used as a grounding for identity. The Gibeonites as *individuals* are *ḥerem* in the sense that the individuals are not being used as slaves; they serve the sanctuary as woodcutters and water carriers (Josh 9:21). However, their community *identity* as the people of Gibeon remains intact: "The Gibeonites were *not a part of Israel* but were *survivors of the Amorites*" (2 Sam 21:2 NIV). In 2 Samuel 21, we learn that King Saul tried to annihilate the Gibeonites "in his zeal for Israel and Judah" (2 Sam 21:2), presumably in a self-motivated effort to complete the conquest. What he should have done, which would also have respected their treaty with Joshua, was destroy their identity as the people of Gibeon and make them a part of Israel. Instead, he kills individuals, which serves no purpose since the individuals are already removed from use, and also violates the treaty, which in turn brings only the wrath of Yahweh (2 Sam 21:1).

The purpose of the military action that expels the Canaanites is so that they will not "become barbs in your eyes and thorns in your sides" (Num 33:55). Similar injunctions in Exodus 34:12-15 and Deuteronomy 7:2-4 indicate that the reason Israel is not to make treaties (as they do with the Gibeonites) is ultimately for Israel's sake, and the decision to obey (or not) constitutes part of their choice between "life and prosperity" or "death and destruction" (Deut 30:15). William Ford notes that, if Yahweh's objective were the death of the Gibeonites, he could easily rain down rocks on them, treaty or no treaty; instead, he rains down rocks on their enemies (Josh 10:1-11).[1] Although Joshua 9 does not use the word, the assignment of the Gibeonites to the sanctuary indicates that they are indeed *ḥerem*; nobody in Israel is using them (as slaves). However, because they are *also* not a part of Israel they give Israel trouble (immediately in Josh 10:6-7, but continuing all the way to 2 Sam 21).

Rahab stands in contrast to the Gibeonites, whose persons are *ḥerem* but whose identity is not. Rahab "lives among the Israelites" (Josh 6:25), and that she marries into an Israelite family (Mt 1:5) indicates that her person is not proscribed from use. Because Rahab abandons her Canaanite identity and becomes an Israelite, the identity she represented is gone, and therefore to *ḥerem* her personally would serve no purpose. It is worth noting that the negative foil of Rahab in Judges 1:25 does not assimilate but goes and builds a city, which of course cancels out the accomplishment of the *ḥerem* of the original occupants of Bethel, since their identity survives.[2] Rahab is not an exception to the *ḥerem*; she is the embodiment of it.

---

[1] William Ford, "What About the Gibeonites?," *Tyndale Bulletin* 66, no. 2 (2015): 197-216.

[2] Barry Webb notes that the name of the new city (Luz) is the same as the former name of Bethel. The identity of the Luzites therefore remains intact: "What is clear is that the informer has not become an Israelite. He remains a 'Luzite,' and therefore a Canaanite, at heart." Barry G. Webb, *The Book of Judges*, NICOT (Grand Rapids: Eerdmans, 2012), 115.

Of course, converting everyone is not the actual objective of the *ḥerem* any more than killing everyone is; conversion would have accomplished it, but it is not expected (see Josh 11:20). As discussed in proposition sixteen, the objective is to remove the various Canaanite identities from the use of every individual who remains in the land, by one way or another.

THE AMALEKITES IN 1 SAMUEL 15

Ḥerem against communities is intended to destroy identity, not to kill people. We see this further in the case of the Amalekites, whose destruction is promised in the Pentateuch and carried out in 1 Samuel 15. That the target is the identity is specified in Exodus 17:14 and Deuteronomy 25:19 by the idiom "blot out [the name]," which is the same fate that awaits the tribe of Benjamin in Judges 17 (even after Israelite wives are found for some of the survivors). Therefore, as discussed in proposition sixteen, being blotted out cannot possibly mean having one's genetic legacy die out. The same applies to a micro-identity within Israel in Deuteronomy 25:5-6: "If brothers are living together and one of them dies without a son, his widow must not marry outside the family. Her husband's brother shall take her and marry her and fulfill the duty of a brother-in-law to her. The first son she bears shall carry on the name of the dead brother so that his name will not be blotted out from Israel." Here it is the family *identity*, not genetics, that is preserved, since of course levirate marriage does nothing to pass on the genes of the deceased. We should also note that Samuel in 1 Samuel 15 makes no attempt to kill the animals but only kills the king (1 Sam 15:32).[3] This is because the king is the

---

The land of the Hittites, where he settles, is within the territory of Israel (the Hittites are on the list of nations in Ex 3:8, etc.). See Jack M. Sasson, *Judges 1–12*, AB (New York: Doubleday, 2014), 169: "There may also be a lesson in that the man chose to set roots in . . . territory that God had promised the Hebrew people."

[3]Saul's claim in 1 Sam 15:20 that he "destroyed the Amalekites and brought back Agag their king" is oxymoronic, since by *not* destroying the king he has not, in fact, destroyed

embodiment and personification of the community identity, as also demonstrated by the promise in Deuteronomy 7:24, where the names of the kings will be wiped out, and by the (talionic) proclamation of Samuel in 1 Samuel 15:33 that "[Agag's] mother [will] be childless" (that is, Agag's family line will end). Samuel thus carries out the intent of the *ḥerem*, not by killing every last ethnic Amalekite and all of their animals (which he does not do) but by terminating the final marker of Amalekite community identity. Thus the *ḥerem* in 1 Samuel 15 has nothing to do with offering the Amalekites as sacrifices to Yahweh, as some interpreters are inclined to propose; as with all *ḥerem* against communities, it has to do with destroying the identity (or failing to do so).[4]

As discussed in proposition five, the punishment against Amalek is carried out in retribution for offenses against the Israelite community (1 Sam 15:2), not for moral or cultic offenses that have invoked the wrath of deity and must be propitiated. The *ḥerem* against community identity is ultimately for the sake of Israel, not for the sake of Yahweh (see proposition sixteen), and in Judges 2:3 Yahweh denies this benefit to Israel (see also Judg 2:22-23; 3:1). Thus, when David fights the Philistines and Jebusites, there is no command to *ḥerem* them. The Amalekites in Saul's day are an exception to the new "allow the nations to remain and test Israel" policy because of "what

---

Amalek. As with his erection of a victory monument (see proposition nineteen) and attempt to destroy the Gibeonites (see proposition eighteen), he misunderstands fundamentally how the Israelite covenant is supposed to work, and this (rather than a generic "attitude" or an aggregate of individual offenses) is the reason why he is ultimately rejected as king over Israel.

[4]For example, David Gunn tries to use Saul's claim that he is going to sacrifice in 1 Sam 15:15 to argue that Saul is indeed intending to carry out the *ḥerem* because "clearly, *ḥerem* was something akin to sacrifice." David M. Gunn, *The Fate of King Saul*, Journal for the Study of the Old Testament Supplement Series 14 (Sheffield, UK: Sheffield Academic, 1980), 46. In contrast, see V. Philips Long, *The Reign and Rejection of King Saul*, SBL Dissertation Series 118 (Atlanta: Scholars Press, 1989), 145: "[The statement "willing to destroy" in 1 Sam 15:9b] would be an odd way of expressing things if Saul had intended all along to fulfill the ban order."

they did to Israel when they waylaid them as they came up from Egypt" (1 Sam 15:2 NIV). Blotting out an identity *can* be a punishment (as in Ps 9:5; 34:16; 106:13-15), but that does not mean that it is a punishment every time it happens (the dead brother in Deut 25:6 was not punished) or that *herem* is the only way to carry it out (Yahweh intends to do it himself in Deut 9:14, and none of David's enemies in the Psalms are ever *herem*). But even when it is a punishment, there is no indication that it occurs specifically for offense against deity; offense against humans is far more common. Thus there is no basis for understanding the *herem* of the Amalekites as propitiation for offense against deity.

EXCURSUS: *Herem* and the Removal of Impurity

In Leviticus 18:24, the land is impure; thereafter, the land is *herem* and thereby inducted into Yahweh's constellation ("holy"). However, it does not appear that *herem* is thereby a mechanism for the removal of impurity. As discussed in proposition ten, making something holy is not the same as making something clean (*thr*, removing its impurity). In Leviticus 27:28 the things that are *herem* are most holy, but causing a thing to become holy is something that God does, not something that humans do. Additionally, "holy" means "co-identified with deity," not "free of impurity [and thereby suitable for ritual use]." Unclean animals that are devoted are both holy and unclean, and *herem* sites do not become temples suitable for ritual. Indeed, as we discussed in proposition fifteen, *herem* means "remove from use," so the idea of a thing being removed from use (*herem*) in order to make it suitable for ritual use (clean) is somewhat oxymoronic.

In addition to the misguided conception that *herem* represents the process by which a thing can become most holy, some interpreters believe that *herem* removes impurity as a kind of propitiation for the wrath of deity against the object. This interpretation is normally supported by citing Deuteronomy 13:15-16: "You must *hrm* it, both its people and its livestock. You are to gather all the plunder of the town into the middle of the public square and completely burn [*śrp*] the town and all its plunder as a whole burnt offering [*kālîl*] to the LORD your God."

Interpreters often combine this verse with Leviticus 27:28 ("every *herem* is most holy to the LORD") to freely intersperse the concepts of holiness, sacrifice, and *herem* whenever any one of the three is mentioned: "Joshua's *herem* on Jericho implies that not only have its people and property been consigned to God, but also their very land—all are 'most holy.'"[5] Likewise, "in Biblical Hebrew it [*herem*] bears a one-sided relationship to the verb *qadaš*, expressing solely the negative aspect of sanctification."[6] A closer examination of the text, however, indicates that the free exchange of concepts is not entirely warranted.

The word for "burnt offering" when it refers to a sacrifice is *ʿōlâ*, not *kālîl*. *Kālîl* is an adverb (or adjective) that means "entirely." The two words (*kālîl*, *ʿōlâ*) are used together in 1 Samuel 7:9 (also translated "whole burnt offering"), but in Deuteronomy 13 the word for "offering" is not used, so the phrase means "burn all of it." More importantly, the word here for "burn" (*śrp*) never refers to sacrifice; the word for a burnt sacrifice is *qṭr*, as in Exodus 29:13, "take all the fat . . . and burn [*qṭr*] them on the altar." Significantly, this burning is immediately *contrasted* with the disposal by fire of that which is *unsuitable* for sacrifice: "burn [*śrp*] the bull's flesh . . . outside the camp" (Ex 29:14). The purpose of *herem* is not to kill or destroy things, either to make them clean or to please Yahweh as a form of sacrifice. The purpose of *herem* is to remove that thing from use.

This is consistent with the examples of *herem* elsewhere in the ancient Near East. In the Hittite document described in proposition fifteen, the land is offered and made sacred—generic terms that also

---

[5]Jacob Milgrom, *Leviticus 23–27*, AB (New York: Doubleday, 2001), 2392.
[6]Baruch A. Levine, "The Language of Holiness," in *In Pursuit of Meaning*, ed. Andrew D. Gross (Winona Lake, IN: Eisenbrauns, 2011), 1:321-33, quote on 325.

describe rituals—but the purpose of the action is different from that of the sacred offerings presented in temples. In the ancient Near East, ritual offerings were intended to meet the needs of the gods (usually by feeding them) so that the gods would in turn bestow their favor. However, while ritual offerings are presented to the gods because the gods need food, Mursili does not present his conquered site to the storm god because the storm god needs a pasture. Rather, the offering is a gesture of royal piety signifying the king's gratitude to the god for aiding him in the victory. In Israel offerings serve different purposes than they do in Mesopotamia. Their purpose is to represent Yahweh favorably because proper cultic behavior is an indication of order and thereby of divine competence (see proposition eleven). Likewise, Joshua's *herem* of the Canaanite cities is not to demonstrate piety but to carry out the obligation to surrender the right to administer territory in the context of a vassal treaty (see proposition nineteen). However, the point still stands that ritual offerings serve a different purpose from *herem* in both the ancient Near East and Israel, and therefore the two concepts cannot be freely exchanged.

There are several secondary objectives of the *herem* documented in various places throughout the text. In Judges 20 it serves as a means to an end to procure wives for the Benjaminites. It is used to intimidate enemies in 2 Kings 19:11, and it is used as punishment for aggressive actions toward Israel in 1 Samuel 15 and Isaiah 34, and for Israel's covenant infidelity in Zechariah 14:11. These secondary objectives are not all interchangeable in any given circumstance, but none of them involves purifying the object for ritual use. However, as we discussed in proposition fourteen, though the land is figuratively described as a temple to identify it as a locus of order, it is not literally a temple where literal rituals are performed. Consequently, the removal of impurity is likewise figurative, signifying the change in status from a place of nonorder to a place that embodies order. The impurity itself is real, but the removal of the impurity is mechanically accomplished by the *kpr* of the sanctuary on the Day of Atonement, which "is among them in the midst of their uncleanness" (Lev 16:16), not by the *ḥerem* of the territory during the conquest.[7]

---

[7]The natural impurity generated by Israel as a result of ordinary usage is absorbed by the sanctuary and purged on the Day of Atonement. This is what it means to *kpr* the sanctuary after it has been "among [Israel] in the midst of their uncleanness," e.g., Lev 16:16; also Lev 16:19. In contrast, the natural impurity generated by Canaan as a result of ordinary usage has no mechanism for removal and remains in the land. Their participation in the land's uncleanliness is included for the sake of rhetorical comparison to Israel's potential (re)de-filement, but the emphasis is on the *fact* that the land is unsuitable to represent the covenant order (and therefore in need of a change in status before it can be used), not on the details of how it got that way.

Proposition 19

The Logic of the *Ḥerem* in the Event of the Conquest Operates in the Context of Israel's Vassal Treaty

The Israelite covenant functions as a vassal treaty, and in the event of the conquest Yahweh assumes the role of an ancient Near Eastern emperor. The word *ḥerem* refers to removing something from human use. In the case of territory or cities, it normally implies giving that thing to a deity for the deity to use. In ordinary circumstances a conqueror would only ban a single city as a gesture of pious devotion (see excursus in proposition eighteen), but Joshua, in accordance with Yahweh's command, effectively bans all of the land he acquires. This deviation from normal practice is because of what Yahweh intends to do with the land, which is described in Deuteronomy as "the place I have chosen to set my name."

KINGS AND GODS IN THE ANCIENT NEAR EAST

The idiom "place my name" is known from Assyrian royal ideology. Specifically for our purposes, it is found on monumental inscriptions that signify the king's lordship over a vassal state: "As had the great kings and heroes of Mesopotamian history and legend, YHWH states that he has 'placed his name' in the Promised Land. The king has captured this new territory; he has claimed it as his own."[1] The imagery of the land as vassal territory is everywhere throughout the canon; one of the most blatant is Malachi 1:14, where Yahweh refers to himself as "a great king," the epithet of choice for ancient Near Eastern emperors.[2] More significantly, the covenant document itself in Deuteronomy (especially Deut 4; 32) is universally acknowledged to mirror the form and structure of a treaty between a suzerain and a vassal.[3] The geopolitical domain of Israel is a vassal territory of Yahweh, whose homeland and capital city is in the divine realm (when Elijah travels to Horeb in 1 Kings 19:8, he is essentially paying a visit to the capital), while Israel's human monarch serves as the ruling regent.[4] The imagery of the king serving as a vassal of the gods and receiving delegated authority from the gods is not unique to Israel; in both Israel and the ancient Near East the concept is demonstrated by the language of "divine sonship," a status extended to the Davidic dynasty in 2 Samuel 7:14.[5] Where Israel's ideology differs is in regard to what the divine sovereign expects the regent to do. Kings in the ancient Near East were charged with maintaining order in the earthly realm so that ritual activity could

---

[1] Sandra L. Richter, *The Deuteronomistic History and the Name Theology: lᵉšakkēn šᵉmô šām in the Bible and the Ancient Near East*, Beihefte zur Zeitschrift für die alttestamentliche Wissenschaft 318 (New York: de Gruyter, 2002), 217.

[2] "Great king" is the title of ancient Near Eastern emperors from Assyria to Persia. Anthony Petterson notes that the construction "great king" is never used to refer to Israelite kings but is used for Sennacherib in 2 Kings 18:19, 28 (Anthony R. Petterson, *Haggai, Zechariah & Malachi*, Apollos Old Testament Commentary [Downers Grove, IL: InterVarsity Press, 2015], 336). Andrew Hill says that the expression refers to a suzerain or overlord (Andrew E. Hill, *Malachi*, AB [New York: Doubleday, 1998], 195).

[3] See, for example, Peter C. Craigie, *The Problem of War in the Old Testament* (Grand Rapids: Eerdmans, 1978), 69.

[4] Contrary to some interpretations, the various titles for Israel's rulers (*špṭ, ngyd, mlk*) are all titles for the regent; the difference is the physical structure of the administration and their relationship to Israel's tribal confederacy, not their relationship to the divine sovereign. Specifically, the title "king" (*mlk*) does not indicate the human ruler's desire to gain independence from the divine ruler (Jonathan H. Walton, "A King Like the Nations," *Biblica* 96 [2015]: 196-99).

[5] John H. Walton, *Ancient Near Eastern Thought in the Old Testament* (Grand Rapids: Baker Academic, 2006), 282-83.

proceed efficiently and the needs of the gods could be met. As discussed in proposition eleven, however, Yahweh demands representation, not service and pampering. The Israelite regent is therefore responsible for maintaining order in the land such that Yahweh is properly represented. Yahweh's name in the territory signifies that he is responsible for it, and anything that happens in it is accountable to him: "When [the Deuteronomist] adopts this same idiom, he does so to speak of YHWH's ongoing suzerainty over Israel."[6]

In accordance with the concept of representation, the idiom "placing a name" entails more than a declaration of ownership. According to Sandra Richter, placing a name involves establishing reputation, specifically by celebrating fame through the commemoration of heroic deeds.[7] Whereas these deeds generally consisted of glorious military victories or heroic feats of derring-do (Gilgamesh's battle with the monster Huwawa is offered as a prime example), Yahweh's deeds consist of his ongoing maintenance of the covenant order as manifested through the nation of Israel, with whom he is co-identified.[8] Nonetheless, the basic objective of *legacy* remains the same, and legacy is simply a temporally projected identity; legacy signifies what people think you (were) like. Yahweh does not pass away and leave a legacy, so for him placing a name is simply a declaration of identity (as a commemorative monument would also do even while the ruler who placed his name on it was still alive). Yahweh's monument is not fixed in stone, however, but is ongoing and acted out in real time: "Look here at this nation in this land and see what I have done." This use of the land, through the placement of the name, as a vehicle for identification is why the territory is associated with Yahweh intimately enough to be properly called holy, while the territories merely ruled

---

[6]Richter, *Deuteronomistic History and the Name Theology*, 205.
[7]Ibid., 180-81.
[8]Ibid., 182.

by ancient Near Eastern gods are not closely associated enough to be dingirized (see proposition eleven).

The act of a king placing his name in vassal territory formalizes his status as overlord and represents his reputation and presence in the land. "It is the conquering king who is demanding [Israel's] obedience; it is the *new sovereign* of the region who is awarding Israel her land grant."[9] Israel in many ways conceived of its God similarly to how other nations conceived of their deities, but it also conceived of its God in the same way that a vassal kingdom conceived of its suzerain.[10] The second half of the book of Joshua is a land grant, representing the bestowal of territory to faithful underlings. The preceding conquest narrative, which is written to emphasize the *ḥerem*, describes the process by which Yahweh becomes the new sovereign.

Israel's conquest of the land is therefore comparable to ancient Near Eastern practice, wherein an appointed general or vassal ruler would procure territory for a human emperor, who in turn would place his name there. In the biblical conquest account, Israel (designated as a vassal of Yahweh through the covenant) is procuring territory, not for themselves but for their (divine) emperor, who will likewise place his name there. Once the emperor's name is established in the territory, his reputation will be contingent on what happens there, which includes the conduct of his vassals and their appointed regent. Similarly, Yahweh's reputation—that is, his identity—will be represented through the conduct of his vassal nation Israel and through his relationship with them.

Ḥerem in the Context of Israel's Vassal Treaty

A treaty concerns the actions and obligations of the vassal, while a grant concerns the actions and obligations of the suzerain.[11] Joshua

---

[9]Ibid., 205 (emphasis added).

[10]Craigie, *Problem of War in the Old Testament*, 69-70.

[11]Moshe Weinfield, "The Covenant of Grant in the Old Testament and in the Ancient Near East," *Journal of the American Oriental Society* 90 (1970): 184-20, on 185.

1–11 is the record of Israel carrying out the terms of the treaty; this is the thrust of the repeated phrase "[he did] . . . as the LORD commanded Moses." Joshua 12–24 then describes the land grant awarded by the suzerain in return. The exile, when it occurs, represents the emperor removing rebellious vassals from his land and putting its nation to *herem* (that is, destroying their national identity), as emperors would commonly do (see 2 Kings 19:11; Zech 14:11; and discussion in proposition sixteen). However, as discussed in proposition eight, this motive cannot be extrapolated to Yahweh's treatment of the Canaanites. Since the treaty (represented by the covenant) is made with Israel and not with Canaan, it is not possible to imagine the Canaanites as rebellious vassals being disciplined for insurrection, as was also the case in the Hittite example of the *herem* (see proposition fifteen). The purpose of the conquest is to carve out new territory, not to repatriate rightful territory. This is part of the effect achieved by the portrayal of the Canaanites as invincible barbarians (see proposition twelve); they owe no allegiance to the overlord and are simply enemies.

Israel accepts the covenant of its own volition (Ex 24:7; Josh 8:30-35). While vassals in the ancient Near East were often subjugated through conquest (or as an alternative to conquest; see 2 Kings 12:18; 15:19-20), there are examples of vassals submitting themselves voluntarily. Gyges patriated himself to Assurbanipal in order to defeat the Cimmerians (likewise depicted as invincible barbarians),[12] and a Hittite treaty describes a king named Mashuiluwa voluntarily submitting to Hatti in order to gain military assistance against usurpers in his homeland.[13] Whether voluntary or not, vassal treaties normally impose obligations or restrictions as part of their terms. These obligations, however, are not

---

[12]Sellim Ferruh Adalı, *The Scourge of God: The Umman-Manda and Its Significance in the First Millennium BC*, SAAS 20 (Helsinki: The Neo-Assyrian Text Corpus Project, 2011), 121. Ahaz similarly patriates himself to Tiglath-Pileser in exchange for military aid in 2 Kings 16:7.

[13]Gary Beckman, *Hittite Diplomatic Texts*, SBL Writings from the Ancient World (Atlanta: Scholars Press, 1996), 69.

random and arbitrary metrics to determine the vassal's degree of loyalty. Sovereigns do not test their vassals with unseemly demands in order to discover whether the vassal is loyal enough to carry them out.[14] Rather, the demands placed on vassals are eminently pragmatic. As discussed in proposition eight, this probably extends to Israel's cultic obligations as well; a stipulation in the aforementioned Hittite treaty—"you shall not desire any other power over you"[15]—is reminiscent of the Israelite prohibition on worshiping other gods or idolatry. But for our present purposes, this means we should assume that the command to *ḥerem* the territory of Canaan also served some pragmatic purpose in the context of the suzerain-vassal relationship between Yahweh and Israel. An examination of such relationships in the ancient Near East suggests that this purpose was a symbolic divestiture of Israel's right to administer its own territory, instead acknowledging the supreme authority of the sovereign.

THE SURRENDER OF THE RIGHT TO ADMINISTER TERRITORY

One common obligation placed on vassals was the acknowledgment of their submissive status through symbolic actions. Emissaries from subjugated territories are known to have presented model cities, representing their countries, to the suzerain.[16] Some scholars suggest that this ceremony was specifically part of the establishment of a new capital city.[17] As discussed in proposition fourteen, Israel's counterpart to the thematic imagery of "capital city" is the land under the covenant, so it seems reasonable that the inauguration of the covenant as a functioning center of order would recapitulate that ceremony in some way. Thus Israel as a vassal is expected to present its territory to their sovereign as recognition of its vassal status.

---

[14]The conquest is not a recapitulation of the sacrifice of Isaac; there is no "God tested Israel" at the beginning (cf. Gen 22:1), nor is there a "now I know that Israel fears God" (cf. Gen 22:12).

[15]Beckman, *Hittite Diplomatic Texts*, 71.

[16]Charles K. Wilkinson, "More Details on Ziwiye," *Iraq* 22 (1960): 213-20.

[17]Stephanie Dalley, *The Mystery of the Hanging Gardens of Babylon* (New York: Oxford University Press, 2013), 111.

One of the conditions of being a vassal was the admission that the ownership and distribution of the territory belonged to the sovereign, not the regent. This is probably what the symbolic presentation of territory was supposed to affirm; the region belonged to the emperor, and the regent was given authority over it at the king's discretion, not by their own inherent right. The Hittite treaty emphasizes repeatedly that the king could have made *anybody* regent instead: "I could have made someone else lord in the land . . . [but] I have given . . . your land back to you, and I have installed you in lordship for the land."[18] Israel, as Yahweh's vassal, is likewise reminded of its subordinate status (e.g., Lev 25:23, "the land is mine and you reside in my land as foreigners and strangers") and required to symbolically divest its own right to administer its territory. It does not present model cities because its sovereign is a deity, not a human; instead, the symbolic yielding of the right to control territory takes the form of the action used to turn control of a territory over to a deity. That action, as described in proposition fifteen, is the *ḥerem*.

ERECTING A MONUMENT AND PLACING THE NAME

Once a treaty was ratified, the overlord typically would erect a monument in the territory to signal that the region belonged to him and was under his authority and control. This type of monument, which glorified the king and signified his control and authority over the territory, is the source of the idiom "to place the name."[19] Yahweh does not erect a physical monument; the monument is the physical embodiment of the sovereign's presence and authority, and, since Yahweh is a deity, his monument takes the form of the embodiment of a *deity's* presence and authority, namely the temple (referenced throughout the

---

[18]Beckham, *Hittite Diplomatic Texts*, 70-71. See also Dennis J. McCarthy, *Treaty and Covenant* (Rome: Biblical Institute Press, 1978), 53.

[19]Richter, *Deuteronomistic History and the Name Theology*, 163: "The language of setting up victory stelae is also the language of 'placing the name.'"

Deuteronomistic History as "the place where Yahweh has set his name"). But this lack of a monument does not mean that the regents themselves are allowed to set up monuments of their own, because the territory does not belong to them. This is what Saul does in 1 Samuel 15:12.[20] Saul's actions regarding the *ḥerem* of the Amalekites are enlightening because they contrast ordinary ancient Near Eastern royal logic with what is expected from covenant Israel.

Ancient Near Eastern kings generally conceived of themselves as the vassals of the gods, though in their understanding the relationship was more metaphorical than literal. Normally, kings would acknowledge their dependence on the support of the gods by crediting their assistance in inscriptions on monuments erected by the kings to themselves. *Ḥerem* might be enacted against a single city, as Mesha does to the town of Nebo in the Moabite Inscription, or as Mursili does in the Hittite *ḥerem* text discussed previously (see proposition fifteen), but doing so was a token gesture of royal piety signifying gratitude and honor for the gods. In the ordinary royal logic of the ancient Near East, such behavior was proper and commendable and would be expected of any pious monarch.

As the text implies, this is exactly what Saul thinks he is doing. He has won a glorious victory and taken territory (1 Sam 15:7) and built a monument to himself (1 Sam 15:12), probably crediting Yahweh with the victory.[21] Spoils are taken, not for themselves, as Achan did, but "to sacrifice to the LORD" (1 Sam 15:15). From a typical ancient Near Eastern perspective, Saul has acted with full propriety, as he himself states in 1 Samuel 15:13. However, by sparing the king, Saul has defeated the entire purpose of *ḥerem* against a community (see proposition eighteen); he may as well have done nothing at all. More severely, however, he has effectively declared independence from his suzerain

---

[20]It also may be what the Transjordan tribes are suspected of in Josh 22.

[21]V. Philips Long, *The Reign and Rejection of King Saul*, SBL Dissertation Series 118 (Atlanta: Scholars Press, 1989), 142.

by honoring *himself* in place of the emperor and by taking a vassal[22] of his own (Agag's thinking in 1 Sam 15:32 indicates that he expects to be subjugated rather than executed). This explains Samuel's odd reference to divination and idols (lit. *tərāphîm*, NIV "idolatry") in 1 Samuel 15:23; in covenant ideology, these represent breaches of political loyalty to the divine sovereign (see proposition eight). The divine sovereign's retribution against Saul likewise follows standard procedure; the rebellious regent is dethroned and replaced.

Israel under Saul perhaps serves as a negative foil for Israel under Joshua; where Saul now failed, Joshua had succeeded. After the conquest Israel makes no monument to itself; it accepts its status as a vassal under the jurisdiction of Yahweh, whose authority and control are demonstrated by placing his name. However, the name of the sovereign is also supposed to enhance the king's reputation. If a king raised a victory stele over a land that was not conquered and claimed rulership over a land rife with anarchy, the king would look extremely foolish. The *herem* of the cities turns control of the territory over to Yahweh, but the order in the land that represents the king's stable and functioning rule has not yet been established, and indeed is not established until the time of Solomon. This, incidentally, is why David is not allowed to build the victory stele, which is represented by the Jerusalem temple. It is not because the blood of his wars has made him somehow ritually impure; rather, his tumultuous reign is not indicative of the stability, order, and prosperity that the suzerain's monument should represent (see 1 Kings 5:3). David is the warlord who completes the conquest, but it is Solomon who is appointed regent to preside over Yahweh's territory as the representative of the established

---

[22]Although David and Solomon receive tribute, it is not unheard of for vassals to rule domains of their own, if properly authorized. An inscription from Shalmaneser III (which may be literary rather than historical but nonetheless shows the point) describes a Tartanu (commander in chief) being granted ownership of a territory and authorized to receive tribute (Raija Matilla, *The King's Magnates*, SAAS 11 [Helsinki: The Neo-Assyrian Text Corpus Project, 2000], 114).

covenant order. But before Yahweh can celebrate the triumph over chaos by erecting his monument, chaos has to be brought under control. The process of replacing the existing chaos with the covenant order is represented by the *ḥerem* not of the Canaanite cites but of the Canaanite communities, as discussed in proposition sixteen.

PART 6

HOW TO APPLY THIS
UNDERSTANDING

The Old Testament, Including the Conquest Account, Provides a Template for Interpreting the New Testament, Which in Turn Gives Insight into God's Purposes for Us Today

As we discussed in proposition two, our response to the biblical material is based not only on what it says but also on what we think the Bible is. Our study thus far has examined what the text actually says so that we can properly translate the ideas represented by the words, logic, and imagery into English. What we have seen is that the conquest account tells the story of the origin of Israel in terms of cosmogony, using imagery recognizable from ancient Near Eastern creation narratives. In doing so, the author is telling us what the nation of Israel is, and therefore what the covenant is, and therefore giving us an idea of what God is doing through Israel and the covenant. But in order to apply the content, we still have to know why this story is important enough that it was preserved for future generations to read. In order to answer that question, we first have to understand the purpose of the Old Testament. As discussed in proposition two, many people assume that the purpose of the Old Testament is to provide its readers with a list of moral or social imperatives. However, we have also seen that this assumption about what the Bible is should not be accepted uncritically.

WHY ARE THERE TWO TESTAMENTS?

As discussed in proposition three, we should not think of God's work in the world in terms of progress; therefore we should not assume that the two covenants were each independently trying to achieve the same goal. Rather, we should think of the two covenants as two different steps in a process. That process includes God's actions in both steps and also the preservation of the record of those actions as Scripture, but for our purposes, in our ongoing examination of what the Bible is, we are interested primarily in the latter. God's actions in the old covenant served a different purpose from God's actions in the new covenant, because the two covenants are different steps in a process. But this also means that *reading about* God's actions as recorded in the Old Testament serves a different purpose from *reading about* God's actions in the New Testament. This is simply a logical extension of reading the text in the context in which it was written.

Normally when we think of the two Testaments, we think of them as two books in a series (that is, a story and its sequel), or perhaps as individual volumes of a single two-volume work. However, these conceptions assume that the two parts should be approached in more or less the same way. A better understanding of how the two Testaments should be viewed might be found by considering the difference between a bilingual dictionary (say, German → English) and the *Oxford English Dictionary*. Although both of these books are dictionaries and both of them therefore exist to describe the meanings of words, the ways we use them are quite different. In the same way, both the Old Testament and the New Testament are Scripture, and both of them therefore serve as the means for God to reveal his purposes, but they do so in different ways.

That the Old Testament should be read differently from the New Testament does not therefore make it somehow inferior or obsolete. To continue the metaphor, we might imagine a native German speaker who knows no English but who (for whatever reason) is trying to read the *Oxford English Dictionary*. The bilingual German → English dictionary will not give her the same information as the Oxford dictionary—that is, it will not tell her the definitions of words—but nonetheless, she will not be able to get to the definitions of words without it. Similarly, the Old Testament will not give us the same information as the New Testament; that is, it will not tell us how we can participate in God's purposes in the context of the new covenant. Nonetheless, we will not be able to get to that information without it. The Old Testament, through its description of the old covenant, provides us with a conceptual framework that we can use to understand the logic of the new covenant. We don't read the Old Testament just so that we can know what the Old Testament says; we read the Old Testament because we need to know what the Old Testament says if we want to be able to make any sense of what the New Testament says. That is what we mean when we say that the Old Testament is a *template*.

READING THE OLD TESTAMENT AS A TEMPLATE

A discussion of all of the details of the Old Testament template would be a book in itself and is beyond the scope of this study. What we are specifically interested in is the application of one specific component of the template—the conquest account—and the significance for the new covenant that results from it. Accordingly, we will examine the elements that we have already discussed as critical to a proper understanding of the conquest—the community of Israel, the land, and the presence of God—and use them as examples to demonstrate how reading the Old Testament as a template ought to work.

In the Old Testament, God's purposes are carried out through the nation of Israel, which is a specially selected community with whom God chooses to co-identify. Therefore, we should look for a similar community to be established in the New Testament through which God's purposes will be carried out. That community is, of course, the *ekklēsia* (the church). The community of Israel in the Old Testament is co-identified with Yahweh by virtue of being declared holy (see proposition ten). The church is likewise commonly referred to as being God's holy people (*hagios*). However, it is critical for a proper understanding of how the template works to recognize that the church *recapitulates* Israel but does not *reproduce* Israel in terms of its particular details. Thus, for example, Israel is defined by an ethnic identity marker, but the church is not. Likewise, we should not use the New Testament to figure out what it means for a thing to be *hagios* in first-century Rome and assume that whatever that was (*hagios* in Greek literature means "devoted to the gods") should be read backwards and assigned to Israel in the Old Testament.[1] We should also not assume that the word is being used to define a property of the New Testament community (though it incidentally might be). The term *hagios* is used to describe the church because that was the word used to describe Israel when the Hebrew Bible was translated into Greek, and the purpose of the word is to thematically link the church to Israel in the Old Testament template. The connection tells us that we should expect the church community to be co-identified with God and serving as a medium through which to carry out his purposes. The actual property of divine co-identification is established not by the Greek word *hagios* but by the idiom "in Christ" (e.g., Rom 8:1) or, less often, "bear[ing] that name [of Christ]" (1 Pet 4:16). Because divine co-identity with the chosen community is present in the Old Testament template, we can have some confidence that this particular interpretation of those idioms is correct.

---

[1]Henry George Liddell and Robert Scott, *A Greek-English Lexicon with a Revised Supplement*, 9th ed. (Oxford: Clarendon, 1996), 9.

In Israel, it was the overarching abstraction of the community that was co-identified with Yahweh, not each particular individual. Individuals participated in divine identity *by means of* their membership in the community. The use of Israel as a template indicates that the Christian community works this way as well. (This, incidentally, is probably the significance of the later idea that "no one can have God as their father who does not have the church as their mother."[2] It is also what Protestants mean when they refer to the church universal.) Like Israel, membership in the community requires the adoption of an identity marker. For Israel the marker was circumcision; for the Christian community it is the baptism of water and the Spirit. The gift of the Holy Spirit does not co-identify an individual with God; it identifies the individual as part of the community that is co-identified with God. This distinction is important because it helps us identify the new covenant recapitulation of the temple and the land.

Because of Paul's metaphor in 1 Corinthians 6:19 ("your bodies are temples of the Holy Spirit"), many interpreters assume that the temple is recapitulated in the new covenant by individual Christians. However, we recall that in the Old Testament the Temple Mount is occasionally used as a metaphor for the entire land (just as the priesthood is used as a metaphor for the entire community in Ex 19:6, repeated for the Christian community in 1 Pet 2:9). This does not, however, mean that the land is literally a temple or that all of the people are literally priests. As discussed in proposition fourteen, the land is a metaphorical temple (and those who live there are metaphorical priests) because the land is a locus of divine presence, but God is not present in the land in the same way that he is present in the temple. God's fully manifested presence and the symbolism of his dwelling among his people (which is what a temple represents) is found not in individual Christians but in the person of Christ, whose name, Immanuel, means "God with us"

---

[2]Cyprian, *On the Unity of the Catholic Church* 6.

(Mt 1:23) and who explicitly identifies himself with the temple (Jn 2:19-22; cf. Jn 1:14). The presence of God in individual Christians is obviously very different from the presence of God in the person of Christ.

According to the Old Testament template, the land is the place where the community is located in order to do its work. The superficial counterpart to this would be the buildings where the church meets: the houses, the basilicas, and the cathedrals. However, that interpretation takes the recapitulation too literally. The parallel is truly found in Israel's functional and symbolic relationship to the land, not its literal relationship to the land. That is why it is so important to understand the Old Testament's logic, imagery, and symbolism rather than only its words. Israel is a political entity, and so its kingdom is a geographical domain. The church, however, is a "kingdom . . . not of this world" (Jn 18:36), and so it is not located in a physical place. Rather, "where two or three gather in my name, there I am with them" (Mt 18:20). The work of the church community is done wherever its members are. The community itself is an abstraction; the bodies and persons of the individuals who collectively constitute it recapitulate the land. Paul's metaphor still stands because in the Old Testament the land can be metaphorically compared to the temple. This understanding will allow us to understand what exactly is the significance of the *herem* in the new covenant, which we will discuss in the next proposition.

The Application of *Ḥerem* in the New Covenant Is Found in Putting Off Our Former Identity and Surrendering to the Lordship of Christ, and Therefore *Ḥerem* Has Nothing to Do with Killing People

The commands given to Joshua to *ḥerem* the people of Canaan are not intended to be commands of any kind to anyone today. They are not orders to be obeyed or examples to be followed. However, this does not mean that we ought to simply snip those passages out of the Bible. As discussed in proposition sixteen, the conquest of Canaan was intended to accomplish something specific in the context of the overall process of the old covenant, and that intent, in turn, informs our understanding about the process of the new covenant. If we want to understand what the conquest means for readers of the Bible today, we have to understand how it works within the Old Testament template. That is what we will examine in this proposition.

As discussed in propositions fifteen and sixteen, there are three primary targets for *ḥerem* in the Old Testament: the territory of the land itself, the identities of communities within the land but outside the covenant, and the identities of smaller communities of Israelites within the larger community of the people of the covenant. Notably *not* subject to *ḥerem* are the territories or communities outside the boundaries of the land. In order to understand how the *ḥerem* is supposed to be recapitulated in the new covenant, we need to remember how the elements *land* and *community of Israel* are recapitulated in the new covenant, and also remember what specifically the *ḥerem* was intended to achieve in its original context. Only then will we finally be able to answer the question we have had since the beginning: What exactly am I personally supposed to do based on the story I read in Joshua?

Ḥerem as the Surrender of Territory

Ḥerem means "remove from use." When the object of the *ḥerem* was land, the purpose of enacting the ban was to forfeit the right to administer the territory and instead turn the site over to the deity for the deity's own use. In the new covenant, the land is not recapitulated as physical territory. Nonetheless, a new covenant parallel to the old covenant's element of land does exist. What the *ḥerem* of the Canaanite cities by Joshua tells us is that the new covenant's equivalent of land must also be removed from use and turned over to God for God to use as he sees fit. In the new covenant, the element of land is recapitulated by believers themselves. As described in proposition twenty, the common ground of association is that in the old covenant the land was most importantly the place of God's presence. In the new covenant believers both individually and communally become the place of God's presence. Christians are supposed to surrender the right to make use of *themselves* as they turn themselves over to God for his own use.

In the New Testament's own language, the *ḥerem* of the self is represented by such phrases as "crucified with Christ": "I have been crucified with Christ and I no longer live, but Christ lives in me. The life I now live in the body, I live by faith in the Son of God" (Gal 2:20). Likewise, the argument of Romans 6:3-4, 13: "Don't you know that all of us who were baptized into Christ Jesus were baptized into his death? We were therefore buried with him through baptism into death. . . . Rather offer yourselves to God as those who have been brought from death to life; and offer every part of yourself to him as an instrument of righteousness." Similar statements are found in Galatians 5:24 ("Those who belong to Christ Jesus have crucified the flesh with its passions and desires") and 2 Corinthians 5:15 ("And he died for all, that those who live should no longer live for themselves but for him who died for them and was raised again"). A similar idea is expressed in the phrase "you were bought with a price" (1 Cor 6:20; 7:23) and the epithet "servant of Christ" (e.g., Rom 1:1). Christians are not allowed to make use of themselves; their persons and their lives belong to God to do with as he pleases.

But if the Christian's self recapitulates the land, what recapitulates the Canaanites? What needs to be driven away in order for the land to be given to God?

The thing using the Christian's self that needs to be driven away is referred to by Paul in Romans 6:6 as the "old man" (NIV "old self"). Like the Canaanites in Leviticus and Deuteronomy, the old man is rhetorically associated with all manner of horrible vices: "Put to death, therefore, whatever belongs to your earthly nature: sexual immorality, impurity, lust, evil desires and greed, which is idolatry . . . anger, rage, malice, slander, and filthy language from your lips. Do not lie to each other, since you have taken off your old self with its practices" (Col 3:5, 8-9). Likewise, "[The Gentiles] have given themselves over to sensuality so as to indulge in every kind of impurity, and they are full of greed . . . [but] you were taught, with regard to your former way of life, to put off your old self, which is being corrupted by its deceitful desires. . . . Get rid of all bitterness, rage and anger, brawling and slander, along with every form of malice" (Eph 4:19, 22, 31); "The acts of the flesh are . . . sexual immorality, impurity and debauchery; idolatry and witchcraft; hatred, discord, jealousy, fits of rage, selfish ambition, dissensions, factions and envy; drunkenness, orgies, and the like" (Gal 5:19-21). Because we read these New Testament vice lists through the template of the Old Testament, we know that they are rhetorical and are not intended to be a technical exposition of the unregenerate human condition. They are not indictments, just as the list of Canaanite vices that they recapitulate are not indictments. They are *certainly not* intended to describe the actual condition and practice of *nonbelievers*, because the template is clear that the rhetorical depiction of the Canaanites did not extend to the people outside the land (see proposition eight). Rather, the template indicates that they are a rhetorical deprecation of conditions outside the community, written for the purpose of idealizing the community to the current members of the community (see proposition twelve).

We have proposed that the Old Testament template is not overly concerned with the condition of the actual historical Canaanites. It certainly does not teach that their condition and subsequent fate should be extrapolated even to people outside the land (who are recapitulated in the new covenant by non-Christians). The Old Testament template is concerned with the conditions under which Israel will serve God's purpose; the Canaanites and foreign nations are held up rhetorically as counterexamples. Israel was not supposed to feel vindictive toward the Canaanites; they were supposed to feel motivated toward themselves. The same is true of the imprecations of the flesh and the former self in the New Testament. We don't destroy our former selves because they committed crimes and deserve to be destroyed; we destroy them because they are in the way of God using us for his purposes.

Table 4. *Ḥerem* Template Comparison

	Old Testament Element	New Testament Recapitulation	Objective
Territory Subject to *Ḥerem*	Canaanite cities captured; captives and spoils destroyed (in accordance with the established procedure of the ancient Near Eastern devotion ritual)	The personal selves of members of the Christian community ("crucified with Christ"), represented by baptism	Place where the presence of God is located is turned over to God to use as he sees fit
What Is Driven Out of the Territory in Order to Remove It from Use	Canaanite armies defeated, people displaced	The "old self," "former nature," "the flesh," etc.	Removal of elements currently using the territory that prevent or impede intended divine use
Identities Outside the Community Subject to *Ḥerem*	Canaanite nations within the boundaries of the land	Personal or corporate identities other than "Christian" within the church or its members (Jew, Greek, slave, free, male, female, etc.)	Removal of elements that will lead to identity contamination of the community through syncretism
Identities Inside the Community Subject to *Ḥerem*	Individuals or communities within Israel who defy the covenant order (typically idolaters)	Self-identified members of the Christian community who deviate from the parameters the community has established for itself (heretics)	Restoration of the health of the community from identity contamination that has already taken place
Not Subject to *Ḥerem* of Any Kind	Cities and nations outside the land	Persons or identities outside the membership of the church (nonbelievers, other religions)	

HEREM AS IDENTITY DESTRUCTION

The *herem* of the cities of Canaan was designed to remove the territory from human use, both by the Israelites and by the previous occupants, and to turn the territory over to God for God to use. The *herem* of the Canaanite communities served a different purpose; it was intended to remove all identities from the land that were not the identity of the people of the covenant. In the new covenant, the people of the covenant are the community of the church, those who are "in Christ." The land is parallel to the selves of believers. Yahweh was in the land, and now he is in his people. What the Old Testament template tells us, then, is that in order to serve God's purposes we are supposed to purge ourselves—our personal allotment of "land"—of all identities other than "in Christ," just as the Israelite tribes were supposed to purge their allotted territory of all identities other than the people of the covenant (which the book of Judges makes a point of demonstrating that they did not do).

"There is no Gentile or Jew, circumcised or uncircumcised, barbarian, Scythian, slave or free, but Christ is all" (Col 3:11). Likewise, "There is neither Jew nor Gentile, neither slave nor free, nor is there male and female, for you are all one in Christ Jesus" (Gal 3:28). Most modern interpreters generally read these passages as instructions not to apply these labels to other (Christians), but the template (and the context) indicates that a far greater concern is for Christians not to apply the labels to *themselves*. Each of those demographic labels represents an identity that an individual could claim. As discussed in proposition sixteen, community identity is manifested in personal affinity and vicarious solidarity. These passages, read through the Old Testament template, teach that we should not have these sentiments toward anything other than the Christian community. I happen to be an American male, but if I feel a greater sense of affinity and solidarity with any American atheist than I feel with (say) any central African

Christian (because we are both American), or with any male atheist than with any female Christian (because we are both male), it means I'm doing it wrong.

As we discussed briefly in proposition sixteen, there is a difference between adopting an identity and incidentally possessing identity *markers*. I am not supposed to identify as American or as male (that is, feel a sense of vicarious solidarity with other members of those demographics simply because we are both members of the same demographic), but that does not mean I am supposed to renounce my citizenship and castrate myself. It also does not mean that I can avoid any duties or responsibilities that these markers entail (unless, of course, those duties entail something that is forbidden to a member of the Christian community). For example, in the United States, male citizens of a certain age are required to register for the military draft. I would not be allowed to circumvent this duty on the grounds of "I am not an American male, I am a Christian" (even though that is how I am supposed to think of myself).[1] On the other hand, any *privilege or status* that accompanies the identity markers is not to be asserted. Paul has the identity of apostle, but he repeatedly refuses to assert the rights that accompany that identity (1 Cor 9; 1 Thess 2:6). An even better example is Christ in Philippians 2:7. The act of "emptying himself" (NIV "made himself nothing," Greek *ekenōsen*, also called *kenosis*) is sometimes thought to be a stripping off of metaphysical divinity, but in fact is a stripping off of divine *status* (KJV "made himself of no reputation"). Status is a form of identity, though of course the identity marker of divinity (the divine essence) remains. At the same time, the presence of identity markers in certain members can even be a benefit to the Christian community, as Paul's Roman citizen identity marker is on numerous occasions. Individual

---

[1] That is, unless I happen to belong to a sect whose membership entails conscientious objection, since in that case my duty as a citizen would contradict my obligation to represent the community.

Christians bring different resources to the community; just because the community has a common single identity does not mean that all members should be interchangeable (in fact, that is true of any community). This is the metaphor of the body of Christ: "For we were all baptized by one Spirit so as to form one body—whether Jews or Gentiles, slave or free—and we were all given the one Spirit to drink. Even so the body is not made up of one part but of many" (1 Cor 12:13-14). The hand needs to realize that it is in fact a hand, so that it knows it is supposed to do hand things instead of nose things. At the same time, it is not to think of itself in terms of "I am a hand and not a nose"; it is supposed to think, "I am a part of the body of Christ, and that part that I am happens to be a hand." Adopting an identity is not the same thing as assuming a function.

Ḥerem of identity in the new covenant means removing from use all identities (which recapitulate the Canaanite nations) other than Christian from the self (which recapitulates the land). That means that the Christian community as a whole is not allowed to require any identity marker for its members other than Christian (in other words, the baptism of water and the Spirit). This issue is the source of the conflict with the Judaizers in (especially) Galatians. The question they need to resolve is: In order to receive membership in the Christian community (and thereby co-identity with God through the community and the ability to participate in the divine purpose, that is, salvation), is it *also* necessary to become a member of the *Jewish* community and adopt Jewish identity markers of circumcision and Torah? The Judaizers said yes; Paul and the Jerusalem Council said no. The debate was not about the mechanism of salvation (keeping the law versus professing faith in Christ); it was about the identity of the people of the covenant under the new covenant. The Second Temple community assumed that the people of the new covenant would be the remnant of Israel. Instead, it turned out that not only were the Gentiles allowed in the covenant community without becoming Jewish, the Jewish people had to surrender their own Jewish identity (as Paul rebukes Peter for not doing in Gal 2). Being a Christian means not being able to retain any identity other than Christian.

The Jewish identity (usually referred to in the New Testament text as "the law," e.g., 1 Cor 9:20; Gal 4; or "the circumcision," e.g., Gal 2:12) is not done away with because it is inherently inferior or inherently deserving of disposal. The Old Testament template indicates that there was no attempt to destroy the non-Israelite identities of anyone outside the land; therefore in the new covenant there should be no attempt to destroy non-Christian identities of people who are not Christians. Likewise, in the Old Testament, the rhetorical descriptions of those communities are not intended to indict, or even depict, the actual behavior of actual people. Following the template, then, the various descriptions of the Jewish law (in Galatians, Romans, and to a lesser extent Hebrews) are not intended to describe or indict the actual doctrines or practices of Second Temple Judaism. The point is that, in the new covenant, being Jewish does not help one participate in the purposes of God, just like being Canaanite did not in the Old Testament. But within the Christian community, keeping the law (that is, adopting the Jewish identity markers) does not mean that a person is participating in God's purpose more fully or more completely than someone who does not; it actually means that the person is doing it wrong. Membership in the Christian community, and thereby participation in the purposes of God that are carried out through the community, means the setting aside of all other identities.

ḤEREM AS COMMUNITY SELF-CENSORSHIP

The third use of the *herem* in the Old Testament template is the community of Israel removing deviant individual or community identities from within itself. In the Old Testament, the duty of censoring the community was assigned to the priests, who determined who was or was not allowed into the camp (e.g., Lev 14). In the Second Temple period, this duty belonged to the rulers of the synagogue, who could throw people out (e.g., Jn 9:22). In the Christian church this responsibility eventually falls to the ecclesiarchy, the leadership of the church (perhaps following 1 Tim 5:17). Most Protestant churches have a membership status of some kind that can be conferred or revoked by whatever process is specified in the church's constitution. The point here is not to discuss whose responsibility the self-censorship is but rather why it is done.

The Greek word used by the Septuagint to translate the Hebrew *ḥerem* is *anathema*. The word occurs in four occasions where context indicates that it is in reference to the template; all of these take members of the community as the object and probably are intended to conceptually recapitulate the *ḥerem* of Israelite idolaters in the Old Testament.[2] The referents are: Paul himself (Rom 9:3); "anyone who does not love the Lord" (1 Cor 16:22); and "anyone who preaches a [different] gospel" (twice in Gal 1:8-9). Paul parallels the word with the phrase "cut off from Christ" in Romans 9:3, which apparently indicates removal from the community. A similar concept is described in 1 Corinthians 5:2, 11-13: "Shouldn't you rather have gone into mourning and have put out of your fellowship the man who has been doing this? . . . Do not even eat with such people. What business is it of mine to judge those outside the church? Are you not to judge those inside? God will judge those outside. 'Expel the wicked person from among you.'" The last line of 1 Corinthians 5:13 references Deuteronomy 13, which in context concerns the self-censoring of Israel (see proposition sixteen).

The Old Testament template indicates that the *ḥerem* of Israelite individuals and microcommunities was not intended to purge the

---

[2]The word occurs a total of six times in the New Testament: the last two occurrences are 1 Cor 12:3 and Acts 23:14, which probably intend the ordinary meaning of the word ("cursed"). First Corinthians 12:3 is a quote that in context has Christ as the object and is paralleled with the statement "Jesus is Lord." Acts 23:14 is also a quote, with the speakers as the object (NIV "taken" [a solemn oath], lit. "cursed [*anathema*] with a curse") in collocation with a word used twice in the same chapter (Acts 23:12, 21) to refer to calling down curses (on oneself for failure to carry out a sworn action).

world of a particular offense; it was rather to ensure the health of the Israelite community and the integrity of the Israelite identity. As is the case for all communities, the identity of the community is defined by its collective participants. For ancient Israel, participation in the community was based on an inherent identity marker (namely ethnicity), and the only way to remove an individual with an inherent identity marker from the community was to kill them. The Christian community, however, has no inherent identity markers; nobody is a Christian by default. Because membership in the Christian community is conferred, it can be revoked. This revocation eventually became known as excommunication and is signified in the declarations of the church councils by the word *anathema*.

The ancient Israelite community cut off its own members in order to protect the rest from the covenant curses. In the new covenant, however, the community receives no particular blessings or curses; under the new covenant, participation in God's purposes is its own reward, and failure to participate is its own consequence. The immediate purpose of the new covenant (that is, the function of the particular part that is being made in this step of the assembly line; see proposition three) is transformation of the members of the community through the regeneration of the Holy Spirit (called *glorification* or *theosis*). How exactly this element will be worked into God's final product we are not told, just as ancient Israel was never told what exactly would be accomplished by their receipt of blessings (or lack thereof). However, in order to accomplish this purpose, the community must have members. Israel had an ethnic identity marker and so could sustain itself simply by reproducing. Christianity, on the other hand, has no inherent identity markers, so if Christians want to sustain the community, they have to recruit. This is the purpose of the command to "go and make disciples." However, in order to make disciples, two factors are necessary. First, people have to want to join your community voluntarily. Coercion makes conscripts, not disciples.

Second, there needs to be something for them to convert *to*. The purpose of self-censorship of the community is to make sure that both of these requirements are met.

The first of these objectives is addressed by 1 Corinthians 5. Importantly, membership in the Christian community (salvation) does not carry an identity marker of moral performance (works). A church community with its membership closed to sinners is not worth much to anybody. Vice (or immorality) is detrimental to the health of the person who practices it and obstructs the transformation process, and therefore it is doubly its own consequence, but that is not the source of this particular concern.[3] The immorality that needs seeing to in 1 Corinthians 5 is a problem because it is of a kind that even pagans do not tolerate. The problem is that the Corinthians are making the community look bad. Making the community look bad is to be avoided even if the cause is not immorality. Titus 2:1-10 discourages social impropriety for this explicit reason, "so that in every way they will make the teaching about God our Savior attractive" (Titus 2:10). This objective applies not only to the community's membership but also to the distribution of its altruism (1 Tim 5:3-12). If the community is a laughingstock, or otherwise despised, it will not be able to recruit anyone and will die out.

On the other hand, if the community simply panders to those who are not a part of it, it will become indistinguishable from them and will likewise vanish. This is the importance of the other objective, described by Galatians 1; attractive or not, the community must not compromise the integrity of its identity (preach a different gospel). Christians are called to make disciples of Christ in keeping with the tenets of true *Christianity*, not of just any old ideology that happens to be floating about (or even of any old ideology that happens to call itself

---

[3]The consequence is further amplified if the individual has sacrificed the benefits of ordinary worldly life in the hope of receiving the benefits associated with transformation; this observation is essentially the point of the argument in 1 Cor 15:19.

Christianity). In the context of religious communities, a person who tries, through their own participation, to change a community's identity to be something that the community does not wish to adopt for itself is called a *heretic* (as distinct from an *apostate*, who wishes to abandon the community and its identity altogether, or an *infidel*, who is outside of the community and has nothing to do with it whatsoever). What exactly does or does not constitute Christian heresy, and who exactly gets to decide, is irrelevant for this study; indeed, we would not expect the template to give us that kind of information. What the template does tell us is that, in order to serve its purpose, the integrity of the community's identity must remain intact; the community cannot serve its purpose simply by conforming to whichever way the wind happens to be blowing. The decision of whether to be all things to all people (that is, be attractive to potential converts) or to not be conformed to the pattern of this world (that is, remain distinct at any cost) does not default in either direction. Deciding which is more pressing in which context at any particular place and time is part of the responsibility that is delegated to the leaders and shapers of the community. The template only tells us that both factors need to be considered.

However, just as the template does not give us any specifics in identifying heretics, it does not specify what to do with them, either. The purpose of the new covenant *anathema*, like the old covenant *ḥerem*, is to remove the subject from the community for the sake of the community. It is not to punish the subject or discipline the subject. Israelite idolaters had to be killed because that was the only way to remove the inherent identity marker. Historically, those labeled heretics by various parochial institutions were also killed for a variety of reasons. However, the killing of heretics is not part of the template. The template only says that they need to be expelled from the community so that the community might be preserved. The penalty of expulsion is applied to those within the community who fail to properly adopt the identity of the community, as demonstrated by 1 Corinthians 16:22 ("If anyone does not love the Lord, let that person be *anathema*"). The word translated "love" (*philei*) refers to community solidarity, and "the Lord [Jesus Christ]" as the head of the community is a figure of speech to indicate the entire community that is "in Christ." This failure might perhaps take the form of adopting a Jewish identity through circumcision (i.e., Gal 5:2), or perhaps by having "a part in . . . the table of demons" (1 Cor 10:21; see excursus in proposition eight). The problem is not anything inherent in the action itself but the identity contamination that the symbolic gesture indicates. We might compare to Deuteronomy 7:26; "Do not bring a *tôʿēbâ* thing into your house or you, like it, will be *ḥerem*." As discussed in proposition thirteen, *tôʿēbâ* refers to things that do not belong in the community. Identities other than "in Christ" are effectively *tôʿēbâ* to the new covenant community. If a member of the community fails to put those identities to *ḥerem* (removed from their use), then that person themself will be *ḥerem* (cut off from the community) instead.

All of this indicates that all of the targets of the *ḥerem* in the new covenant are members of the Christian community. Christians are not supposed to *ḥerem* infidels and nonbelievers for the sake of purging the world of apostasy. They are not supposed to conquer territory and subject it to theocratic rule, and they are not supposed to pass murderous judgment on out-group individuals because of their immorality. Instead, they are supposed to *ḥerem* themselves for the sake of the integrity of the Christian community, not as punishment but in order to make space for God to carry out his purposes through their lives. That is what the conquest of Canaan did within the context and purpose of the old covenant, and that is what Christians are supposed to do within the context and purpose of the new covenant.

Conclusion

Now we return to the issue with which we began. When we try to understand what the Bible says, it is of utmost importance that we approach the text consistently. We cannot take individual passages or verses in isolation and apply whatever particular logical process is necessary to make them say what we want them to say or think they should say. This is true whether we are apologists trying to defend the Bible or anti-Christian critics attempting to defame it. Inconsistent interpretations are of no value, and their conclusions should not be seriously considered by anyone.

Accordingly, the purpose of this study is not to dredge up a line of logic that we can apply to a few select passages to argue that they do not advocate killing people. The objective of this study has been to read the biblical text consistently as an ancient document within its ancient context. As it turns out, the text in context does not emphasize the killing of people nearly as much as modern critics of the Bible would like us to think. However, when killing does occur, the text in context demonstrates much less antipathy toward the process, and offers much less of what we would consider acceptable justification for it, than modern apologists would like us to think. More importantly, though, a careful reading of the text in context indicates that the Bible's depictions of killing people (or lack thereof) are not as significant as many of us are inclined to think. This is because, as we have suggested, we are inclined to misunderstand what the Bible is for.

When we approach the conquest narrative, the question we should ask ourselves is, why is this in here? We should not ask, how can I possibly construe this event to make it seem good? Both critics and apologists generally assume that the Bible's purpose—the reason behind God's revelation—was to teach the Israelites and thereby also teach future readers of the documents how to be good. Apologists try to argue that what the Bible portrays as goodness really is good, while critics argue that what the Bible portrays as goodness really is horrible. Both of these arguments are misguided for the same reasons. God's revelation was not written to teach the Israelites how to be good, and it was not written to teach us how to be good, either. The Israelites already knew how to be good; their moral knowledge was derived from their surrounding culture, what we termed the cultural river or cognitive environment. The Bible's text assumes this knowledge and writes in its terms, but it does not attempt to revise their thinking. Neither, however, was it written to stamp the ancient conceptions of goodness for all time with the seal of divine authority. Some of what the ancient world considered to be good happens to correspond to things that we in the modern world also consider to be good; some of it does not. Apologists for the Bible tend to focus on the former; critics focus on the latter. However, the Bible does not exist in order to help us imitate ancient Israelite culture, for good or bad. Some of the aspects of ancient culture may incidentally be worth imitating, but they have to be judged on their own merits, and this is true of any literature, philosophy, or scriptures and is not particular to the Hebrew Bible.

Since the content of the text is not supposed to describe or demonstrate goodness, the question of whether it actually *does* describe or demonstrate goodness is irrelevant. A far more useful discussion concerns what it is describing or demonstrating instead. The Old Testament is the record of God's actions for and through the nation of Israel in the context of the Sinaitic covenant. However, the text does not simply record activities passively and impartially, as if it were making a documentary. Rather, the text is designed to offer an interpretation of those events and thereby not only record that the covenant existed but also describe what it was and what it was for. The purpose and significance of the old covenant was different for the ancient Israelites than it is for us, because they were subject to its conditions and we are not. Nonetheless, it is important that we understand what that purpose and significance was, because the Old Testament is not useless or meaningless even to those under the new covenant. The record of God's actions through Israel describes what the covenant was and how it served to carry out God's purposes in its own ancient context. This knowledge provides us with a template that we are supposed to use to understand what the new covenant is and how it served to carry out God's purposes in the Greco-Roman context of the New Testament. That in turn allows us to understand what we should be doing in order to participate in those purposes in our own modern context today.

The Old Testament describes the covenant in order to demonstrate what it is and how it works, but it does so using language, logic, and imagery that had meaning in the context of the ancient cognitive environment. Since that cognitive environment is foreign to us, however, that language, logic, and imagery will necessarily be somewhat obscure. Consequently, in order to access the text's teaching, that language, logic, and imagery need to be translated. We have to understand what the events described would have meant to the original Israelite audience; we cannot arrive at a proper interpretation by translating only the words and speculating about what the event may have been based on what those (English) words mean to us in our own cultural context.

If the Bible as Scripture is the authoritative word of God, then its interpretation of the events it describes carries that authority. As a result, if we wish to respect that authority, we need to adopt the text's own interpretation as our own; we cannot impose our own interpretation onto its description of events. If the logic and imagery, properly translated, do not depict an event as an atrocity, then we cannot claim that it was an atrocity. Likewise, however, if the logic and imagery do not depict an event as divine judgment, as punishment for crimes, or as divine mercy in extending the benefits of the covenant to the inhabitants of the land, we cannot claim that these are occurring, either. We cannot interpret the text to say what we think it should say; we can only try to understand the interpretation it offers for itself.

The text in context, when properly translated, does not describe the conquest as judgment on the Canaanites for their sins. None of the normal Hebrew words indicating crime or punishment are ever used to describe the Canaanites or their actions. The descriptions of Canaanite nations in Leviticus 18 and Deuteronomy 9 are, in context, invoking a well-established ancient Near Eastern literary trope about hordes of invincible barbarians who are established by the gods to cause trouble for the servants of the gods before being destroyed by the gods. The purpose of the trope is not to justify attacking the barbarians and exterminating them, because the trope is normally used to describe enemies that the documents' sponsor either cannot defeat or does not wish to fight. In Leviticus and Deuteronomy, the trope is not intended to describe the actual qualities of the historical people of Canaan. Rather, the imagery is employed to portray the conquest event as God driving away the forces of chaos in a recapitulation of the biblical creation story. This in turn is designed to interpret the conquest event as the establishment of a new created order and to interpret the covenant as the manifestation of that order. Finally, Genesis 15:16 does not say that the conquest was delayed so that the Canaanites could build up a balance of enough sin to warrant their destruction; it says that the conquest was delayed so that the violence and turmoil would not occur during the lifetime of either Abraham or his Amorite allies.

The actions of Joshua and his armies are not intended to be imitated, but they are intended to be understood. In order to understand, we must be cautious with our translation not only of the Hebrew words but also of the imagery and logic of the ancient culture that gives those words their meaning. When we translate the event as holy war or jihad or genocide, or even conquest, we are not translating the event properly, because those words and ideas do not mean the same thing to us that the logic and imagery used to describe the conquest would have meant to the original audience, either in terms of their connotations or their objectives. When we hear words such as *genocide* we interpret them as "a thing that should never be done." But the text does not depict the conquest event in terms of a thing that should never be done. Order was highly valued in the ancient world, comparable to the value we place on things such as human rights, liberty, or democracy. That does not mean the text demands us to value order as well; the point is translation, not adoption. What it does mean is that, when we translate the event, we should do so in terms, not of wars that were fought for reasons we revile (such as the Crusades), but rather of wars that were fought for goals that we consider noble or valuable, as, for example, we commonly think of the American Revolution, the American Civil War, or World War II. That does not mean that we should ascribe the objectives of those wars back onto the conquest, either (as is done, for example, by those who portray it in terms of revolution). The conquest is not a story of bigotry and butchery; neither is it a story of mercy and grace. It does not tell us that the Israelites valued the same things that we do, and it does not tell us that we should value the same things that the Israelites did. It tells us what God did so that we can understand what God is doing today, not so that we can do the same things today that God did then or argue that what God did then was the same thing that we think (or prefer) that God is doing today.

Understanding the Bible as what it is and according to what it actually says does not solve all our problems. It does not help us work out a philosophy of ethics, or of war, or to somehow vindicate God and his undertakings described in the Bible. Being faithful interpreters requires careful reading. Questions remain about how we should think about war today, but we cannot force those answers from the text. We hope that this book has helped the reader gain information that paves the way for such faithful interpretation. Above all, we hope that the information we have provided about the text and about the ancient world is useful to help Christians today better understand the text and in so doing feel less anxiety about the book of Joshua and about the God whom we serve.

Subject Index

Scripture Index